D0467210

A PRISON
AND A
PRISONER

Books by Susan Sheehan

A PRISON AND A PRISONER

Susan Sheehan

HOUGHTON MIFFLIN COMPANY BOSTON

1978

The material in this book originally
appeared in *The New Yorker.*

Copyright © 1978 by Susan Sheehan

All rights reserved. No part of this work may be
reproduced or transmitted in any form by any means, elec-
tronic or mechanical, including photocopying and recording,
or by any information storage or retrieval system, without
permission in writing from the publisher.

Library of Congress Cataloging in Publication Data
Sheehan, Susan.
A prison and a prisoner.
1. Green Haven Correctional Facility.
2. Prisoners—New York (State)—Case studies.
I. Title.
HV9475.N72G737   365'.9747'33   78–2728
ISBN 0–395–26684–X

Printed in the United States of America

P 10 9 8 7 6 5 4 3 2 1

For Catherine Fair Sheehan

ACKNOWLEDGMENTS

Because most of the hundreds of people who helped me during the time that I spent writing this book prefer to remain anonymous (I am thinking especially of prisoners and guards at Green Haven), it gives me particular pleasure to thank the few people whom I am able to address publicly: Jerry Ducie; Robert Lescher; Sergeant John P. Hues, Lieutenant Kenneth F. Roden, Captain Hylan T. Sperbeck, and Deputy Superintendent of Security (subsequently Superintendent) Walter T. Fogg of Green Haven; Herbert Sturz, president and director of the Vera Foundation; Mitchell Sviridoff and Robert B. Goldmann of the Ford Foundation, and the Ford Foundation for its generous financial assistance; William Shawn, Charles Patrick Crow, Milton Greenstein, Richard S. Sacks, Patti Hagan, Martin J. Baron, Harriet Walden, Janet Groth, Pearl Bsharah, Carmine Graziano, Barbara Solonche, Eleanor Gould, and Ann Goldstein of *The New Yorker* magazine; and Austin Olney, Helena Bentz Dorrance, Linda Glick, Louise Noble, Carolyn Amussen, and Betty Sudarsky of Houghton Mifflin.

My greatest thanks go to the New York State Department of Correctional Services: for approving my idea of writing about one of its prisons and one of its prisoners in late 1975; for introducing me to Green Haven, the prison of my choice, in

January, 1976; and for leaving me to my own devices from then until late 1977, when my work was done. I was taken to every part of Green Haven I asked to see at a moment's notice. I was able to spend countless sixteen-hour days (and an occasional twenty-four-hour day) there. I was permitted to interview prisoners on their tiers and in their cells, a floor or two from the nearest guard. Without the proper combination of the department's cooperation and welcome neglect, it would have been impossible to do this book the way I thought it should be done.

●

The names of most people in this book, including George Malinow's, have been changed.

A PRISON
AND A
PRISONER

George Malinow is a pleasant-looking man of fifty-seven with wavy gray hair and light-blue eyes. Most of his friends are twenty or thirty years younger than he is, and once, when he tried dyeing his hair black, he was gratified by the compliments that his friends paid him upon his youthful appearance. Sometimes it amuses him to grow a mustache, but he rarely keeps it for long; he tries to bring as much variety into his life as possible. Malinow has a soft spot in his heart for children. He refers to his friends' daughters as "princesses," and always advises his friends against spanking them. The accent in which Malinow gives this advice testifies to his Brooklyn upbringing. "You better don't be hitting dem two princesses of yours," he recently told a friend, with an admonitory shake of the head.

Although Malinow left Brooklyn almost forty years ago and has rarely been back, much of Brooklyn remains in him. He dropped out of school at the age of fifteen, shortly after completing the eighth grade at Public School 126. He has an I.Q. that is above average, and a few years ago he took and passed his high-school-equivalency examination. While most of his acquaintances watch television in the evening, Malinow prefers painting pictures on glass, or letter writing, or reading. When

Malinow is asked his occupation, he replies that he is a professional criminal. Like most professional criminals, he might be said to be a specialist; his specialty is payroll robbery.

Malinow is telling the truth as he perceives it when he describes himself as a professional criminal, but it would probably be more accurate to describe him as a professional prisoner. He has been behind bars for all but three of the last thirty-nine years. He was first sent to prison in 1938; he was released in 1942 and remained at liberty for almost twenty months. When he was next released from prison, in 1952, after serving nine years, he stayed out for about sixteen months. He was arrested again in October, 1953, convicted some months later, and eventually sent back to prison for thirteen years. When he was last released, in 1966, he stayed out seven weeks to the day.

Malinow has been locked up in the jails of three of New York City's five boroughs — Brooklyn, Queens, and the Bronx. He has done time in five New York State prisons — Wallkill, Ossining (it was still called Sing Sing on the four occasions he was there), Clinton, Attica, and Green Haven. He is currently a prisoner at Green Haven, in Beekman — one of New York State's five maximum-security prisons.

There were 17,790 other people in prison in New York State along with George Malinow on January 1, 1977. All but 479 of the 17,791 were men. Most of the women were in New York's only large prison for women — Bedford Hills, in Westchester County. The men were confined in an assortment of thirty prisons scattered around the state. New York has several reception-and-classification centers, where men are sent from local jails and courts immediately after they have been sentenced, to be evaluated and then sent on to other prisons to serve their time; a good-sized prison primarily for young men (Elmira, population 1129 on January 1, 1977, all but two of whom were between the ages of sixteen and twenty-nine); a number of medium-sized, medium-security, general-confinement prisons (such as Eastern, Coxsackie, and Wallkill); and an increasing number of small, minimum-security conservation camps in rural areas and community-based facilities in and around New York City, for prisoners who are within a year or so of being released. The majority of the men in prison in New York, however, are confined in the state's five maximum-security prisons, which hold between fourteen hundred and two thousand prisoners each. They are Attica, in the northwestern part of the state, twenty-five miles from Buffalo, best known for the riot of September 1971, in which thirty-two prisoners and eleven prison employees lost their lives; Auburn, in central New York, between Syracuse and Rochester, where all the state's license plates are produced; Clinton, in northeastern New York, sixteen miles from the Canadian border, which is celebrated for its endless winters (there is a ski jump and sometimes a bobsled run in the prison yard); Great Meadow, in Comstock, seventy miles north of Albany, long known as "the garbage dump" of the maximum-security prisons; and Green Haven, in Dutchess County, eighty miles north of New York City, the newest and supposedly the most innovative of the lot. Ossining, formerly Sing Sing, is still designated a maximum-security prison but is now primarily used to hold prisoners in reception status and parole violators awaiting parole-revocation hearings. It has only a small maintenance cadre of about a hundred regular state prisoners.

New York's five maximum-security prisons differ from maximum-security prisons in other states and, in minor ways, from one another. Nightsticks, once carried by every guard at every one of the state's maximum-security prisons, became optional a few years ago. At Green Haven in 1976, all but two or three guards chose not to carry them; at Great Meadow, all the guards still carry sticks. Green Haven went through a time of trouble after the Attica riot. In December 1972, the prison was shut down and searched. Hundreds of sharpened mess-hall knives were found throughout the prison. Since then, prisoners

3

have not been allowed to use knives in the mess hall. Great Meadow doesn't permit the use of knives in the mess hall, either, but Clinton, Auburn, and Attica do. Green Haven and Great Meadow have shut down their bathhouses, which prisoners once had to walk to for weekly showers, and have built showers in all the cellblocks; the bathhouses at Attica, Auburn, and Clinton are still in use. When the New York State Special Commission on Attica studied that prison in the months following the riot, it found Attica sufficiently representative of the prisons in New York State and elsewhere to justify generalization, concluding, "Attica is every prison; and every prison is Attica." Six years later, one might paraphrase the commission and say that Green Haven is every prison, and every prison is Green Haven. Or one might say, as Malinow does, in unknowing imitation of Gertrude Stein, "A prison is a prison is a prison."

Like all of New York State's maximum-security prisons, Green Haven is surrounded by a wall. Green Haven's wall, which is made of steel-reinforced concrete, is a mile long and thirty feet high. At its base, it is twenty-eight inches thick. Midway up, it is twenty-four inches thick. At the top, it is eighteen inches thick and is rounded, so that no one can walk on it or throw a rope with a grappling hook up and shinny over. There are twelve guard towers spaced evenly around the top of the wall. Guards, armed with an array of shotguns, rifles, and tear-gas guns, occupy eight of the twelve towers around the clock. (Four towers have been closed in an economy move over the past few years.) No one has escaped over the wall of Green Haven since it was opened as a state prison, in 1949. This is not to say, however, that there have been no escapes from Green Haven in the last twenty-eight years. "Maximum," according to one dictionary, is "the greatest quantity or amount possible, assignable." Green Haven may seem to have maximum-security possibilities — sturdy steel-barred cells for most prisoners, in sturdy red brick cellblock buildings behind the formidable wall — but it is debatable whether Green Haven meets this definition of maximum security. There are fifty acres inside Green Haven's wall. It would presumably be possible to keep all of Green Haven's prisoners confined to these fifty walled acres, but this is not the practice. About a hundred of its prisoners are assigned to spend the day working outside the wall. A few men work on the outside-grounds gang, a few work in the prison garage, one man drives the prison's fire truck around the grounds, but most of the hundred or so work on the prison's farm, milking cows, driving tractors, and cleaning barns. Here they are supervised by nine or ten guards and civilians, but the farm occupies four hundred and forty acres, and the guards and civilians cannot keep their eyes on all their charges all the time. The prisoners assigned to the farm and to the other outside jobs must meet certain criteria. They must, for example, be within three years of appearing before the parole board, the theory being that these men will have less incentive to flee than, say, a man just beginning a life sentence, who would have no hope of appearing before the parole board for fifteen or twenty years. The theory is probably sound, but nowadays one or two men take off from the farm just about every year anyway.

On July 29, 1976, a rainy Thursday, Duane Nelson and Earl Franklin, two farm workers, were seen at the farm mess hall between 12:15 P.M. and 12:30 P.M. Around 12:45 P.M., when a guard was told to round up his men, he couldn't find Nelson and Franklin. A search was made of all the farm buildings. No Nelson, no Franklin. About forty-five minutes later, they were declared missing. The state police were notified. Green Haven's prisoners, who ordinarily were not confined to their cells to be counted between the 6:30 A.M. count and the 5:30 P.M. count, were locked up at two o'clock for a count. The prison's power-house whistle was blown three times — the signal that an escape had taken place. Prisoners who knew the missing men were questioned, roadblocks were set up, photos of Nelson and Franklin were sent out. Prison guards, state policemen, and state police bloodhounds, which were given clothing from the missing men's cells to sniff, searched the farm and the surrounding area for Nelson and Franklin for hours. They didn't find them. The search — except for eight cars — was called off at 7:10 P.M. Franklin was caught several days later at a tavern in New York City, Nelson shortly thereafter in New Jersey. When Franklin was brought back to Green Haven, he said that he and Nelson had hidden in the woods while the men and dogs looked for them. They had worn plastic bread wrappers over their shoes and had previously washed the clothes they were wearing and those they had left in their cells with spices from the kitchen, in the hope of confusing the bloodhounds. They had waited quietly until the search was called off, had stayed in the woods all night, and then had made their way to a local dump, where they came upon an old man in a pickup truck. They had got him to drive them into New York City that morning. When they were apprehended, they were charged not only with escape but also with kidnapping the driver of the pickup. They were found guilty of escape and not guilty of kidnapping. Donald Baden, the last man to walk away from the farm before Nelson and Franklin, had enjoyed his freedom a little longer. He was last seen at Green Haven around eight o'clock on the morning of Sunday, December 14, 1975, near the dairy barn. He turned himself in on January 22, 1977, in Oregon — he said he was "tired of running" — and was brought back to Green Haven.

Most people might assume that if a prisoner is sentenced to serve time in a maximum-security prison like Green Haven, he is kept on the premises — whether inside the wall or outside the wall — for the duration of his stay. This is no longer the case. A few years ago, New York State (like most other states) began a program called Temporary Release, whereby certain prisoners are selected to be let out on furloughs of up to seven days for various purposes, among them seeking post-prison employment, maintaining family ties, and solving family problems.

Although the prisoners selected for furloughs must be within a year of meeting with the parole board or completing their sentences, and the return rate from furloughs is high — it was 98.9 percent for the state last year — it is never 100 percent. In 1976, there were 199 furloughs from Green Haven. Five men failed to return on time. One man simply returned nine hours late. One came back after six and a half weeks, attributing his late return to "family pressures." One was arrested while he was on furlough, and was charged with several new crimes, including burglary. Two are still at large.

In recent years, four men who were not eligible to work on the farm or to be given furloughs have also succeeded in escaping from Green Haven.

In the early spring of 1974, Neil Shea and Lee Gregory were working in the prison kitchen. Shea, a fifty-five-year-old man with a silver tongue and a long record — his most recent conviction was for killing a state trooper — and Gregory, a thirty-eight-year-old robber, passed part of their time watching the trucks that entered the prison's rear gate, unloaded supplies at a platform near the kitchen, and then left the prison by the rear gate. They had noticed that one truck was different from all the others: the delivery truck that brought cans of milk in from the prison farm had no window between the cab and the body. If two men could get their hands on a piece of plywood, cut it to approximately the same size, paint it the same color as the inside of the body, and sneak into the truck, they could conceal themselves behind their false partition. Neither the driver of the milk truck nor the Green Haven guard whose job it was to look inside the truck before it went out the rear gate would be likely to detect them. Shea and Gregory had also observed that security in the loading-platform area was lax, especially on weekends. The truck driver, a civilian, didn't stay with the truck while it was parked — he usually went into the kitchen to pick up empty milk cans or food for the farm workers — and the storehouse clerk, a prisoner, whose desk overlooked the loading

7

platform, was off on weekends and holidays. In May 1974, Shea, whose sentence was thirty years to life, went before the parole board. He had already been denied parole once, and in May he was denied parole a second time. "They ain't never going to let me out," he later admitted saying to himself, and he decided to let himself out in the windowless truck, which struck him as an opportunity that might never come along again. Gregory didn't have much time left to do at Green Haven, but because he faced some federal bankrobbery charges later he also decided to escape.

The two men were able to scrounge up, in the vicinity of the kitchen, all the materials they needed to make their partition: a piece of plywood, paint, some hinges and handles, and some cardboard in case the plywood was too small. They hid the finished partition, which folded up neatly, on top of a refrigerator in the nearby prison flour room. They were ready to leave in June, but didn't want to mess up such traditional big visiting days as the Fourth of July and Labor Day for their fellow prisoners, so they bided their time, worrying as they waited for an opportune moment to depart that the milk truck might break down and be replaced by a truck with windows. On the morning of Saturday, October 4, 1974, while no one was looking, they carried their partition into the milk truck, stood behind the cab, pulled their false partition up in front of them, and rode out the rear gate undetected. After the truck had been parked at the farm for a while, they got out, hid the partition in the hay barn, where, they hoped, it wouldn't be found for at least a day, and walked a short distance to the Stormville Airport, where they phoned for a cab. Shea and Gregory were wearing green prison uniforms, which they had bleached a little yellow, and old blue coats with fur collars. The coats had "Green Haven" stamped on them, but the men had covered the name of the prison with shoe polish. "If you looked real close, you could see it," Shea said later. No one looked close. They asked the cab company for a cab to take them to Poughkeepsie, eighteen miles away. When the cab arrived, they asked the driver to take them to New York City instead, and he did.

Shea had plenty of money to pay the fare. Over the years in prison, he had accumulated a lot of cash (which is contraband at Green Haven but is always around) by wheeling and dealing in liquor (also contraband, also always available) and cigarettes. He had buried the cash in the garbage area in back of the kitchen. Shortly before he left, he dug up his savings, which amounted to about twelve hundred dollars, and concealed the money — it was mostly in hundred-dollar bills — in the hollowed-out heel of one of his shoes. Shea also had some identification, which he later found useful for registering at motels. Three years earlier, a civilian in the kitchen had given some of the prisoners a hard time. To settle the score, someone had stolen his wallet, put it behind a loose tile in the kitchen bathroom, and plastered over the wall. The wallet, which contained a driver's license, stayed there until Shea was ready to use it. The license had expired, but Shea correctly surmised that no motel clerk would check its expiration date. Shea and Gregory were already in New York City when their absence was discovered, during the five-thirty count. On Saturday evening, the prison authorities believed that the two men were still hiding on the Green Haven grounds. They were actually at a topless go-go joint in Times Square. Late Saturday and all day Sunday, prison guards and state police went out looking for them. They didn't find them or the partition, and had no idea how the two men had got out. On Monday evening, October 6, Shea and Gregory were sitting in a "gin mill" getting "bombed," Shea later said. They got drunk enough to decide to return to Green Haven and retrieve the partition, so that the prison personnel would never discover how they had escaped. They drove Gregory's father's car from New York City to the Stormville Airport, parked, walked to the prison hay barn, picked up the partition, carried it to the airport, and put it on the roof of the car. Gregory drove, holding the steering wheel with his right hand, the partition with his left; Shea sat next to him, holding the partition with his right hand. After about three miles, they dropped the partition along the side of the road. The men then returned to the city.

Gregory was arrested in New York City a short while later, as a result of a tip from a woman. Shea went south after Gregory's arrest, figuring that New York City was too "hot." He took a Greyhound bus to Philadelphia and traveled around for a while — to Baltimore, Washington, and parts of Virginia. In December, he drove through a red light in Pennsylvania, and, after a high-speed chase, was picked up by police in what proved to be a stolen car. He was brought back to Green Haven, where he agreed to discuss the escape, on tape, at a long, friendly session with one of the sergeants and one of the lieutenants he had temporarily outwitted. After Shea had described the Monday-night return-to-Green Haven caper — the way he and Gregory, both "stoned," were staggering around, falling down, dropping the partition, getting lost on the roads, and arguing which way to go — the sergeant said, "I wouldn't believe that in a movie." Shea replied, "I know it." Shea was transfered to Clinton; Gregory was sent to Attica; the cab of the milk truck was immediately provided with a rear window. Green Haven officials say they have tightened up their security procedures at the rear gate since October 1974.

On June 22, 1975, Michael Gaynor and Floyd Wilkes, two Black Muslims who were serving life sentences for murder, went to the visiting room to receive visits. One went on a genuine visiting-room pass, one on a forged pass. Among the people in the visiting room were some women dressed in long Muslim robes. Apparently, the women were wearing street clothes under their long robes. Apparently, the women were able to slip off their robes. Apparently, Wilkes and Gaynor were able to put on the long robes and discard their green prison pants, unobserved by the visiting-room guard. Apparently, they walked out the front gate a short while after their visitors left.

The adverb "apparently" is necessary because Gaynor and Wilkes are still at large. Green Haven officials say they have tightened up their visiting-room and front-gate security procedures since June 1975.

George Malinow was pleased that four fellow prisoners made it out the front and rear gates of Green Haven in a period of less than a year. "The guards and officials are arrogant," he says. "They seem to think they have a monopoly on intelligence. I take the position that where there's a will there's a way. It's good to see them being outsmarted. Escapes give me a great deal of vicarious pleasure."

The guards at Green Haven like to tell visitors — especially visitors they suspect of having pro-prisoner sympathies — "No one is in here for taking candy from a baby." A booklet published annually by the New York State Department of Correctional Services, called *Characteristics of Inmates under Custody,* confirms the accuracy of this saying. Almost every person in state prison is a convicted felon; the few who are not are "youthful offenders." The latest year for which complete facts and figures are available for New York State's prisoners in general and Green Haven's in particular is 1975. There have been no dramatic changes in these figures in 1976 and 1977, nor do Green Haven's figures differ significantly from the figures for the state's other prisons. On December 31, 1975, there were 1626 men at Green Haven. Of those, 556 were there for robbery, 213 for homicide, 193 for murder, 153 for drugs, 142 for burglary, 89 for felonious assault, 70 for possession of dangerous weapons, 38 for grand larceny, 64 for rape, 25 for sex offenses other than rape, and 10 for forgery; 24 were youthful offenders, and 49 fell into the "all others" category, which includes kidnapping, arson, and criminal possession of stolen property. By December 31, 1976, the number of prisoners at Green Haven had increased by 229 men, bringing the total to 1855, but the distribution as to categories of crime remained approximately the same. Professional criminals like Malinow frequently express their disdain for rapists and child molesters and will not associate with them, but since there are not very many rapists and other sex offenders at Green Haven, the disdain is perhaps out of proportion to the numbers. Although Malinow is a robber, the charge for which he is currently serving time at Green Haven is attempted felonious possession of a loaded gun, which puts him in the dangerous-weapons group. On October 25, 1966, he was picked up by the police with a loaded revolver in his pocket, several blocks from a factory whose payroll he had planned to rob that day but had, at the last minute, because of unforeseen circumstances, decided against robbing.

The violent crimes for which most men are sent to prison in New York State are the sort that, if they occur in New York City, get a one-day splash in the *News* or a line or two in the *Times'* "Police Blotter" listings. A grocery-store owner in the Bronx was killed during a holdup. A man was stabbed by another man on a street in upper Manhattan as a result of an argument. A night gas-station attendant in Brooklyn was robbed and shot. Between 1949 and 1977, only a few men whose names would be recognized by a substantial percentage of newspaper readers have served time at Green Haven. Joey Gallo, who was convicted of attempted extortion and conspiracy, was at Green Haven from October 1966 until May 1970; some oil paintings he did to pass the time there can still be seen in the homes of several of Green Haven's guards and former officials. Ted Gross, Youth Services Commissioner in Mayor John Lindsay's administration, who was convicted of bribery, was at Green Haven from September 1973 to June 1974. In June 1976, he was murdered. Gross had met Kenneth Gilmore, the man subsequently convicted of his murder, at Green Haven. Mark Fein, a rich young man who was convicted of murdering his bookmaker in 1964, served the last nine years of his sentence at Green Haven; he was paroled in July 1976. H. Rap Brown, once the chairman of the Student Nonviolent Coordinating Committee, served the last part of a five-to-fifteen-year sentence, for robbery and assault, at Green Haven, where he played quarterback on the prison football team; he was paroled in the fall of 1976. The names of the overwhelming majority of Green Haven's inmates would be familiar only to their friends and relatives, to their victims (if they survived) and the victims' families, and perhaps to members of the specific communities in which the crimes occurred.

Of all the men in prison in New York State, 69.1 percent are from New York City. An even higher percentage of Green Haven's prisoners — about seventy-five percent — are from the city, as Malinow is, because Green Haven is the maximum-security prison closest to New York City, and the Department of Correctional Services attempts to house prisoners close to their homes, especially toward the end of their sentences. Many men begin their sentences at upstate prisons, like Clinton and Attica, and work their way downstate to Green Haven.

Fifteen percent of New York State's prisoners are between the ages of sixteen and twenty; 72.7 percent are between the ages of twenty-one and thirty-nine; and only 12.4 percent are forty or over. Just as young men outgrow reckless driving, young men outgrow crime. Thus, automobile-insurance rates for men over the age of twenty-five go down, and prison is a young men's place. When Malinow is asked why he is one of only forty-seven Green Haven prisoners over the age of fifty-five, he makes no apologies for his recidivism. Instead, he compares himself to a mustang. "I'm like a wild horse that you'll kill before you'll break it," he says with pride.

Of the state's male prisoners, 52.5 percent are single, 23.1 percent are married, and 11.4 percent have a common-law marriage; as for the remaining 12.7 percent, either they are divorced or separated or widowed or their marriages have been annulled. Malinow was married in a Catholic church in July 1953, thirteen months after he was released from his second prison term. He has a son, Arthur, who was born in April 1954, when Malinow was back in jail and awaiting sentence for his third crime. Malinow saw his wife a few times during the seven weeks he was next out, in 1966, and also saw his son, then twelve years old, for the first time. His wife, whom he has described as "a nice, loving, religious woman," hadn't divorced him. He hasn't been in touch with her since he was arrested for his fourth crime, and has no idea whether he belongs among the married men or the divorced men, but he has certainly been separated a lot from his wife since three months after their marriage.

Fifty-eight percent of the men imprisoned in New York are users of drugs. Of the drug users, 80.9 percent have committed major crimes other than drug-law violations — usually robberies or burglaries to get money to support their drug habits. Malinow has never used drugs and has contempt for drug users. "When I'm robbing a joint, I'm not desperate for a fix, like dem young addicts," he says. "I can take a place or I can leave it if it don't look right. I won't be hopped up, so I won't do nothing foolish." He has no such contempt for drug pushers. "They're businessmen," he says.

Like Malinow, over 78 percent of the men in prison in New York did not graduate from high school. Fewer than 7 percent went to college or received special vocational training. Over half listed their occupation as "unskilled laborer" upon commitment. State prison has traditionally been a place for the uneducated working-class street criminal rather than for the college-educated white-collar criminal. Green Haven's prisoners are resentful of the long sentences they receive — for stealing five hundred dollars from a supermarket cashier in an armed robbery, say — in comparison to the short sentences stockbrokers receive for stealing millions of dollars from old ladies who have put their savings in mutual funds. "Look at Bernard Bergman, the nursing-home operator, who was responsible for more human misery than I've ever caused," Malinow says. "His sentence for running all those terrible nursing homes was four months. And look at Nixon. He tried to steal the Bill of Rights and he got a pardon. I only wish to God that when I was younger I'd had someone to teach me economics and banking. Then I could have stolen millions of bucks with a few strokes of the pen and maybe been sent away only once for a couple of years."

Of the men in Green Haven, 1119 have been in prison before; 507 have no prior institutional commitment. Many of these 507 — like Malinow when he was first sent away, in 1938 — had committed crimes before but had received probation or suspended sentences the first couple of times before they were imprisoned. Most genuine first offenders at Green Haven are there for crimes of passion, like murdering a wife or an in-law. Malinow doesn't look down on murderers as he does on sex offenders — he readily admits that he "might have had to kill someone" in the course of a robbery — but he regards the wife killers as amateurs and says they are apt to have a harder time in prison than the professionals, who are street-wise and find it easier to become prison-wise.

All the men in prison in New York State are serving indeterminate sentences (two to four years, say, or five to ten) rather than flat sentences (say, seven years). More than half have maximum sentences of over five years, but few men serve their maximums. The median time a man spends in prison in New York is twenty months. Fifty-seven percent of the men get out on parole, for which they first become eligible after serving two-thirds of their minimum sentence (if, like Malinow, they were sentenced for crimes committed before September, 1967) or after serving their entire minimum sentence (if they were sentenced for crimes committed after September 1, 1967). Twenty-six percent get out on conditional release; in prison language, they "C.R." Every man in New York receives ten days' "good time" for each thirty days served in prison. If he does nothing in prison to forfeit his good time (Nelson and Franklin each lost a hundred and eighty days of good time for their escape), he gets out on conditional release after serving two-thirds of his maximum sentence. In New York State, men who C.R. are required to do the balance of their sentences on parole. The prisoners consider this unfair. They believe that good time should be genuine good time, for behaving well in prison, as it is in many other states. Only 2.8 percent "max out" — serve until the maximum expiration dates of their sentences. Malinow is among 11.7 percent of New York State's male prisoners who have life sentences. He is doing fifteen years to life for attempted felonious possession of a gun because when he was last arrested, in October 1966, he had previously been convicted of three felonies. In 1966, the law mandated that all fourth-felony offenders be given life sentences. A year after Malinow's last arrest, a new penal code went into effect, and all felonies committed before 1967 were counted as one felony. If Malinow had been arrested in October 1967, he might have received the same sentence that Patrick Halloran, the man he was arrested with in 1966, got then as a third-felony offender — three and a half to seven years — and, like Halloran, been long out of prison.

In 1970, the state's only electric chair was moved from Ossining (where it had last been used in 1963) to Green Haven. In 1974, the New York State Legislature passed a law making the death penalty mandatory for those convicted of intentionally killing police officers or prison guards, or for prisoners already sentenced to life who murdered anyone. In 1976, a New York State Supreme Court justice ruled that the law was unconstitutional, but while the state appealed his ruling, the two men in New York who had been convicted under the law and had received the death sentence remained on Green Haven's death row.

New York's prison population is 56.6 percent black, 26.7 percent white, 16.3 percent Puerto Rican, and four-tenths of 1 percent other (Asian, American Indian, Eskimo). Except for four of the state's smallest prisons, blacks are in the majority in every prison in New York, including Green Haven. In 1938, when Malinow first went to prison, whites — especially Italians and Irish — were a sizable majority. The white majority dwindled during the forties and fifties. In 1963, blacks outnumbered whites (by a hundred and sixty-seven men) for the first time. Since 1972, there have been more than twice as many blacks as whites in the prisons. In recent years, the number of Puerto Ricans imprisoned in New York has also been increasing steadily. Racial segregation was never an official policy in the state, but until the 1960s most of New York's prisons were segregated de facto: there were black ball teams and white ball teams, black cheering sections and white cheering sections for the ball teams, black barbers to cut blacks' hair and white barbers to cut whites' hair. Malinow admits that being white was formerly an advantage in prison: the guards were overwhelmingly white and often gave whites better jobs. To some extent, they still are and still do, but Malinow is increasingly conscious of being a member of a minority group — one that he feels is being discriminated against. He often sounds like a longtime Irish resident of South Boston talking about how nice the neighborhood used to be. Two prisoners were murdered at Green Haven in 1976. One victim was black, one was white. The whites are bitter when they compare the immediate aftermaths of the two murders.

At about 10:15 on the morning of August 23, 1975, a fight broke out between two white prisoners and several black prisoners in one of Green Haven's four large yards. A day earlier, Cyril Kolesar, a white man, had lost his wristwatch. He suspected a black man of stealing it and asked if he could search him. The black man consented to the search. Kolesar didn't find the watch on him. The black man's friends were upset that he had allowed Kolesar to shake him down, and vowed revenge. Kolesar must have suspected he was in for trouble, because he went to the yard on the twenty-third prepared for a fight; he was armed with a knife and was wearing a homemade chest-and-stomach shield fashioned out of cardboard. Several guards assigned to the yard saw the fight. They saw a man lunging at Kolesar with a sharpened broomstick handle, but they didn't see the man who hit Kolesar over the head with a two-by-four before they could break up the fight. Kolesar was taken by ambulance to a hospital in Poughkeepsie, where he died three days later of brain injuries. Months went by, and no one was charged with the crime.

At about 10:15 on the morning of October 30, 1976, a black man, Eli Walker, was stabbed in the chest and abdomen in his cellblock. He was taken by ambulance to a hospital in Poughkeepsie, where he was pronounced dead at 12:13 P.M. Two black prisoners who had witnessed the stabbing identified Walker's killer as Roger Filippi, a white man to whom Walker had possibly made homosexual advances. Soon afterward, Filippi was indicted by a Dutchess County grand jury for first-degree murder. Bruce Serafino and Adam Caldera, two white men who had accompanied Filippi to Walker's block and who were identified by the black prisoners as witnesses to the stabbing, refused to testify before the grand jury, even though they had been granted immunity; they were also indicted. Serafino and Caldera, who are acquaintances of Malinow's, could have had many years added to their sentences if they had gone to trial and been found guilty. One of Malinow's friends served as the head of a group that raised money for a defense fund for Serafino and Caldera, to which many white prisoners contributed. The two men eventually pleaded guilty to contempt. Caldera received a one-and-a-half-to-three-year concurrent sentence, Serafino a two-to-four-year concurrent sentence. The whites at Green Haven are convinced that the prison administration was afraid to let a black man's death go by, because of possible repercussions, but was quite willing to let a white man's death go by, because the whites now lack the strength of numbers. They may be wrong. Prison officials say that in late 1976 they found two witnesses to the Kolesar murder who were willing to testify, and that there is a better chance of eventually prosecuting

Kolesar's murderer, who is sane, than there is of ever putting Filippi on trial. Filippi had a history of mental illness before Walker's murder and has cracked up since. Even if the murderer of Kolesar is convicted, however, the white prisoners will not change their minds, because of the lapse of time and the sense of vulnerability they feel as a result of their minority status.

There are other facts about New York State's prisoners not covered by the booklet *Characteristics of Inmates under Custody* but known to those familiar with its prisoners. One is the significant number of men who are missing teeth — visual evidence of the fact that it is the poor rather than the rich who are usually convicted and sentenced to state prison. Another is the small number of Jews; in 1976, there were only about thirty Jewish prisoners (and about a thousand blacks) at Green Haven. There are about two million Jews and two million blacks in New York State. Others are the large number of men who, like Malinow, are tattooed and the large number who have nicknames (Malinow's is Popeye). Still another is the number of men who have relatives in prison. When Cyril Kolesar was murdered, his brother Joel Kolesar was fighting at his side. There are a few pairs of brothers at Green Haven now (some are serving time for the same crime), and until recently there were three brothers there. One former Green Haven official remembers identical-twin brothers at the prison, and another remembers nine members of a family who were in prison at the same time, including one — the wife and mother — at Bedford Hills. There are some fathers and sons at Green Haven, and Malinow has a nephew there. In 1976, only one man died of natural causes at Green Haven. On November 23, Reuben Griffith, sixty, who was serving a fifteen-to-life sentence for robbery, died of a heart attack in the prison hospital. The Catholic chaplain was given the assignment of notifying the next of kin. He did not have to make many long-distance phone calls. After he called the common-law wife and the sister of the

dead man, in New York City, he notified Griffith's stepson and
nephew. The stepson was at Green Haven serving a short sentence for attempted robbery in the first degree; the nephew was
at Green Haven serving fifteen-to-life for murder.

No one is sure how many homosexuals there are at Green
Haven, but both prisoners and guards estimate the number of
men there who practice homosexuality at twenty percent. There
are only a handful of "queens" at Green Haven at any one time
— men with feminine characteristics they do their best to en-
hance. The queens are usually given women's nicknames or the
names of Hollywood actresses (recent Green Haven prisoners
have answered to Angie, Ruby, Diane, and Marilyn) and are
referred to by the feminine pronoun. They dress as much as
possible like women, within the limits imposed upon them by
the prison's clothing regulations. All prisoners must wear the
state-issued green prison pants and are forbidden to alter them;
the queens wear altered pants nevertheless — tapered and tight
fitting. Instead of the state-issued black shoes and green shirts
(the wearing of which is optional), they wear platform shoes
and angora sweaters. Makeup is contraband, but the queens
improvise, using Coricidin to redden their lips and black shoe
polish around their eyes in lieu of mascara. A Green Haven
guard was caught taking ten dollars from a homosexual to bring
in a makeup kit a few years ago. Until the 1960s, the known
homosexuals were housed separately and worked in a separate
area. Later, they were allowed to live and work with the rest
of the prisoners. The queens usually lead charmed lives at
Green Haven, with many men vying and paying dearly for their
favors, although they are occasionally abused. One queen's
"husband" asked her to "produce" for four of his friends and
stabbed her when she declined. A number of men who are
heterosexual on the street practice homosexuality in prison,
some by choice, some not. The involuntary homosexuals tend
to be good-looking young men, who are usually forced into
becoming jailhouse "punks" by older men serving long sen-

tences. Hardly a year goes by without a gang rape at Green Haven. On New Year's Eve, 1976, for instance, a twenty-three-year-old man was forcibly assaulted and sodomized. Some years, there are also fake rapes. On June 12, 1976, a man named Ira Wilson claimed he had been assaulted and raped by four other prisoners. An investigation showed that Wilson had made a false accusation. He had on many previous occasions lent himself willingly to those he accused, and he had apparently been cooperative this time as well. Prison authorities frown on homosexuality, because it is one of the major causes of trouble in prison, often resulting in stabbings or pipings, and occasionally, as in the case of Eli Walker, in death. They are, however, unable to prevent it. Most men at Green Haven take care of their sexual needs by masturbating. If one of his young friends says to Malinow, "Come on, Popeye, how many times a week?" he may or may not tell him. Old-timers like Malinow speak disparagingly of the "homos."

Still another fact not dealt with in *Characteristics of Inmates under Custody* is the guilt or innocence of men in prison in New York State. It is likely that a few men at Green Haven are innocent of the crimes for which they have been convicted, as many maintain themselves to be, since no legal system in history has been free of error. Like every legal system, ours is made up of fallible human beings. It has been known to include prosecutors who are more interested in convictions than in justice, lazy judges, credulous or prejudiced juries, incompetent defense attorneys, police who have coerced confessions or faked evidence, and mistaken eyewitnesses. One man at Green Haven says he is certain that another man there is innocent, because he himself committed the crime for which the other man was convicted. It is just as likely that most of the men at Green Haven are guilty of the crimes for which they have been convicted. Some eighty percent of the convictions obtained in New York State are the result of plea-bargaining — pleading guilty to a lesser offense than the original charge, in the hope of obtaining leniency in exchange for sparing the state the expense of a trial — and the majority of the men in Green Haven wouldn't have pleaded guilty to anything if they had believed the evidence against them was insufficient to convict them. As a former superintendent of Green Haven says, with irony, only a "select few" of New York's felons ever wind up in state prison at all — the least skillful and the least lucky. In 1975, in New York State, 93,363 robberies were reported to the police (and additional robberies probably occurred that weren't reported). In 1975, in New York State, there were 23,908 arrests for robbery, 5288 convictions for robbery, and 3293 sentences to state prisons for robbery. Almost no one at Green Haven ever says plainly that he is guilty of anything, no matter what the circumstances of his arrest, no matter what his plea. After Earl Franklin was caught and charged with escape, in the summer of 1976, he said, "I admit the charges, but I was under extreme duress. My life was being threatened by a crime partner, so I had to escape." Or, as Malinow, who admits to being guilty of three of the four crimes for which he has been convicted, puts it in owning up to each one, "I'm guilty — with an explanation."

Green Haven is situated in the scenic mid–Hudson Valley region of New York State. Its mailing address is Stormville, New York. Stormville, an unincorporated hamlet in the township of East Fishkill, consists of a few houses, a fire department, a small, run-down hotel, and a general store, in which there is a post-office window. The prison takes its name from its site, in the unincorporated hamlet of Green Haven, one of four hamlets that make up the town of Beekman (pop. 5701). To compound the geographical confusion, neither Stormville nor Green Haven has a telephone book of its own, and the prison is listed in the phone book under Hopewell Junction, another unincorporated hamlet in East Fishkill. As far as the town of Beekman is concerned, Green Haven is one of its principal employers; over a hundred local residents work at the prison, as guards, supervisors, or civilian employees. As a state agency, the prison is exempt from paying property taxes, but it performs a few useful services for the community. It has, on occasion, built some cabinets and cooked some turkeys for a church in Beekman. When Nelson and Franklin walked off the prison farm in July 1976, an irate local citizen and two town officials came to call on the prison's superintendent to express their displeasure and to demand that Green Haven's security be upgraded. Except when there is an escape or a difference of opinion between the prison and the town over a matter like waste disposal, however, the attitude of the townspeople toward the rather self-contained prison is one of apathy.

Green Haven is on a two-lane road in a setting of rolling hills, old farms, and modern, low-lying split-levels and ranch-style houses. Though it doesn't dominate the landscape to quite the extent that the cathedral at Chartres soars over its environs, it is an incongruous sight to come upon. The road dips, and suddenly the prison wall is there, looking rather like a dam — if dams were punctuated by guard towers. A sign near the entrance spells out GREEN HAVEN CORRECTIONAL FACILITY in metal block letters. Until 1970, the sign read GREEN HAVEN PRISON. In 1970, the state legislature decreed that prisons in New York were thenceforth to be known as correctional facilities. The prisoners and the guards still call Green Haven "the prison" or "the joint" or "the jailhouse." In 1970, in what appears to have been an epidemic of wishful thinking by nomenclature, the state introduced a number of other euphemisms. The guards — there are 479 of them at Green Haven — became correction officers. Men like George Malinow call their keepers "guards," "officers," "C.O.s," "hacks," "screws," "police," "cops," and various obscene terms, rather interchangeably. They never call them correction officers. The officers are the first to admit that they do far more guarding than correcting, just as Green Haven still does more imprisoning than correcting. Old-timers like Malinow refer to themselves as convicts or cons, but most of the men at Green Haven call themselves inmates or prisoners. Collectively, the inmates are referred to as "population." At one time, the Department of Correctional Services (which one New York-prison critic has described as "probably the most glaring misnomer in state government") was called the Department of Prisons. An Albany spokesman for the department has no idea when that time was. When recently asked, he said he was too upset about an argument he had just had over a policy matter with a department commissioner to find out. "The commissioner doesn't know too much about our prisons, uh, our correctional facilities," the spokesman said. "He keeps saying he's going to visit Great Haven and Green Meadow."

Behind Green Haven's damlike wall, and invisible from the road, are twenty-five red brick buildings. The first one to which a prisoner is taken when he reaches Green Haven — in handcuffs chained to a belt and in leg irons — is H block, the prison's reception block, where he is unshackled, strip-frisked, and assigned a temporary cell. He spends anywhere from a few days to a few weeks in H block, going through the reception process. One of the first things he receives at Green Haven is a number: there are apt to be several James Smiths and Victor Hernandezes at Green Haven at the same time. The first man sent to Green Haven when it opened as a state prison, in October 1949, received the number 1. Numbers have been dispensed in chronological sequence ever since. Green Haven's total population is fairly constant (it may be 1840 one day, 1862 the next, and 1845 the day after) but also, as the number system shows, fairly transient. The first man to arrive at Green Haven in January 1976 received the number 22,988. The last man to arrive there in December 1976 received the number 24,600. As men are paroled from Green Haven, or get out on C.R., or max out, or are transferred to other prisons in the state, other men take their places. All these men are returned parole violators, returned C.R. violators, or transferees from other prisons or from reception-and-classification centers. No one comes to Green Haven directly from court. Malinow has been at Green Haven twice. The first time, he asked to be transferred from Clinton; the second time, he came to Green Haven from Attica, after the riot.

The reception process, a haphazard one, usually involves having a photograph taken, getting an identification card, being given a blood test, being issued green prison uniforms from the state shop, and obtaining certain other basic supplies, such as bedding and a set of earphones for the prison radio system. A Green Haven *Inmate Handbook of Rules and Regulations* was published in 1975 but has long been out of print as well as out of date. "Green Haven's rules change with the weather," Malinow says. New arrivals gradually pick up the latest prison rules, and how best to go about breaking them without getting caught, from inmates who have been at Green Haven for a while. Each new arrival is asked whether he has any enemies in the prison population. If he does, he is transferred elsewhere. There are a number of prisoners in the state who might find it fatal to be in the same prison as their enemies. One man at Green Haven in 1976, a former bodyguard of Malcolm X who was serving time for a string of assaults and robberies, had been at Clinton in 1972. When one of the three men convicted of murdering Malcolm X was transferred from Green Haven to Clinton, in September 1972, a few days after a big fight in a Green Haven yard between two rival groups of black inmates — the People's Party and the followers of Elijah Muhammad (of which he was a leader) — the former bodyguard was dispatched to Green Haven.

By far the most important step in the reception process is an interview with the three-man Classification Committee, which makes job assignments. In addition to the hundred-odd men who work outside the walls (as Nelson and Franklin did) and the hundred-odd who work in the kitchen and the mess halls (as Shea and Gregory did), about three hundred are assigned to work in prison industry. Green Haven has a knit shop (which makes men's, women's, and children's underwear), an upholstery shop, a furniture shop, and an optical shop. Industries seem to come and go at Green Haven, just as prisoners do: in times past, the prison produced brushes and had a thriving textile industry, which employed over six hundred inmates and turned out bolts of cloth, sheets and pillowcases, and American flags. Another three hundred men are assigned to the academic school. Classes include elementary reading and arithmetic (the average prisoner entering Green Haven has an I.Q. of 95 and reads at a fifth-grade level), high-school history and English, and such college subjects as business law and social psychology. About a hundred and eighty men are assigned to the vocational school. Among the trades offered are printing, drafting, and welding. About two hundred and fifty men have jobs as porters, cleaning the cellblocks, the other prison buildings, and the yards. A hundred and fifty hold jobs as clerks. Each cellblock has a clerk, as do various departments — among them the commissary and parole clothing — and certain civilian employees — for example, the Protestant chaplain and the recreation supervisor. Fifty prisoners hold assorted prison-maintenance jobs (as painters, plumbers, masons, electricians, carpenters, sewermen, and repairmen), about twenty work in the prison hospital as nurses and technicians, about twenty are runners (prison messengers), about a dozen work in the tailor shop and the laundry, eight work in the officers' mess, six are assigned to the prison band (it plays before the movie that is shown in the auditorium every Saturday, and at special events sometimes held on Sundays and holidays), and a few men have one-of-a-kind jobs: Green Haven has one cobbler, one man to tend flowers, and one identification-room technician. Despite a considerable amount of featherbedding — it is difficult to imagine how the prison could be dirtier if it had only half the number of porters — Green Haven has an even more serious unemployment problem than the outside world: on a given day, anywhere from ten to twenty percent of the inmates are unemployed. It can take a man a month or two after his arrival at Green Haven to find a job.

The Classification Committee is composed of a sergeant and two civilian prison employees. The classification sergeant is its dominant member. The job a man is given — or, in Department of Correctional Services bureaucratese, the "program" to which he is "assigned" — depends on whom he knows and what he is willing to tell. The sergeant may remember and like a man from a previous stint at Green Haven and give him a good job. A new prisoner whom the sergeant is not acquainted with is likely to be assigned to whatever mundane work position is available that day. His job assignment can be changed later, however. Like all prisons, Green Haven is run with the help of informers — "rats." In 1976, the classification sergeant, a man with a strong personality and a husky build, who is respected by fellow officers, by supervisors, and by most inmates as well, was also known at Green Haven as a one-man C.I.A. When a Neil Shea was caught, he interrogated him; when an Eli Walker was murdered, he was asked to help find the "perpetrator." One way he has of rewarding rats is with jobs.

A man who is an invalid (there are usually about a dozen men at Green Haven suffering from serious heart conditions or crippling arthritis) or one who is unemployed is paid $0.25 a day — or, rather, $0.25 is credited to his inmate account. The other prison jobs, except those in industry, pay from $0.35 a day to $1.15. There are four pay grades, with four or five steps within each grade. A porter's job is a Grade 1 job that starts at $0.35 a day and goes up $0.05 every so often to a maximum of $0.50. A porter may advance to Grade 2 (from $0.55 to $0.70 a day) if he becomes a "feed-up" man — one who transports food from the kitchen to the block for the invalids and to those who are "keeplocked," or confined to their cells for disciplinary reasons. A clerk's job is a Grade 3 or a Grade 4 job that starts at $0.75 a day and increases $0.05 every so often until it reaches the $1.15 maximum. The Department of Correctional Services gives the schools and the kitchen an allotment of jobs in all four grades to distribute — theoretically, according to seniority and merit in the schools and seniority and job importance in the kitchen. In still another D.O.C.S. euphemism, the amount of money an inmate earns a day isn't his pay; it is his "work-incentive allowance." The average salary at Green Haven is $0.55 a day. Malinow is classified as a clerk and earns $1.15 a day in the parole-clothing department.

The best-paying jobs at Green Haven are industry ("the in-dustrial-training program"), where men earn between $0.0625 and $0.2875 an hour. A prisoner can make as much as $11.10 a week in industry. Some men work in the industrial shops during the day, and others during the evening. (Industry is one of only a few jobs done in the evening as well as in the daytime.) A few men at Green Haven regard the prison wages as slave labor and refuse to work. They are locked up in a special area and are paid nothing — not even the minimum $0.25 a day.

Men's motives for taking different jobs vary. Some men work on the farm because they like being outdoors all day rather than cooped up inside. Others, who are afraid of cows, hate fresh air, and plan never to live in the country, work on the farm because they think it will impress the parole board, which seems to regard outside-the-wall workers as "trusties." Some men care about earning money and take day jobs as clerks and evening jobs in industry; their combined earnings can amount to $16.85 a week. Some men choose a job according to the job's fringe benefits. A kitchen worker can eat as much as he pleases and can bake loaves of soft bread for himself every day. (The bread baked daily at Green Haven and served to the prisoners in the mess halls is coarse.) "The most sought-after job at Green Haven is a porter's job," the classification sergeant says. "A porter spends fifteen minutes a day mopping and sweeping. He's free to hang out on the block or go to the yard for the rest of the day. It's a lazy man's job."

As soon as a man has completed the reception process, he is assigned a cell, whether he has been given a job or is still awaiting assignment to one. Although the number of prisoners in New York State has been increasing at the rate of about a hundred a month in the last two years, New York has thus far been able to deal with its inmate population explosion by taking over former Office of Drug Abuse Services treatment centers that have been closed down and converting them into prisons. In all of New York's maximum-security prisons, inmates are housed one to a cell. In states like California and Maryland, inmates have had to double up in cells originally built for one. In numerous southern states, inmates are sleeping in even more crowded conditions — in tents, or on mattresses placed close together on corridor floors, or five men to a one-man cell. The United States began 1976 with more people behind bars than ever before in its history. There were 250,042 people in state and federal prisons on January 1, 1976. By January 1, 1977, the number had increased to 275,578 — the largest one-year jump ever. The increase would have been even greater — to 283,268 — if 7690 men sentenced to prison hadn't been backed up in county jails.

The most imposing buildings at Green Haven are the eight cellblocks, which are 300 feet long, 50 feet wide, and three stories high. Until 1976 (when two of the blocks were renovated), the cellblocks contained 252 cells — 84 per floor, with two rows of 42 cells stacked atop each other on each of the three floors of the block. The rows of cells face in opposite directions, and are separated in back by a five-foot space containing a catwalk. A set of 42 cells is known as a company, and six companies, numbered 1 to 6, make up a block. Although all eight blocks were built at the same time, the four blocks on the west side of the prison, which are lettered A, B, C, and D, are "closed," with twelve feet of floor space between the bars of the cells and the enormous barred windows of the cellblock. The four blocks on the east side of the prison, which are lettered E, F, G, and H, are "open;" that is, only the cells on the ground level have the twelve feet of floor space between the cell bars and the windows. The second and third tiers have five-foot walkways in front of the cells, and these lead to a staircase that goes down to the ground floor. Open blocks, which are rather reminiscent of aviaries, are usually preferred by prison administrations, for security reasons: a guard on the ground-floor tier can hear all the way up to the third-floor tier. Closed blocks are almost invariably preferred by inmates. They are quieter; if an inmate on the first tier is playing his bongo drums, an inmate on the third tier isn't part of his captive audience. They also provide twelve feet of usable space between the cells and the cellblock windows on all three tiers, which the prisoners can take advantage of for various activities. On closed blocks, inmates on the upper tiers (which are also called decks or galleries) can open or shut the windows if the temperature is too hot or cold for their liking, and they can dry their clothes on the steam pipes that run beneath the windows. Until the winter of 1976, a man's job determined his cellblock: farm workers and other outside workers locked on A, a closed block; those attending academic classes locked on B, also closed; kitchen workers locked on D, likewise closed; the six members of the band locked on G, an open block; and the men who worked in industry locked on one of the four east-side blocks, all open. If a man changed his job, he changed his cell location. Until 1976, A and D were considered the prison's honor blocks. (J block, a smaller block added to Green Haven in 1966 and originally intended to house old and infirm prisoners, was also an honor block. It bears little physical resemblance to the eight other blocks. In 1976, most of J block, a two-story structure with mini-rooms rather than cells, was occupied by inmates participating in an experimental diagnostic-and-treatment program to help them understand the reasons for their criminal behavior. The program was recently phased out at Green

Haven.) Whereas inmates on B, E, F, G, and H blocks had no television sets and locked in at five o'clock for the night (unless they had a special six-to-eight-thirty program on certain evenings — for example, Alcoholics Anonymous or night recreation in the gym or the yard), the men on the A and D honor blocks could remain out of their cells until II P.M., and there were three television sets on each block. TV-watching schedules were worked out in advance by the inmates. One set was usually devoted to sports, one to movies, and one to weekly comedies and dramas or specials. Police shows are especially popular at Green Haven, as they are at most prisons around the country. Quite a few Green Haven inmates say they have upgraded their criminal expertise by watching such programs as "Baretta," "Kojak," and "Starsky & Hutch." A- and D-block inmates were also allowed to keep tables on their tiers, where they did hobby work and cooked meals. Electric frying pans, contraband at Green Haven, were overlooked on the honor blocks. Being out of their cells an extra six hours a night gave the A- and D-block inmates more time for taking showers, for doing their personal laundry in the tier's slop sink, and for lollygagging. In early 1976, when Green Haven's officials closed down D block for renovation, they were reminded of the fact that such privileges mean a great deal in prison. D block's inmates were dispersed to other blocks, as space permitted. Two companies of kitchen workers were sent to F block, an open block. The farm and kitchen workers had originally been assigned to A and D, the privileged blocks, because their work was considered harder and dirtier than most jobs in the prison and their working hours were longer. Most of them worked seven days a week rather than the customary five. At Green Haven, the prison's open east side was always regarded as "the ghetto," its closed west side as "the suburbs." Men like Malinow have always succeeded in doing their time at Green Haven on the west side. The kitchen workers didn't want to go to F block, on the east side. They thought that two companies of B-block students should be moved to F. B-block students locked in at five o'clock anyway and weren't entitled to television, so a change to F block would be less drastic for them. It would simply mean a move from a closed to an open block. For the kitchen workers, a move to F meant giving up all of their cherished privileges. There wasn't space on the walkways of F block's two upper levels for tables or TV sets, whereas B block's tiers could have accommodated tables and television. Prison officials didn't want to disrupt B block, and moved the kitchen workers to F block in March 1976. A few days after the move, the workers staged a work slowdown. The officials ignored the slowdown. The kitchen workers remained on F block. On Friday morning, April 2, the mess-hall forks and spoons were used at breakfast. At 11:15, shortly before the main meal of the day was scheduled to begin, it was discovered that most of the prison's silverware was missing. The main meal was served by rewashing and reusing the small amount of silverware that could still be found. A search of the kitchen and the surrounding area was made. Green Haven officials phoned other nearby prisons in an attempt to borrow silverware, and bought plastic forks and spoons for the evening meal. At one o'clock that afternoon, a guard was told by a reliable informer that the silverware had been put in a huge bin with the breakfast garbage. The company that had taken the garbage out had buried the contents of Green Haven's bins several hours earlier, and it was impractical to go digging for silverware amid all the garbage and refuse. Guards on the 7:20 A.M. to 3:20 P.M. shift and several sergeants and civilians were held overtime to search for the missing silverware in the hope that it might still be in the prison. They spent two hours searching in vain. The silverware was never found. The mess-hall silverware episode cost New York State taxpayers a fair amount of money. The estimated twelve hundred missing forks were valued at $413.50, the estimated twelve hundred missing spoons were valued at another $413.50. The state also paid Green Haven's guards, sergeants, and civilians a total of

529 hours of overtime. Malinow described the missing silver-ware incident as "an inventive form of nonviolent protest." An officer whose overtime pay rate was $10.89 an hour said, "It's an ill wind that blows nobody good." In 1976, Green Haven spent over $750,000 on overtime.

In the winter of 1976, Green Haven officials decided that inmates would no longer be housed according to their jobs. If they were assigned to the kitchen from H-block reception, they could be put on B block or on F block. If they transferred from the kitchen to the vocational school, they did not change cells. The only blocks to which they could no longer be assigned from reception were C and D, which became real honor blocks — blocks to which men could gain access only if they met certain criteria.

Until C and D blocks were renovated, at a cost of $1,509,800, all the cells on both the east and the west sides of the prison were the same size. The original cells measure six feet wide, eight feet four inches long, and seven feet nine inches high. Their backs and sides are made of steel plate; the fronts consist of steel bars with barred doors that slide open twenty-five inches. The state furnishes all of these cells identically. They contain a single bed with a metal frame, a foam-rubber mattress, a small sink with cold running water, a small topless toilet, a small metal locker, a stool, a bare bulb in the ceiling, and a three-channel outlet for earphones. (Music, news, and sports selected by the prison's radio room are played on two channels, television sound tracks on the third. Prison announcements are broadcast daily at 5:30 P.M.) The furniture is inevitably shabby, the painted steel walls are usually peeling, and there is little floor space for walking around, especially by the time the inmates have found ways to acquire extra lockers, stools, and other state property and have crammed them into their cells.

When the renovated C block opened, in March 1976, and D block eight months later, they offered the privileges of the old honor blocks, as well as larger and more attractive cells. The cells were the same height and length as those in the other blocks, but they were nearly one and a half times as wide: eight feet, nine inches compared to the six-foot width of the original cells. The beds were comfortable foam-rubber mattresses on steel platforms, the sinks had hot and cold running water (on the regular blocks, inmates are lucky to get two pails of hot water a day from the company's slop sink), and there were additional furnishings — a large double locker, two modern light fixtures, three shelves, a typing table, a contoured chair, a two-foot-by-three-foot cork bulletin board, a wastebasket, and a sixteen-by-twenty-two-inch mirror. "A little thing like a mirror is a real score in prison," George Malinow says. The cells were freshly painted and clean. With only twenty-two men to each company, the galleries and showers were less crowded.

When applications for C block were distributed to Green Haven's population, in early March 1976, Malinow decided to apply. He enjoys novelty, and C block was "a new toy." He met the various criteria for the honor block: he had been at Green Haven for at least six months, had been in state prison for at least a year, hadn't been caught breaking a prison rule for six months, and had held his job for at least three months. He moved to C block in late March. As luck would have it, he was assigned a cell on the "flats" (as the first floor is called), which pleased him because he is not an avid climber of stairs and because the flats are cooler in summer than the two upper tiers. (Green Haven's buildings are not air-conditioned.) His cell was on the side of the block facing the wall rather than the yard, which he also considered an advantage, because the wall side is quieter. The four blocks on the west side of Green Haven are arranged in the shape of a squarish C. They enclose two square prison yards, with ninety thousand square feet of space in each. One yard, called A&B, has a basketball court, a boccie court, a shuffleboard court, punching bags, areas for weight lifting, a volleyball net, two black-and-white television sets, and "spots," with tables and lockers for small groups of inmates who use their turf to play cards, gamble, and hang out. The second yard, C&D, is sparsely equipped, because it is used primarily for softball, football, and jogging. The prisoners in the four cell-blocks can go to either yard. The four east-side blocks are similarly arranged around E&F yard (A&B's counterpart) and G&H (C&D's counterpart). The yards are in use a good part of the day and evening but are busiest between 3:20 P.M. and 4:20 P.M. — after jobs let out and before supper and the obligatory 5:00 P.M. lock-in.

Malinow also found his tiermates congenial. Although C block's residents are not necessarily more law-abiding than the residents of the non-honor blocks, they tend to break prison rules quietly, as Malinow does. There has been none of the drunkenness and assault-prone behavior on C block which is not infrequent on the east-side blocks, especially G. Six months after C block opened, Green Haven officials were tipped off to "an alarming amount of narcotics" throughout the institution, and they conducted a surprise midnight-to-dawn raid on various cellblocks, among them C block. A few of C block's original tenants — those whose cells contained alcohol, marijuana, commercial yeast, or homemade knives — were evicted and were replaced by men on the C-block waiting list.

Malinow was enthusiastic about C block from the day he moved in. He liked the hot water. He is a fastidious man, and when he washed his coffee cup in hot water the stains came right out. The cups he had washed over the years in his many cold-water cells had never come clean. When he put his "dropper" (prison slang for an electric heating coil) into a cup of hot water, it took less time to boil, which was especially nice when he was preparing his first cup of instant coffee in the morning. There were no rats and roaches on C block, as there had been on the other blocks. Best of all was the extra space. Like most men doing "big time," Malinow has accumulated many possessions. Even his one-and-a-half-times-as-wide cell on C block is cluttered. In addition to his state-issued allotment of bedding, towels, and uniforms, Malinow has a considerable quantity of personal property — extra pillows and blankets and odds and ends left to him by departing prisoners, such as a desk lamp and an alarm clock that tells the approximate time but no longer rings. He has about three dozen dress shirts, turtlenecks, and T-shirts in every color of the rainbow except blue. Inmates are forbidden to wear blue, presumably because the guards wear blue shirts and the prisoners might try to escape by impersonating officers. Malinow's lockers also hold three dozen handkerchiefs and a few pairs of shoes, which he has liberated from the parole-clothing department; a few books on subjects that interest him, such as reincarnation, real estate, and navigation; a generous supply of groceries, plastic bowls, thermoses, and other eating utensils; half a dozen hairbrushes and combs; and an array of toilet articles — shampoos, foot powders, and aftershave lotions. On his shelves can be found a box containing his legal papers, a box filled with newspaper stories he has clipped, and the supplies he requires for his two favorite pastimes, glass painting and letter writing: tinfoil, paints, brushes, jars for mixing paints, pads, and ballpoint pens.

In 1973, Malinow acquired a Philippine pen pal named Liwayway Ona, who is thirty years younger than he is. Divorced or not, he plans to marry her soon after his release. He has a box with all of Liwayway's letters and a photograph album with pictures of Liwayway, a comely young woman of twenty-six, and her family and friends. Malinow also corresponds with a few other pen pals and some relatives of present and former inmate friends, whom he refers to as his adopted sisters and brothers, sons and daughters, and nieces and nephews. To save his correspondents embarrassment, Malinow takes care not to let the world know that he is a prisoner. At Green Haven, one must put a return address on the letters one mails out. The customary way of writing this address is:

George Malinow, #17386
Drawer B
Stormville, New York 12582

That isn't the way Malinow does it. He prefers the dollar sign to the capital "S," and writes:

George Malinow
Drawer B — 17386
$tormville, N.Y. 12582

Malinow doesn't do this just when writing to people he doesn't want to have know he's in prison. He does it when writing to friends and pen pals who know exactly where he is. "I don't want my friends to be embarrassed," he says. "Maybe their mailmen don't know they're writing to a prisoner, and maybe they don't want them to know. The way I do it, it looks like a box number."

A plywood toilet-seat cover, made by a friend and painted aqua, and two bright scatter rugs give his cell a homey touch. Pinned to Malinow's bulletin board are photographs of himself and his friends, palms from the Palm Sunday services held at Green Haven's Catholic chapel, and a button that reads "Attica Is All of Us." Malinow is one of the few men at Green Haven without a centerfold pinup from *Playboy* or *Penthouse* or *Hustler* on display in his cell.

A few men at Green Haven write poems about the physical and psychological horrors of cell confinement. They decry the lack of privacy to go to the toilet, the smells from the open toilets, and the block noises — flushing toilets, despondent men crying out in the night, the guards coming down the galleries rattling their keys when they walk up and down to take the 2:00 A.M. and 4:00 A.M. head counts, less to make sure that an inmate isn't sawing through his bars than to make sure an inmate isn't ill or attempting to commit suicide. Malinow is reluctant to criticize other prisoners, but what he calls their "far

37

out" poems obviously do not move him. He isn't particularly embarrassed by the lack of privacy. "We're all men here," he says. "If you're walking down a tier and a man is using the terlet, you use simple good manners and look the other way." He has no trouble sleeping through the night. "If the guards stopped taking the count in the middle of the night, I'd probably miss their footsteps," he says. "I read somewhere that when the 'el' was torn down, people who lived on Third Avenue had a hard time getting used to sleeping without the noise of the trains." A few men at Green Haven engage in photography. Many of their photographs show men's hands gripping cell bars. Malinow says that bars don't bother him and never have, and points out that the paint on the bars at Green Haven isn't worn off at gripping height. He doesn't refer to his cell as a cage. Like most men at Green Haven, he calls his cell his "house." His C-block cell is so spacious that he describes it as his "cell-room."

Although Malinow hates, as a matter of general principle, to agree with the guards about much of anything, he does in one instance. He believes that punishment should be taken manfully. He says, as the guards so often do, "If you can't do the time, don't commit the crime." With a few exceptions, the men at Green Haven seem to be able to do the time, and there are hardly any men with furrowed brows, bent heads, or plaintive eyes to be seen here. Most of the men look healthy and in reasonably good spirits. A great many retain a sense of humor. Last Labor Day, some men on A block were watching the evening news on TV. The newscaster was discussing the crowded traffic conditions on highways throughout New York State. One inmate said to another, "Aren't we lucky to be in here, not facing all those problems? Here I am, sitting at Green Haven, not having to worry that the cars on the Long Island Expressway are backed up for twenty miles." Late one night on C block, as a guard walked past some cells jangling his keys as he took the 11:00 P.M. count, one inmate said, "Here comes the

Good Humor man." Several of Green Haven's officials think that the reason most men at Green Haven keep their sanity is that the saying "Crime does not pay" has not been true in their experience. For many men at Green Haven, it paid very well — better than the legitimate jobs they could have had. Like Malinow, most men have committed many crimes for which they weren't caught. "Going to prison is to a robber what paying insurance is to a store owner," a Green Haven official says. "It's part of the overhead."

Soon after the C-block officer pushes the button that electrically opens the door to Malinow's cellroom, Malinow heads for the parole-clothing department, which is in the basement of the two-story Administration Building, the first building one reaches after going through the prison's front gate. As its name indicates, the Administration Building contains the offices of the men who manage the prison, some of whose titles were among those changed in the great 1970 renaming process. Until 1970, the person in charge of a prison in New York was called a warden. He is now a superintendent. Wardens were men who had started as guards and came up through the ranks by putting in a certain number of years at each level and then taking (and passing) a civil-service examination to advance to the next — sergeant, lieutenant, captain, assistant deputy warden, and warden. Once a man became a warden, he had tenure. He could be brought up on charges for malfeasance and transferred (though he rarely was), but once he had made warden, he remained a warden. From 1949 to 1970, Green Haven had two wardens, Edward M. Fay (1949–65) and Harold W. Follette (1965–70). They both ran the prison with considerable autonomy, enjoyed their jobs, and died, so to speak, in harness. In recent years, the superintendent's powers have been significantly curtailed by countless directives and phone calls from the central office of the Department of Correctional Services, in Albany. There were some days in 1976 when Green Haven's

39

superintendent spent more of his day answering inquiries from Albany than running the prison. In 1975, a few months after Benjamin Ward was appointed commissioner of the D.O.C.S., he succeeded in getting the state legislature to pass a law that took the superintendent's job out of the civil-service category. Superintendents were henceforth to be chosen from among any people in the Department of Correctional Services at or above Grade 27, were to be appointed by the commissioner, and were to serve at his pleasure. Since 1970, partly as a result of the constant intervention by Albany (which the superintendents did not appreciate) and partly as a result of Commissioner Ward's short-lived pleasure with some of his superintendents, there have been either six or seven superintendents at Green Haven. Six if you don't count a man who was appointed superintendent on July 2, 1977, spent several days at Green Haven, and turned down the job; seven if you do. Some of the recent Green Haven superintendents have resigned and retired, one was transferred to Albany, and one was asked to resign and has gone back to the title he held before he was appointed superintendent.

Until 1972, the person immediately under the superintendent was the deputy warden, otherwise known as the principal keeper, and called the P.K. for short. In 1972, in an attempt to make security (keeping) seem less important, the P.K. was replaced by a triumvirate of deputy superintendents ("deps" for short) — a dep of security, a dep of programs, and a dep of administration. At New York State's maximum-security prisons, some deps are more equal than others. At Green Haven, the dep of security is the most equal. The dep of administration concerns himself with the prison budget and the maintenance of the prison. At a recent administrative meeting, Green Haven's dep of administration was preoccupied with the size of the wet-dry vacuums being used to clean the prison kitchen and with the purchase of rubber mats for the block showers. The dep of programs oversees such activities as a weekly ceramics class and the occasional appearance at Green Haven of outside performers. In 1976, a theatre group, a rock singer, and a circus troupe appeared at Green Haven.

The dep of security in 1976 did not think ceramics class was a good idea. He didn't like the looks of the ceramics tools — he regards all pointed things as dangerous weapons. He especially didn't like the clay cutter, a piece of wire with wooden handles on each end, which could easily be used as a garrote. He didn't like the objects the ceramics students were making, either. The busts or heads, he said, could be used to make dummies, and dummies were not what he needed in a maximum-security prison. The idols the ceramics students produced had hidden cavities for concealing and transporting contraband. The ceramics program didn't last long at Green Haven. "After Attica, there was a lot of lip service paid to programs, but security is still the name of the game," Malinow says. The dep of security is responsible for the day-to-day operation of the prison's custodial services. He is much closer than the two other deps to the superintendent, to the inmates, and to the uniformed staff.

Green Haven's 479 blue-shirted guards are presided over by 39 white-shirted supervisors — 1 captain, 9 lieutenants, and 29 sergeants, a number of whom also have desks in the Administration Building. One of these men, perhaps the most harassed person at Green Haven, is the daytime chart sergeant, who (with the assistance of two chart officers) has to see to it that he has an officer to cover each essential post at the prison. The 479 guards work one of five different shifts — 7:20 A.M. to 3:20 P.M., 9:45 A.M. to 5:45 P.M., 1 P.M. to 9 P.M., 3:20 P.M. to 11:20 P.M., and 11:20 P.M. to 7:20 A.M. — with more men, of course, assigned to the day shifts (when the inmates are out of their cells) and fewer to the evening and night shifts (when most, and eventually all, inmates are locked in). A few officers are fortunate enough to work from Monday to Friday with every weekend off, but most are divided into seven squads, with each squad working a cycle of six days on and two weekdays off four times in a row; then six days on and three days off once; and then five days on and three days off once. The first set of three days off is a Friday, Saturday, and Sunday; the second set is a Saturday, Sunday, and Monday. The cycle is set up to give each man two weekends off every seven weeks. The men follow equally complicated vacation schedules and, in addition to their regular days off (R.D.O.s) and vacation days, are allowed five days a year of personal leave time (P.L.T.) and thirteen days a year of sick leave.

Most men on each shift — say, the busy 7:20 to 3:20 shift — do the same job every working day. The man who has Tower 1 is always on Tower 1, the man who has Tower 4 is always on Tower 4. Two men always ride the same two horses on guard duty at the farm. When they are off, their horses are off. Other men always work on a certain block or in the hospital. One man has the hobby shop, one is assigned to the prison correspondence room. The chart sergeant has only a dozen or so "miscellaneous" officers whom he may assign wherever he needs them. Although the chart sergeant plans relief for all of the men on their R.D.O.s (a third horse is even kept at the farm for the man who relieves the mounted guards on their days off) and although he anticipates that a certain number of men will be out sick or on personal leave, there are always more men out than he anticipates and more spur-of-the-moment jobs that come up than the miscellaneous men can fill. Inevitably, just on the day when a car pool from New York City with five guards fails to reach Green Haven because the car has broken down on the Taconic State Parkway, a doctor orders round-the-clock guards for a man who has attempted suicide, an inmate is stabbed and must be taken to an outside hospital and also guarded around the clock, and a guard is hit by an inmate and leaves the prison to see his doctor. There are some posts the chart sergeant cannot close — there must always be at least two men on a block — and some he can close, like the correspondence room or the hobby shop. After the chart sergeant has closed all the nonessential posts, he still often has to get guards from other shifts to work overtime, sometimes willingly, sometimes reluctantly. There are never more than two hundred officers at Green Haven at any one time — and then only from 9:45 A.M. to 3:20 P.M., when three shifts overlap — and they are spread pretty thin. The chart sergeant's face shows that he has spent too many days robbing Peter to pay Paul.

A good number of Green Haven's 279 civilian employees also work in the Administration Building, among them the prison's seven parole officers, its eighteen Service Unit counselors (whose job, according to the D.O.C.S., is to provide "problem solving and counseling service to the inmate population"), and numerous clerks who work on inmates' accounts, process their legal work, and deal with their yellow (P.K.) record cards and plump record folders. The Administration Building also contains certain important objects — for example, the adding machine on which the prison's various counts are tabulated and the time clock on which the guards and civilians punch in and out, not to mention the impressive collection of keys and weapons kept in the prison arsenal. No employees are permitted to bring guns inside the prison; any weapon they might carry might be seized and used against them. Several generations of newspaper feature writers have likened New York's maximum-security prisons to walled cities; many of them have found it irresistible to call them "cities of hope," with the cities' residents hoping for freedom. Green Haven's most hope-filled room is also in the Administration Building. It is a large room in which three members of New York State's twelve-member parole board meet for a week each month. A New York State judge also holds court in the room one day a month to hear the ever-increasing number of habeas-corpus petitions filed by prisoners (often prepared with the help of "jailhouse lawyers" — inmates who have made themselves knowledgeable in the law) whose hopes have been dashed by the parole board. In

43

these petitions, the inmates contend, sometimes successfully, that they are being illegally detained by the unreasonable decisions handed down by the parole board.

Five rooms in the Administration Building offer Green Haven's prisoners their primary contacts with their families and friends on the outside. In the phone room, inmates are allowed to place two six-minute collect calls each month to people on their approved phone lists. A handful of civilians (and an officer when one is available) in the correspondence room open the inmates' incoming mail and inspect it for cash and other contraband. (Inmates are allowed to seal and mail letters going out of the prison.) Each inmate at Green Haven is permitted to receive two packages a month, weighing a total of thirty-five pounds, from people on his approved visiting list. These packages, which may be mailed in or brought in on visits, are opened for inspection in the package room. They may contain a variety of food, clothes, toilet articles, and sundries (dominoes, pipes, snuff), and up to five cartons of cigarettes and a hundred cigars a month; cigarettes are limited not for possible hazards to the prisoners' health but because they are used as currency — for example, in betting on prison and outside ballgames. "If a prisoner dies of cancer, that's his business, but if he's taken off the count for welching on a gambling debt, it's my business," a Green Haven sergeant says. In April 1977, an inmate was murdered by another inmate at Green Haven as a result of a gambling debt. Until 1975, when the package room got a fluoroscope machine, an officer poked his way through the incoming packages, searching for cash, guns, and drugs. Now he gives the package a once-over-lightly, puts it into the fluoroscope, and looks for objects such as guns and money on the screen. Not long ago, a dollar bill placed on a tinfoil tray that held some homemade Southern-fried chicken didn't show up on the fluoroscope screen. The package-room officer admitted he was far too busy to search the packages properly; he said he didn't have time, for example, to check individual tea bags, because the volume of packages was too great. He simply looks at the cellophane wrapping that encases the box of tea bags to see whether it is intact. "Tea bags are often used for smuggling dope into Green Haven," Malinow says.

Two of the prison's visiting rooms are also in the Administration Building — the "old" visiting room and the "new" visiting room, which was added on to Green Haven in 1976, at a cost of $425,753, to relieve weekend congestion in the old visiting room.

To visit an inmate at Green Haven, a person must be on the inmate's visiting list (getting on the list is a simple matter of filling out a form) and must, some weekends, wait in line for several hours before submitting to an entrance procedure that takes about ten or fifteen minutes. A visitor first walks up the stairs built into the prison wall and enters a large, glassy room that protrudes from the prison wall at the front, or north, side of the prison. The reception room was added on to Green Haven in 1976, at a cost of $325,985. Several guards are assigned to process visitors in the reception room. A visitor must first give the name and number of the inmate he wishes to see and must properly identify himself (a driver's license, a birth certificate, or a current credit card will do). A guard then checks the inmate's visit card to see if the visitor is on his list and if the prisoner is within his allotted number of monthly visits: each inmate at Green Haven may receive fifteen visits a month, no more than four of them on Saturdays and Sundays, the remaining eleven on weekdays. As many as four adults and an unlimited number of children may be counted as one visit, as long as they arrive and depart together. A visitor who has been duly verified will be given a slip of white paper on which he must write his name, his address, his relationship to the prisoner, and his signature — which will be compared to the signature he was required to put on the prisoner's visit card on his initial visit. This slip of paper, which specifies whether the visit is to take place in the old or the new visiting room, must later be presented to the visiting-room officer, and, upon departure, retrieved and returned to the reception-room officer. Visitors may leave packages (which will later be searched in the package room) at a package counter in the reception room. At another counter, known as the frisk table, a guard delves through women's pocketbooks, confiscating whatever contraband he finds. All medication is contraband — even aspirin — and so are daily newspapers, and must be left in the reception area and retrieved on the visitor's way out. Visitors have to remove their coats (which are searched) and walk through a metal detector, which is much more sensitive than the walk-through metal detectors used by airlines to foil hijackers: even a bracelet or the tinfoil in a pack of cigarettes will set it off, so a man usually finds it necessary to empty his pockets of keys, change, and cigarettes, and a woman to remove her jewelry before walking through. When the metal detector is broken, as it occasionally is, the guards pretend it isn't. They send visitors through it, tell them they've set off the machine, suggest they remove their metal-buckled shoes or their earrings, and send them on their way. Visitors who have met the metal detector's high standards — or the guards' imaginary ones — get their left hands stamped by a guard. The invisible-ink stamp varies from week to week. It is sometimes a star, sometimes a smiling face, and sometimes it has a seasonal motif: a turkey in late November, a Santa Claus in late December. A guard who sits behind a bulletproof glass window then presses a button that opens a door leading to a small, enclosed passageway. Visitors are required to put their left hands under an ultraviolet light (they do so again as they leave Green Haven) before the guard will open a barred gate, which takes the visitor into a hallway and then back into the open air, this time inside the prison wall. The visitor crosses a roadway that runs along the inside perimeter of the prison, walks up a flight of stairs, opens an unlocked door, and finds himself in the lobby of the Administration Building, where he may deposit money in an inmate's account if he wishes to. He is then admitted through a locked gate to the old visiting room or through a locked door to the new visiting room. Meanwhile, a reception-area officer has already informed the Administration Building corridor to expect the inmate. Upon receiving the visiting slip from the visitor, the visiting-room officer calls the inmate's block and tells the block officer of the pending visit. The block officer issues the inmate a pink visiting-room pass. The inmate walks from his block to the Administration Building, is pat-frisked at the corridor, and is then free to enter one of the visiting rooms. (Inmates are strip-frisked after they have completed their visits.)

The old visiting room is furnished with a long table in the shape of an M. Visitors sit on the outside of the table, inmates on the inside. A guard seated at a raised desk presides over the room to see that embracing is kept within what he considers reasonable limits and that nothing is passed to and fro. Visitors may bring cash into the prison and may use it to buy food, coffee, and soft drinks from the visiting rooms' vending machines. The new visiting room (which inmates who haven't been caught breaking prison rules for ninety days are eligible to use) is furnished with tables and plastic chairs and has a small, outside fenced yard. Guards assigned to both visiting rooms have described their days as "eight hours of watching R-rated movies." Every so often, an inmate is locked up for an X-rated sexual act. In September 1976, an inmate lost sixty days of good time for "fondling a female visitor" (a G-rated way of putting it) in the new visiting room. In 1977, two television cameras were installed in the old visiting room to further deter the inmates from making love to their visitors or receiving contraband from them. Three television screens were installed in the office of the deputy superintendent of security. If a lieutenant assigned to the dep's office is monitoring the pictures on two of the screens and sees too much exposed flesh, he may push a button and record the scene on videotape. The videotape can be used as evidence in a disciplinary proceeding. "If a guy's mother is visiting him and another inmate is making out with his girl, that causes fights," the lieutenant explains. What the lieutenant doesn't explain is that he also puts the videotape to another use: running and rerunning the sexiest visiting-room scenes on the third screen for his own pleasure.

The two visiting rooms in the Administration Building are the only places open for visiting on weekdays. On weekends and holidays, certain inmates may receive visits in an outside-the-walls visiting room. To qualify for the outside visiting room, which opened in 1974, an inmate either must work outside the walls or must have successfully completed a furlough. Malinow was working inside in 1974 and has never received a furlough, but he had worked in the superintendent's house outside the walls for a while in 1972 and that — or a bureaucratic oversight — got him the outside-visiting-room privilege. Malinow's two faithful visitors are Patrick Halloran, his 1966 "crime partner," and Carl Terra, a former Green Haven inmate, who come up from the city about one Saturday a month. Malinow prefers receiving his visits in the outside visiting room, where he finds the atmosphere more congenial. Visitors are allowed to bring food in, and inmates may eat with their guests at picnic tables. There are swings for children and a yard for strolling. In recent years, picnics have been held at Green Haven on Sundays. In bad weather, they are held in the gym. In good weather, they are held on Warden Edward M. Fay Memorial Athletic Field, which is otherwise used for prison softball and football games. Each block has an annual picnic and so do many organizations, including the Holy Name Society (of which Malinow was elected president in 1976) and the Jaycees (of which Malinow is a member), as well as many ethnic groups: the Puerto Ricans have a picnic to celebrate San Juan Bautista Day, the blacks have one in honor of Black Solidarity Day, the Italians hold an annual Italian-culture picnic. Each inmate is entitled to attend at least two picnics a year. (Some contrive to attend many more.) He may invite two visitors to each picnic and must pay five to ten dollars to defray the cost of the visitors' food and drinks. As many as three hundred inmates and six hundred visitors are packed into Fay Field on Sundays. On picnic days, visitors are processed at the prison's misnamed rear gate (it is actually its side gate) rather than at its front gate. Five or six officers process the visitors in a small shack. Tempers are frequently lost as a result of the two-to-four-hour waits to get in, and there are often unpleasant incidents, with visitors pushing and shoving one another and hurling obscenities as well as punches at the guards.

If the inmates would like a larger rear-gate shack and more guards assigned to process their picnic guests, they are pleased that only seven or eight guards are available to observe them on Fay Field, where many tables covered with tablecloths are set up in advance for small groups of inmates and guests. While the prison band plays for dancing, some men dine at the tables alfresco while others make love under the protective covering of the tablecloths. A number of men at Green Haven become fathers nine months after attending picnics on Fay Field. When the picnics end, the guards are so busy checking departing visitors (to make sure that no inmates have traded places with them) that they rarely have time to pat-frisk the prisoners, much less to strip-frisk them. The post-picnic failure to frisk is one of the many ironies at Green Haven, since prison officials and inmates alike admit that more contraband is brought into Green Haven on picnic days than at any other time.

A small number of men at Green Haven receive all the fifteen monthly visits to which they are entitled. The rest, like Malinow, do not. The families and friends of most of Green Haven's inmates are poor, only a few own cars, and the round-trip bus fare from New York City is $13.75 on weekdays and $7.80 on weekends. Overnight lodgings near Green Haven are limited, and cab fares between the prison and the nearest motels are high. Still, Green Haven is closer to the city than any of the state's other maximum-security prisons. In 1976, Green

49

Haven's inmates received over forty thousand visits — an average of about twenty a year apiece — which was more than twice as many visitors as inmates at either Auburn or Great Meadow received.

In 1976, six women were arrested during routine entrance frisks for trying to introduce contraband into Green Haven; one had brought her husband some vodka, two were trying to smuggle clothing into the prison, and three were carrying marijuana. That this was just "the tip of the iceberg," as inmates and prison officials admitted, became apparent early in 1977. On January 13, two guards assigned to the old visiting room found an inmate and his wife acting in a peculiar manner; they seemed "high." The inmate refused to submit to blood, urine, or breath tests. His wife was searched by one of the three female guards then employed at Green Haven, who found two plastic containers in her pocketbook. One was empty, one had a small amount of alcohol in it. The woman, who was arrested and charged with promoting prison contraband, admitted that she had been bringing alcohol into Green Haven for about two months, and that the containers had been on her person rather than in her pocketbook when she had brought them in earlier that day. The metal detector had, of course, failed to detect them.

On January 6, 1977, while doing a routine entrance search on a Mrs. Cynthia Lawton, who had come to Green Haven to see her husband, Jeffrey Lawton, a reception-room guard found a .25-calibre loaded automatic pistol wrapped in a handkerchief at the bottom of her pocketbook. Mrs. Lawton was arrested and banned from the prison. On January 16, 1977, Jeffrey Lawton received a visit from someone else. After his visit, he stopped to pick up a package his visitor had brought him and was attacked near the package room by "unknown assailants." Prison officials investigated and learned that Lawton was heavily involved in contraband coming in through the visiting room. Mrs. Lawton, it seemed, had been bringing narcotics in regularly on her visits. After her arrest, Lawton could no longer produce reefers from the visiting room, thus the attack. Before the end of January 1977, three more visitors were caught trying to bring marijuana and methadone into Green Haven.

The guards assigned to the reception area, the majority of whom are white, are suspicious of visitors, the majority of whom are black, and are frequently hostile to them. They make no attempt to hide their racism from people who might not share it. One weekday morning in 1976, the daily bus from New York City reached Green Haven. Its passengers, almost all of whom were black women, began to disembark. A guard looked out the expanse of windows in the reception room and said, "The African Queen has just pulled in. Here come the Zulus." The reception-room officers do not care for the two or three rich, elderly white men who visit their sons at Green Haven, either, although they are polite to their faces. They make remarks about them after they have processed them ("He should probably be locked up, too") and on occasion help themselves to some of the expensive cigars, cold cuts, and pieces of fruit the fathers have brought their sons before sending the packages in to the package room. It is harder to tell, as the guards go about their business of rummaging through visitors' handbags and stamping their hands, if they sense the futility of a good deal of their work. Surely they must know the metal detector's limitations, even when it is working. Surely they must suspect that the visitors who provided Wilkes and Gaynor with their getaway robes were apparently able to transfer the hand stamps from their hands to Wilkes' and Gaynor's. If they do, they never let on.

Directly behind the Administration Building — the only building the great majority of visitors to Green Haven ever see — are three buildings, in the space between the east-side blocks and the west-side blocks. The first of these is the four-story Hospital-Segregation Building, the most controversial building at Green Haven.

The prison's seventy-bed hospital is on the second floor. Half of its space is for inmates who are physically ill; there is a large ward and a number of small rooms for those with upper-respiratory infections or other contagious diseases. The other half of the hospital is for inmates who are mentally disturbed. Some are disoriented, some hear voices, others talk to themselves (thereby irritating their cell neighbors and thus endangering themselves), some have attempted suicide. In 1976, fourteen men tried to kill themselves at Green Haven. Their motives were quite specific, as far as the prison doctors, nurses, and officials could determine — not general anguish over being imprisoned, although depression over prison life is not ruled out as a contributing factor. One inmate didn't like the block he was on and wanted to be switched, a second was scheduled to be transferred to another prison and preferred to stay at Green Haven, a third wanted a tranquillizer a doctor at Green Haven refused to prescribe. Each thought that cutting his wrists would be the best way to call attention to himself. None of the attempts was serious. The last two successful suicides at Green Haven occurred in 1973.

In 1976, Green Haven had no full-time psychiatrists; the New York State Department of Mental Hygiene provided the prison with several part-time psychiatrists, who spent most of their time at Green Haven conducting brief, mandatory pre-parole and pre-furlough interviews, or seeing inmates who had attempted suicide or who had behaved violently. Most of the psychiatrists are foreigners; the inmates have trouble understanding them, and vice versa. In one 1976 pre-parole interview, an Indian psychiatrist, who was obviously more familiar with the street argot of Calcutta than that of New York City, asked an inmate to explain the circumstances of his crime. "Me and these cats were sitting in a bar minding our own business," the inmate began. "We don't talk about cats here, we talk about people," the psychiatrist interrupted. One evening, another psychiatrist came in. He was scheduled to see four men for pre-parole and pre-furlough interviews. A sergeant had the men assembled waiting to see the psychiatrist and had their record folders in his hands. The psychiatrist said he had time to see only three men, and took the top three folders from the sergeant. The man whose folder was on the bottom was eligible for a furlough before one of the three others, who offered to give up his interview for the fourth man. The psychiatrist refused to trade folders. The sergeant interceded for the fourth man. The psychiatrist again refused. The five-minute interviews are considered a worthless formality. A man at Green Haven who wants to see a psychiatrist to discuss a problem may have to wait many months.

There are three doctors at Green Haven — an elderly American and two middle-aged foreigners — and they work at the prison from 8 A.M. to 3 P.M. Monday to Friday; one of them is on call after 3 P.M. and on weekends and holidays. Two dentists and a pharmacist also work at the prison on weekdays from eight to three. Two or three of Green Haven's seven nurses work the day shift; one is always on the 3:20 P.M. to 11:20 P.M. shift, one on the 11:20 P.M. to 7:20 A.M. shift.

There are three ways (other than by attempting suicide) that an inmate at Green Haven can be certain of receiving medical attention. If he gets hurt (as a result of a piping, a stabbing, a football game, or a volleyball game), he will be taken to the prison's first-aid room. Inmates with minor injuries are treated at Green Haven. Those with serious injuries are given emergency first aid and are taken by ambulance to a hospital in Poughkeepsie or in one of the other towns near the prison. If an inmate is scheduled to appear before the parole board, he also must be examined by a doctor. These mandatory pre-parole physicals are cursory stick-out-your-tongue, cough, stethoscope-to-the-chest, blood-pressure-taking affairs. A third way for an inmate to see a doctor is to go to sick call, which is held each weekday morning at Green Haven on the first floor of the Hospital-Segregation Building. If an inmate just wants some cough medicine, vitamins, or cold capsules, he can get in line to see the pharmacist. If he is in pain or wants a prescription filled or renewed, he gets in line to see a doctor. Sometimes the doctor prescribes pills without examining the inmate. Sometimes he tells the inmate, "I don't see the pain," and dismisses him. Sometimes he does a physical examination, makes a diagnosis, and either tells the inmate there is nothing the matter with him, or writes out a prescription, or sends him to the prison hospital, or puts him on one of the lists to see an outside specialist. Cysts can be lanced at Green Haven and X-rays can be taken, if the prison's X-ray equipment is functioning (it was broken for many weeks in 1976), but Green Haven has no facilities for performing serious operations. The waiting lists to see an outside specialist or to have elective surgery are long: it can take months for an inmate with a skin problem to get to a dermatologist. No regular checkups are given at Green Haven.

It is the opinion of Green Haven's pharmacist that most of the hundred to two hundred men who come to sick call on an average weekday are in good health. He believes they come to sick call to get out of their work assignments or to meet friends from the other side of the prison whom they don't usually have a chance to see. If a man is keeplocked, he can get out of his cell to go to sick call or to receive a visit — he can't go to the yard or even to religious services — so keeplocks often ask to go on sick call. Whenever the prison is closed down by an inmate strike or for an administration search, the number of inmates who ask to go to sick call rises dramatically. The pharmacist also believes that many men ask to see dermatologists because they are bored at Green Haven and want to take a ride, "to get out and see the trees," and the only way they have of going for a ride is to visit an outside doctor. He says that in a normal community of eighteen hundred people a hundred and fifty people do not ask for medical treatment every day.

Malinow, who rarely goes to sick call, believes that there is a lot of truth in what the pharmacist says. He adds that there are a few men who genuinely need an outside specialist's care, a few who keep going to sick call because the doctors have not pursued and diagnosed the cause of their pains and the pains have persisted, and a few who have died of cancer because they were mistakenly diagnosed as hypochondriacs. For good measure, he suggests that Green Haven is not a normal community.

Medical care has been a sore subject at Green Haven ever since the prison opened. On October 28, 1949, eight days after Green Haven received its first inmate, a diabetic prisoner died as a result of going four days without insulin. There was no insulin on hand at the time of his transfer there. His mother sued and was awarded $23,921. Inmates have been complaining about the quality of the medical care they receive at Green Haven ever since. In 1972, two inmates died within a short period of time. The inmates blamed the deaths on the indifference of a prison doctor. He had been phoned about one man's condition during the night and had said it was all right to leave him in his cell, he would see the man in the morning. The man was found dead in his cell before the doctor got there the next morning. Several hundred inmates showed up at sick call a few days later, thinking that would be the best way to bring about the doctor's resignation. It was. The doctor was taken out of the prison by a back route — to avoid an encounter with the prisoners assembled in the hospital corridor — and never returned. A jury recently awarded five thousand dollars to an inmate who had sued two doctors at Attica for having intentionally disregarded his medical complaints. In 1977, a federal judge ruled that the women imprisoned at Bedford Hills were being denied the medical care to which they were entitled, and that this inadequate medical care constituted "deliberate indifference" to their health needs. He ordered the lawyers in the case to meet to work out an agreement for improved sick-call procedures, follow-up reports on laboratory tests, and speedier access to physicians. There have been no successful lawsuits lately over the medical care at Green Haven, but inmates and officers alike are critical of the attitudes of two of the prison's three doctors. The elderly American is considered a competent diagnostician but a very gruff-natured man. One of the two foreigners is so afraid of inmates that he insists on having a guard in the room with him when he examines them.

Malinow has had no bad personal experiences with the doctors at Green Haven. Perhaps because his sick-call card shows that he goes to sick call so infrequently, he is treated considerately when he does go. He is convinced, however, that prison doctors are for the most part mediocre. If they were topnotch, why would they spend any of their time working for the state instead of in a more lucrative private practice? "You don't get a Cadillac for the price of a Volkswagen," he says. A Green Haven guard's reaction to statements like Malinow's is "If you want topnotch doctors, don't come to prison." Both Malinow and the guard agree that Green Haven's medical care is better than it used to be. It wasn't until 1962 that Green Haven got a nurse on the 11:20 P.M. to 7:20 A.M. shift. Some years later, a relief nurse was hired for the shift on the regular night nurse's nights off. And before 1972, unless they were seriously ill, no inmates were taken to see outside specialists and the trees.

On the third floor of the Hospital-Segregation Building is the Special Housing Unit, commonly referred to by everyone at Green Haven as "segregation" or "seg" or "the box" and sometimes, by inmates, as "the hole." Three hundred ten men spent time in seg at Green Haven in 1976. One hundred ninety-five of them were put there for disciplinary reasons.

If a guard (or, on rare occasions, a civilian) catches an inmate breaking a minor prison regulation, he may give him a verbal dressing down or he may write up an infraction slip. If the inmate doesn't get another infraction slip within ninety days, he usually isn't punished. The infraction is simply noted on his record card for future reference. There were 6422 infraction slips at Green Haven in 1976, for such misdeeds as having an untidy cell, spitting on the floor, and having a tape player on too loud.

If an inmate gets a second infraction slip within ninety days, or if he is caught breaking a more serious prison rule — for example, if he lies to a guard or is found "out of place" (in a part of the prison where he is not supposed to be) — the guard (or again, in rare instances, the civilian) writes up a misbehavior report. In many cases, if the inmate is charged with a second infraction within ninety days or with breaking a serious rule, he is keeplocked in his cell. When an inmate is written up for a really serious offense — if, for example, he has assaulted a guard or another prisoner — he is taken to seg and locked up there. In either case, he will be taken to the next scheduled meeting of Green Haven's Adjustment Committee, the prison disciplinary committee, which meets in a small room in the Hospital-Segregation Building from 1:00 P.M. to 2:30 P.M. on weekdays. The Adjustment Committee is composed of a lieutenant, an officer, and a civilian employee. As prisoners (some contrite, some belligerent) are brought in, one at a time, the lieutenant (who dominates the committee) looks at the prisoner's P.K. card, which lists his previous infractions and misbehavior reports at Green Haven and the other prisons where he has done time. He then reads the current misbehavior report and invites the prisoner to comment. A few (very few) prisoners simply plead guilty as charged. "You got me," a prisoner recently told the Adjustment Committee lieutenant, who couldn't conceal his surprise. A few deny the charges. "Me and Dunn wasn't committing no homosexual act on the cell bars. We was discussing a legal case." Most admit to a variation of the charge: "Yeah, well, the officer found the marijuana in my cell but it wasn't mine, and I didn't know it was there." If the lieutenant asks whose it might have been, chances are that the prisoner "really don't know." If he ventures that it might have belonged to Jimmy, it is invariably the case that Jimmy went home "yesterday."

Sometimes the lieutenant accepts a prisoner's explanation. If, for example, the prisoner is newly arrived from Auburn and was written up for doing something at Green Haven that was permissible at Auburn, he might be let off with a warning to learn Green Haven's rules and ordered released from keeplock, with "reasonable explanation" noted next to the offense on his P.K. card. If the lieutenant finds him guilty as charged of this particular incidence of misbehavior but sees that the inmate has stayed out of trouble for several years, he may be given a break and released. If he is guilty but is one of the lieutenant's informers — or an informer for one of the lieutenant's colleagues — he may also be released. This is especially irritating to a young block officer who has written up a prisoner on a serious offense; it undermines his authority. Most men who go to the Adjustment Committee are found guilty and are punished. Common sentences include a week or two of keeplock or the loss of some privileges or both — for example, no yard for a week. Prisoners complain less about the sentences doled out by the Adjustment Committee than about the fact that they are keeplocked before they see the committee. If an inmate is written up on Friday morning, too late to see the Adjustment Committee that afternoon, he will have spent the weekend in his cell and thus have been punished even if the Adjustment Committee absolves him and lets him loose on Monday. Once in a great while, the lieutenant learns from his informers that the inmate charged with harboring marijuana really *didn't* know that it had been put in his cell by others for safekeeping, and is truly innocent.

The prisoners also complain that Green Haven is a very inconsistent place. An officer will lock a man up on Thursday for something he — or another officer — permitted him to do on Wednesday. Men who have transferred to Green Haven from more rigorous but more consistent prisons, like Clinton, because of Green Haven's proximity to their families in New York City, say that Green Haven's officers are "sometimey" and wish that Clinton could be moved to Dutchess County and Green Haven relocated up near the Canadian border. In 1976, the Adjustment Committee heard 3942 cases and disposed of most of them. Only the most serious offenses — among them the assaults, the escapes, the possession of drugs or cash — were referred to a superintendent's proceeding. A superintendent's proceeding is conducted by the captain or one of the three deps but never by the superintendent. There were 432 superintendent's proceedings at Green Haven in 1976, and most men charged were found guilty. The sentences they received were usually more severe than those given by the Adjustment Committee. Such sentences often included a certain number of days in segregation as well as a certain number of days' loss of good time (Franklin, for example, got sixty days in seg as well as a hundred and eighty days' loss of good time for his escape) and a longer loss of privileges — thirty days' loss of packages, forty-five days' loss of night rec — and perhaps the loss of a job or a transfer to another prison. Some of the most serious offenses — escapes and assaults on officers — also bring outside charges. Franklin was later sentenced to fifteen years to life for his escape.

Malinow is fortunate enough not to have been caught breaking a prison rule since November 1971, when he was found drinking liquor with a friend in one of the prison yards, but in 1976 his nephew, William Muller, was one of the 432 who had a superintendent's proceeding and spent some time in seg. In August of that year, Muller, who was working as the gym carpenter at Green Haven, was accused of stealing wood from the gym lumberyard. Muller hadn't stolen the wood; an unemployed inmate named Jesse Calhoun, who had been hanging out in the gym lumberyard, was the culprit. Muller had given Calhoun a little wood because he felt sorry for him. Calhoun had had his larynx removed, and spoke in a whisper. Muller had also lent Calhoun the key to his workbench while he was keeplocked in late July for getting into a minor scrape. Calhoun had betrayed Muller's trust by stealing more wood than the prison's recreation supervisor could conveniently overlook — fifty two-by-fours, which he had used to make boxes to sell to other inmates for their weightlifting equipment. To add insult to injury, Calhoun had also taken some of Muller's personal belongings from his workbench while he was keeplocked. On Saturday morning, August 14, soon after he was released from keeplock, Muller confronted Calhoun with the thefts in the gym lumberyard and ordered him out of the yard. Calhoun pulled a fifteen-inch screwdriver out of his back pocket. Muller armed himself with a wood chisel but was able to grab the screwdriver away from Calhoun before he could use it. Muller bent the screwdriver over his knee and tossed the screwdriver and the chisel aside. Calhoun then picked up a six-foot two-by-two from the gym woodpile, whereupon Muller rearmed himself with a seven-foot aluminum tent pole. Calhoun swung his piece of wood, breaking it on Muller's aluminum pole. As Calhoun ran to the woodpile to get another piece of wood, Muller let him have it with the aluminum pole. Calhoun went down, hitting the woodpile. Muller jumped on top of him, punched him in the face, and was about to punch him again when a guard intervened, saving Calhoun from very serious injury or worse. Calhoun was taken by ambulance to a nearby hospital. His head, hand, and arms required sixteen stitches.

Muller spent seven days in segregation before he was taken to a superintendent's proceeding. The lieutenant in charge of investigating the incident had learned during that time that Calhoun had been stealing wood, just as Muller had claimed, and that Muller had been catching the blame, so Muller was given a light sentence, considering the severity of the assault: thirty days in segregation, suspended, and ninety days' loss of commissary privileges. He also lost his job as the gym carpenter and was reassigned to work as a yard porter. At his superintendent's proceeding, a stitched-up Calhoun got fifteen days in seg, suspended, lost his commissary privileges for forty-five days, and was referred to the Classification Committee for a job.

In addition to the 195 men who were sent to seg for disciplinary reasons, 115 men were sent to segregation for protection. Seventy-four went to seg voluntarily for protection. Several inmates who couldn't pay off their gambling debts and were afraid of getting beaten up asked to be put in seg, and so did a couple of inmates to whom sexual overtures, accompanied by threats of bodily harm, had been made. One inmate, who had successfully passed himself off as a robber and had been accepted as a friend by other robbers, was recognized by a new arrival as a child molester. The robbers who had befriended him were fighting mad. The child molester sought refuge in segregation. So did an inmate who had passed himself off as a "straight" and was discovered to be an informer. Malinow has never requested protective custody in all his years in prison, and regards those who do as "weak types of individuals — rats or punks who aren't to be trusted." The forty-one other men were sent to seg either for mental observation (for those who are prone to commit assaults, seg is an alternative to the mental side of the hospital) or for involuntary protection. Sometimes an inmate doesn't appreciate the danger he faces within the population and won't agree to go to segregation voluntarily. If the prison administration thinks his chances of staying alive will be enhanced by being put in seg, he will be put there against his wishes.

One of the men who needed the safe refuge of segregation most at Green Haven in 1976 was a black inmate named Scott Besson. On Sunday, May 30, at about 12:30 P.M., Tony Pagano, a white inmate who had been convicted of second-degree murder in 1961, had a visit from Thelma Marino, the wife of one of his friends, in the outside visiting room. Mrs. Marino went to the ladies' room, where she found Scott Besson having sexual intercourse with his visitor, a white woman. Besson cursed her for intruding on him. Mrs. Marino came out of the ladies' room upset by what she had seen and heard, and told Pagano. Pagano waited for Besson to come out of the ladies' room and asked him to step into the men's room, where he punched him in the mouth for having embarrassed and insulted Mrs. Marino. Besson came out of the bathroom with a bleeding lip, went to one of the guards assigned to the outside visiting room, and told him that someone had opened the bathroom door suddenly and that it had hit his lip. This was in the best prison tradition: it is extraordinary how many men incur facial injuries by running into doors or by tripping over their own feet while dancing to "Soul Train" in a given year at Green Haven. Besson was sent up to the hospital for a bandage. He soon came back outside and finished his visit.

Both Besson and Pagano locked on A block — Pagano in 3 Company (the third floor of one side of the block), Besson in 5 Company (the second floor of the other side of the block). When Besson returned to A block, some of the black inmates had already heard that something untoward had occurred in the visiting room. When they pressed Besson for an explanation, he didn't tell his friends what had happened, possibly because he knew that A block's inmates, all of whom were outside workers, valued their outside-visiting-room privileges and didn't want anyone getting caught doing anything that might jeopardize them. He also wanted revenge and lacked the courage to get it on his own. Besson told his friends tearfully that three big white inmates had beat him simply because he had a white girl visiting him. Pagano, he said, was the only one of the three he recognized. From 5 P.M. to 6 P.M., all the cells and cellblock tier gates at Green Haven are locked while the 5:30 count is taken. That evening, shortly after six, when the tier gates and the doors to the individual cells were opened, a group of fifteen to twenty blacks from Besson's side of A block went over to Pagano's company. Some came as participants, some as onlookers. Pagano and most of his friends were still in their cells napping. Besson's friends closed the doors to Pagano's friends' cells and then gave Pagano a bad beating. He was hurt on the face, the nose, and the arms, but the most serious injury was to his head: one inmate hit him over the head with a pipe. A guard discovered him on the floor in front of his cell, unconscious and bleeding. He was taken to the prison hospital for emergency first aid and later to an outside hospital. Prison officials were worried that Pagano wouldn't make it through the night. Their worry was not based just on the extent of his injuries. He was liked by the prison administration and was also considered one of the inmate leaders. They were afraid that the beating itself would lead to retaliatory violence and that if he died there would be greater violence still.

Prison officials think well of men like Pagano because they are men who "do their own time" and don't get into trouble unless provoked. When provoked, however, they respond with physical courage. (Pagano had hurt several other inmates at other prisons during his long years of confinement.) Often these men have personalities that make them natural leaders, and sometimes their leadership abilities in prison are enhanced by their street reputations. (Pagano was said to have been a hit man for the Mafia.) Their followers are usually men of similar racial or ethnic persuasion. These leaders are usually long-termers. Short-termers are in and out of Green Haven before the administration can get to know them, and they don't have much at stake in the prison community. The leaders usually share a common interest with prison officials: they want to keep the prison peaceful for the duration of their stays because they want to get out, not to be killed in a riot. The leaders are not rats in the narrow sense of the word — they won't tell a lieutenant what he wants to know about another inmate as, say, an ordinary homosexual informer will, in exchange for being allowed to lock in a cell next to his lover — but they are helpful in certain situations. They are usually not drug users, and perceive drugs as a threat to the prison's tranquillity, as the officials do, and may obliquely suggest the origin of a certain drug supply. If the wrong man has been blamed for something, they will tell the administration to look elsewhere, without giving up the name of the guilty person.

The leaders understand the prison's tense racial situation and work with one another to keep things cool. Whites and Puerto Ricans regard each other as possible allies against the blacks, who outnumber them both. One day in early 1976, Pagano called on Green Haven's dep of security with a Puerto Rican leader. The Puerto Ricans had just been informed that they couldn't have visitors at their upcoming picnic, and were furious. The Italians had already been given permission to have visitors at their picnic, which was scheduled for a later date. Pagano said that the Italians would give up their visitors if the Puerto Ricans couldn't have theirs. The Puerto Ricans got to have visitors at their picnic, and both the dep of security and Pagano had credit in the bank with the Puerto Ricans to draw on the next time they needed it. One prisoner who works with the administration is a Black Muslim leader. He came to the dep of security one day in 1976, after a white man had hurt a Black Muslim, to tell him that his followers wanted to attack the white man. The quarrel between the white and the black had been over a purely personal matter, the Muslim leader said, and an attack on the white man wasn't called for and would spill unnecessary blood. He didn't want to lose face with his followers, but he didn't want to lead them into battle, either. The dep of security solved the problem by putting the white man in segregation. In exchange for such cooperation, prison officials do the leaders small favors, often to strengthen them. A weak leader cannot control his followers and serves no useful purpose. When the members of the Black Muslim leader's mosque wanted an iron to press their robes, the dep of security saw to it that they got an iron and that the leader was given credit for the acquisition. The leaders rarely ask for personal favors — they are more likely to ask for good jobs for their friends, who are impressed by what they can get from The Man. Prison officials look the other way when such leaders violate minor prison rules. Inmates at Green Haven are not allowed to wear any jewelry except religious medals, plain wedding rings, and inexpensive watches: expensive jewelry can be sold to buy contraband. Pagano had two pinky rings with nice stones, which he had been wearing for fifteen years.

By Monday morning, May 31, the prison administration knew that Pagano was going to survive. Reports of the beating and the reason for Pagano's having punched Besson had been travelling around A block on Sunday night. The inmates gradually untangled the truth, and in the morning, tension on the block was high. Pagano's friends, all of whom were white, wanted to get their hands on Besson and the blacks who had ganged up on Pagano. The black inmates who had beaten Pagano on Besson's behalf now knew that Besson had lied to them, and were angry at him for putting them in such a predicament. By morning, prison officials had also learned, from informers, what had happened and who had done what to whom. Meetings were held with groups of white inmates and black inmates. A Black Muslim leader was allowed to go to the hospital to see Pagano because he wanted the beating kept an isolated incident rather than a racial clash. It was decided to bring Besson to the Administration Building for questioning. At first, he didn't want to leave his tier, and refused to talk. When the extent of the trouble he was in was explained to him, he admitted what had happened and was taken to segregation for protection. Through informers, the names of Pagano's assailants were learned. Seth Morgan, the man who had used the pipe, was also taken to seg. Besson, Morgan, and four other men who had either participated in or watched the beating were transferred to Great Meadow. Pagano had to make several trips to outside hospitals and spent six or seven weeks recuperating. On July 14, he was taken to a superintendent's proceeding. He told the captain, who held the superintendent's proceeding, which was taped, that he had received his injuries falling out of bed. When the tape was off, the captain asked him what had really happened. "You know what happened" was all Pagano would say. Pagano was sentenced to thirty days' loss of outside-visiting-room privileges. The captain took Pagano's pinky rings away in a bit of whimsical one-upmanship, because he did know what had happened. The Besson-Pagano episode was the talk of Green Haven for weeks. "Pagano was absolutely right in what he did," Malinow says. "When something like that happens in the ladies' room, it's an insult to your visitor and is not to be tolerated. But the whole thing was so unnecessary. Besson should have gone into the inmates' bathroom if he wanted to fool around with a woman. Men, especially incarcerated men, are understanding about sex. All Besson would have had to do was get a lookout and warn the other inmates not to use the bathroom for a few minutes. That Besson had no brains and no class."

A couple of months after Pagano's outside-visiting-room privileges had been restored, Mrs. Marino came to visit him again, found it necessary to use the ladies' room, and once more happened upon an inmate having sexual intercourse with his visitor. This time, it was a white inmate named Burke Henley, who locked on Pagano's block, and a white woman. Pagano was about to meet the parole board, so he decided to use a little discretion and waited until they were back on the block to beat Henley up. Henley didn't complain: he knew he deserved what he got. Pagano said nothing, as was his custom, but prison officials learned about the incident through informers. When they asked Henley, a farm worker, how he had got the lump on his forehead, he said he had been kicked in the face by a cow. Henley was considered a poor farm worker, and the classification sergeant, delighted to have an excuse to remove him from the farm, took away his job for "failure to report an accident," and assigned him to the school to work as a porter. In the process of punching Henley, who occasionally ducked, Pagano had hit his hand against a wall. It had been his misfortune, he told anyone who inquired, to get his hand caught in a door. He went to the parole board, was granted parole, and left Green Haven with his hand in a cast.

Another man who was put in segregation at Green Haven in 1976 went there not simply because he deserved it but also because the prison administration had put him in peril to use him for its own purposes. In addition to the strong prisoners like Pagano, the administration also finds weak men useful in its efforts to run the prison.

On the afternoon of September 22, Edith Alpin, a woman employed at Green Haven as a clerk, was approached by Jack Finando, an inmate who was doing twenty-five to life for rape and murder. He told her she could earn three to four hundred dollars a week if she would bring drugs into the prison. Miss Alpin said no thank you. Finando advised her to think his offer over before she declined it. Miss Alpin immediately reported the proposition to the sergeant in her area, who reported it to the office of the deputy superintendent of security. The sergeant and the classification sergeant went to speak to Miss Alpin about the proposed bribe. They asked her if she would be willing to wear a tape recorder and turn it on if Finando attempted to bribe her again. She was willing. The following morning, Miss Alpin was outfitted with a tape recorder. At nine o'clock, she was again approached by Finando, who offered her fifty dollars to bring drugs into the prison for him; he said a friend of his had a thousand dollars in cash that could be used to buy more drugs. Thirty-five minutes later, Miss Alpin took the tape to the Administration Building and gave it to the classification sergeant, who instructed her to ask Finando for "front money." Later that day, Finando gave Miss Alpin forty-five dollars in cash with which to buy an ounce of marijuana on the street. Still later in the afternoon, Finando was called to the Administration Building. He was told that the administration was aware of his attempt to bribe Miss Alpin, and was in possession of the forty-five dollars he had given her. At first, Finando feigned innocence, but when he was told that the attempted bribe would be turned over to the state police for prosecution, he decided to turn informer and offered to lead prison authorities to drugs and cash within the prison. On the morning of September 24, Finando gave the names of three other inmates who were involved in the trafficking of contraband at Green Haven — Eric Humphrey, Godfrey Owens, and Howard Brick. Finando was taken to segregation, and so were the three other men. There were twelve cases of arson at Green Haven in 1976. One of the twelve occurred at four-thirty that afternoon, in Finando's cell, on G block. It was set by inmates who had correctly surmised that Finando had become a rat. Finando was sentenced at a superintendent's proceeding to sixty days in segregation for attempted bribery and possession of currency. He was transferred to another prison. He has never been told that the tape with Miss Alpin was of very poor quality and that prison authorities didn't think they could have got an outside conviction.

When Owens was frisked, as all men are when they reach seg, a hypodermic needle was found concealed in his undergarments, and fresh injection marks were noted on his left arm. Owens wouldn't talk. He was sentenced at a superintendent's proceeding to sixty days in segregation and ninety days' loss of good time and was later transferred to another prison. Humphrey had nothing on him, but when his cell, on J block, was searched it was found to contain eleven marijuana cigarettes, a small package of marijuana, half a quart of whiskey in a Hawaiian Punch can, and various other contraband items. Humphrey wouldn't talk, either. He was sentenced at a superintendent's proceeding to forty-five days in segregation and ninety days' loss of good time and was later transferred to another prison. Brick's cell contained an ounce of marijuana, a homemade marijuana pipe, a ten-dollar bill, five blank institutional passes, and assorted papers with three names and addresses that looked as if they might be useful. The names were those of Jennifer and Peter Nicolosi and Douglas Lyons, three residents of White

Plains, New York. By this time, Brick was under investigation for another matter. He had swindled an illiterate inmate named Derek Hunter out of forty-nine hundred dollars that were in Hunter's account by claiming he knew a lawyer who could get Hunter's sentence shortened. An inmate named Leroy Mason, who felt sorry for Hunter, had ratted Brick out. Brick agreed to cooperate with prison officials on the contraband that was coming into the prison, in the hope of getting leniency in the matter of the swindle. Brick first told them where they could find $779 in cash — some of the money he had made peddling marijuana and liquor — that he had stored in another inmate's cell. He also gave up a pair of shoes with hollowed-out heels, used for transporting money and drugs to and from the visiting room and all around the prison, and the name of the inmate who had hollowed them out for him.

When Brick was questioned about the whiskey in Humphrey's cell, he betrayed an inmate named Reed Pastore, who had often been in trouble for dealing in contraband. The three names and addresses in Brick's cell proved to be those of three people on Pastore's visiting list. The Nicolosis and Lyons had been buying forty-six-ounce cans of Hawaiian Punch, steaming the labels off, drilling two holes in the sides of the cans, replacing the contents with six or seven dollars' worth of whiskey, soldering the holes over, filing the soldered parts smooth, replacing the labels, and then either mailing the cans to inmates, using a return address of a member of the inmate's family, supplied by Pastore, or bringing the cans up to Pastore on visits. The Nicolosis and Lyons got thirty dollars a can from Pastore, who got ninety to a hundred dollars from the inmates at Green Haven who received the whiskey. Pastore had introduced Brick to the Nicolosis in the visiting room, and Brick was about to start dealing in marijuana with them when he was ratted out by Mason and then by Finando. Pastore was taken to seg ostensibly for protection — prison officials wanted him to take some of the weight that might otherwise have fallen on Brick by giving the impression that Pastore had turned informer. Pastore is the sort of inmate prison officials like least. When he is caught "dirty," he will disclose the minimum amount of information necessary to stay on at Green Haven — usually the names of his competitors, because if they are caught the price of his marijuana goes up. He then keeps wheeling and dealing until he is caught again. "Pastore's the kind of guy who likes to walk down both sides of the street," a Green Haven sergeant says. "This time, a bus ran over him. We transferred him out." Brick was sentenced at a superintendent's proceeding to forty-five days in segregation and ninety days' loss of good time for possession of marijuana and cash. He had been offered leniency only in the swindle case, which he apparently received: Hunter was eventually transferred and never pressed charges against Brick. He did not get his forty-nine hundred dollars back. It is a Department of Correctional Services rule that money confiscated from prisoners be turned over to a state general fund. Brick's $771 didn't go into the general fund. "We need money like that to work with for future setups," a Green Haven official explains. Brick is still at Green Haven, where he is considered a very helpful inmate. Whether by bureaucratic inadvertence or indifference — the reason is unclear — Finando and the two men he had ratted on who had refused to turn informer, Humphrey and Owens, were all transferred to the same prison.

When the state police came to see Nicolosi, he admitted that he had brought in the Hawaiian Punch and took sole responsibility. On October 26, a month after the contraband-whiskey operation was halted, Nicolosi was arrested and charged with promoting prison contraband, a felony. (The charge was later reduced to disorderly conduct, a violation, and Nicolosi was fined fifty dollars.) On October 27, the *Times* carried a brief story on Nicolosi's arrest and on the smuggling operation, in which Green Haven's superintendent was quoted. He might have been expected to express mild jubilation at the discovery and halting of the Pastore-Nicolosi-Lyons contraband operation. He didn't. Instead, sounding as if he had his finger in the dike but could feel the water seeping around it and making the hole larger, he said that ever since the Hawaiian Punch whiskey operation had been halted, Green Haven's guards had been having trouble controlling the manufacture, by inmates, of homemade brew. On October 7, one inmate had stabbed another in a dispute over a booze-and-drug dealership. On October 8, the prison riot squad, armed with tear gas and gas guns, had to be called out to put a group of drunken inmates back into their cells. On October 14, two guards were punched and kicked by an inmate in whose cell they had found five gallons of booze and whom they were trying to lock up. On October 23, a drunken inmate tried to kiss two female volunteer workers.

Things got worse the following week. A drunken inmate assaulted another drunken inmate on October 29, and on October 30 Eli Walker was killed. On November 1, Green Haven's superintendent complained to a newspaper reporter that a number of Green Haven's better-behaved prisoners were being transferred to the newly opened smaller prisons in and around New York City and that they were being replaced by some of the most disruptive prisoners in New York State. Formerly, these prisoners — many of them young first-felony and second-felony offenders originally sent to Coxsackie and Eastern — had been routinely sent to Great Meadow and Attica after stirring up Coxsackie and Eastern. In an attempt to improve the reputations of Great Meadow and Attica, they were now being sent to Green Haven, Clinton, and Auburn. The problem prisoners were having a bad effect on Green Haven. In addition, many experienced officers were transferring to the new minimum-security and medium-security prisons that were opening up, and were being replaced by unseasoned officers. The superintendent was under increasing pressure from the officers to conduct a prison-wide search for weapons and contraband. The next day, he succeeded in getting Albany to authorize the overtime that would be necessary to close down and search the prison. On November 3, at nine in the evening, the superintendent announced over the prison radio system that all the inmates would be locked in their cells so that the officers could conduct a cell-by-cell search for weapons, drugs, money, and unauthorized state material. The cells and tiers were cluttered with extra furniture, and the papers and magazines the inmates had accumulated were a fire hazard. It was the first time Green Haven was shut down since December 1972.

The inmates' cells, the prison yards, and the various prison buildings were searched over the course of the next three days. Only sixty gallons of booze were found: one reason for announcing the search ahead of time was to give inmates a chance to flush the liquor down their cell toilets. The superintendent simply wanted to be rid of it; he didn't want to turn off the prison plumbing and have the Adjustment Committee bogged down in booze misbehavior reports for the next two months. Only $285.26 in cash was found; with just thirty minutes allotted to search each cell (because of the ceiling Albany had put on overtime), few of the good hiding places (bookbindings, mattresses, the space between the glass and the cardboard backing in glass paintings) could be properly explored. In the Great Frisk, as it came to be known, fifty-eight knives were found and about five hundred pipes and clubs that could have been used as weapons. One hundred twenty-five stools and 250 lockers and various other extra cell furnishings were confiscated. The biggest haul was about five thousand pounds of extra state blankets, sheets, and uniforms. One hundred two truckloads of trash were taken to the prison dump. Some of the lockers and stools that were confiscated were also taken to the dump. Some of the lockers and stools that were in excellent condition were taken to a small shed known as Building 29.

The Great Frisk was a success from the officer's point of view. The 674 hours of overtime required by the three-day search made its way into their paychecks in time to be spent on

Christmas shopping. Officers and civilian employees were observed carting off lockers, stools, and other items from the dump, which rather mysteriously caught fire in a lightning storm on November 5. The better lockers and stools vanished from Building 29. If the homes of certain prison guards and civilian employees were more crowded, the emptied-out prison looked tidier for a while. The morale of the officers soared — for the short time the inmates were locked up. As for the effect of the Great Frisk on the assaults and drinking, it was described by some officials at Green Haven as "fleeting" and by others as "nonexistent." On November 13, a drunken inmate set fire to his cell and kicked and hit an officer. On November 25, one inmate stabbed another with a knife. That same day, two drunken inmates refused to lock in. One of them pulled a knife out of his sock and tried to stab a lieutenant. He also threatened and pushed the deputy superintendent of security. The other struck the lieutenant on the right side of the head. Three other officers were also hurt in the fray. Both inmates eventually landed in seg. One went quietly, one went kicking and screaming.

December began quietly enough — one inmate was assaulted by another with a razor blade, the Catholic chaplain's prayer book was stolen — but ended noisily. On December 31, one inmate was sodomized, two inmates were stabbed, and seg was crowded.

Malinow can remember the decades when men were sent to seg without the "due process" of an Adjustment Committee hearing or a superintendent's proceeding, two innovations resulting from inmate lawsuits of the 1960s. Prisoners were sent to seg for such offenses as helping one another with their legal work or refusing to take a certain prison job, and often stayed in seg for months or even years. Malinow once spent almost two years in seg at Clinton in the 1940s after refusing to work in the prison's cotton shop. Inmates who went to seg in those days were usually beaten on the way there. For the first thirty days, they were put into cells furnished with nothing but mattresses and toilets; they weren't given light bulbs, earphones, or tobacco. Sometimes their punishment included being fed limited rations — two days of bread and water alternating with one day of more or less regular meals, perhaps for thirty days.

Segregation at Green Haven in the 1970s is relatively benign. Most men who went to seg in 1976 went quietly, as William Muller did, and say they were not touched on the way up. The few men who still do get beatings at Green Haven are those who go to seg kicking and punching. There is a staircase in the Hospital-Segregation Building, but it is not commonly used for trips to segregation. Most men are taken to seg by elevator. The inmates are escorted onto the elevator on the first floor, near the hospital clinic, often by members of one of the prison's three riot squads, which are officially called CERT teams (correctional emergency-response teams), and are known by inmates as direct descendants of the "goon squads" of the pre-CERT-team years, since some of the members of the former eagerly volunteered to be on the latter. If the inmate offers no resistance, the elevator goes right to seg, on the third floor. If the inmate offers resistance, one of his escorts stops the elevator between two and three and places the man's nose against an "X" that has been put on the elevator wall with a Magic Marker; then he and his teammates return the inmate's punches, with interest. Sometimes inmates in the hospital witness a beating when the elevator stops at two, instead of between two and three. Sometimes the elevator can be heard rattling on its cables. Most of the members of the CERT teams believe in the "lumps and bumps" school of behavior modification and wish they could get away with more beatings, but they say there is too much paperwork involved and too many questions asked by the D.O.C.S. Office of the Inspector General, the equivalent of the New York City Police Department's Internal Affairs Division. The Inspector General's Office came into existence in 1972. There were forty "use of force" forms filled out by officers at Green Haven in

1976. The prisoners and the guards say that in most cases the amount of force used was minimal.

Most of the cells in seg resemble cells on the regular blocks, with the addition of peepholes in their ceilings so that the officers assigned to seg can take a count from an overhead walkway without getting hit by the food and other unsavory things a few disturbed men in seg sometimes throw at anyone who passes in front of their cells. There are three sturdier cells in seg, each of which has a bed and a combination toilet-sink-and-drinking-fountain secured to a wall. They are used to house the men who tear up their regular seg cells, which Filippi did after he was accused of Walker's murder.

In recent years, every man sent to seg at Green Haven except one was given the same three daily meals served to the men who ate in the prison's mess halls. New York State still has the right, according to the penal code, to feed men in segregation limited rations. This is rarely done, because it is considered an archaic punishment, potential bad publicity, and vulnerable if challenged in court. Every year, one or two men at Green Haven choose to spend their time there in segregation. They assault someone, serve their sentences in seg, are returned to population, and soon assault another inmate or officer and are taken back to seg. One man who went to seg often in 1975 and 1976 was Dwight Harvey. At a superintendent's proceeding held on November 16, 1975, Harvey complained about the prison food. The captain, who was in charge of the proceeding, had long since given Harvey every punishment he had to give, with no result. At that proceeding, he put him on special meals for two weeks. The captain went to one of the prison's doctors, asked him to check off all the items on the day's menu Harvey required for his health, and had a nurse assemble the ingredients in a blender, pour the blended mixture into a loaf pan and bake it. Harvey was served twelve ounces of the loaf three times a day. The captain said the loaf looked dreadful but tasted it, out of curiosity, and said it tasted all right. Harvey refused to eat

75

for four days. He took two paper plates, on which his meals had been served, and one loaf, and asked the captain to mail the loaf and the plates to the commissioner, in Albany. No inmate may be denied the right to communicate with the commissioner. The captain called Albany for advice. Albany told the captain to put Harvey back on regular meals. To save face, the captain told Harvey he was being put back on regular meals because his mental condition had obviously deteriorated, whereupon Harvey said, "Give me the loaf." The captain said no, that he was in terrible mental shape, and ordered regular meals for him. For a day, Harvey refused to eat the regular meals and continued to demand the loaf. After that, he ate his regular meals. Harvey returned to his regular misbehavior when his time in seg was up.

In 1976, most of the men who were sent to seg spent thirty or sixty days there or, as in Muller's case, less. A Green Haven official may sentence a man to thirty days in seg without notifying Albany. If a man is sentenced to sixty days in seg, Albany must be notified. Longer sentences or renewed sentences must be approved by the commissioner. Men whose behavior has resulted in their spending six months in seg may be transferred to another prison for a "fresh start." They usually succeed in getting themselves sent to seg at the new prison shortly after their arrival.

Most men behaved well in seg in 1976 and say they were not mistreated in any way. Their primary complaint was the unaccustomed confinement and boredom. Men in seg are locked in their cells for twenty-three hours a day. They are allowed out for exercise for an hour, under an officer's supervision. They are permitted to take few personal possessions to seg, there is no television there, and they are soon weary of listening on their earphones.

Until December 1975, segregation had fifty cells — two galleries of twelve cells and two galleries of thirteen cells. In 1975, Joseph Eli Davis was convicted of murdering a policeman in

Yonkers. He was brought to Green Haven on December 15, 1975, and put in a cell in one wing of segregation that had been designated as K gallery but was referred to as death row. Until 1973, it had been used to hold some condemned prisoners until they had been resentenced to life imprisonment. Davis's presence on K gallery again reduced seg's capacity to thirty-seven. Davis was alone on death row until November 22, 1976, when Joseph James, who had been sentenced to death for killing a Riker's Island prison guard, was brought to Green Haven. He was put in a cell near Davis's so they could share Davis's television set and round-the-clock guards.

Death row at Green Haven is, dictionarily speaking, real maximum security. Men on death row are not permitted to have certain objects — for example, belts, shoelaces, forks (much less knives), or matches — at any time. (Guards light their cigarettes.) Some objects, such as safety-lock razors, unbreakable mirrors, pencils, pens, toothbrushes, bowls, cups, and spoons may go into their cells briefly, but come out as soon as they have served their purpose. A death row inmate's cell is frisked every day, usually during his daily hour of supervised exercise. His immediate family, his physician, his attorney, or a minister of his faith may visit him without a court order; no one else may visit him without a court order. He is in one locked room and his visitors are in another; they are separated by a bulletproof glass window set in the wall, and speak through a metal grate opening. A log is kept of everything that happens in seg and on death row — razors are logged in and out, and so are visitors, including officers assigned there. Every effort is made to prevent a man on death row from committing suicide. Green Haven's guards were unfavorably impressed with the apparently lax security at Utah State Prison, where Gary Gilmore was able to take two overdoses of barbiturates in the two months preceding his death by firing squad in January 1977.

One floor above segregation and death row, on the fourth and top floor of the Hospital-Segregation Building, is the electric chair. The chair, a symbolic presence at Green Haven, sits on a rubber mat in a good-sized fluorescent-lit room several yards away from the four dark wooden benches provided for the twenty-five state-mandated witnesses to the execution and the two clergymen the victim may request. The benches resemble church pews and face the chair as they would a pulpit. The electric chair is a surprisingly comfortable, boxy-looking oaken armchair with rubber padding on its seat and sloping back, and numerous straps to restrain the victim's arms, feet, and body. Six hundred ninety-five people were electrocuted in New York between 1890 and 1963, but no one would know it to look at the chair.

In January 1976, shortly before Davis was scheduled to be executed, some of Green Haven's guards staged a rehearsal of the event, at the request of the superintendent. One guard was assigned the role of Davis. He was ordered to struggle as the others, playing themselves, struggled to get him into the chair. Davis's stand-in broke the worn leather straps. The guards participated in the rehearsal with obvious pleasure. "The policeman ain't here. Why should Davis be?" one said. "Davis got to do his thing. Now we get to do our thing," another said. The execution was later stayed, pending appeals. News of the rehearsal travelled swiftly to the inmates at Green Haven, who disapprove of the death penalty and the eagerness of almost all of the guards to see it applied. "We're criminals and they're cops," Malinow says. A few days before Christmas 1975, boxes with placards reading FOR DAVIS ON DEATH ROW had been put in the mess halls. Few of Green Haven's inmates knew Davis, but they were sympathetic to his situation of isolation and uncertainty. They donated many dozens of cartons of cigarettes and cans of food, which were placed in a cell adjoining Davis's. At Christmas time in 1976, another large collection was taken up for Davis and James in the mess halls.

In November 1977, New York's Court of Appeals ruled that two of the three sections of the state's death penalty statute were unconstitutional—the two that mandated the death penalty for those convicted of intentionally killing police officers and prison guards who were performing their duties. (The court did not rule on the constitutionality of the third section of the law, which mandates the death penalty when a murder is committed by a prisoner already serving a life sentence.) The decision spared the lives of Davis and James. Both men were resentenced to life imprisonment and were taken off death row. Davis was sent to Attica, James is in population at Green Haven. At Christmas time in 1977, there were no condemned men to take up collections for in the mess halls.

The buildings right in back of the Hospital-Segregation Building are Green Haven's twin, high-ceilinged mess halls, one (painted blue) for the cellblocks on the east side, one (painted orange) for those on the west side. The mess halls are separated by the prison's kitchen, which was described as "spotless" by newspaper reporters who toured it in the 1950s and 1960s. "Filthy" would be a more accurate adjective in the 1970s. A white sergeant who lives in Dutchess County recently cast a cold eye on the kitchen's slippery, slimy, garbage-covered floor and said, "You've got to understand something. Most of the kitchen workers are blacks and Puerto Ricans. To these people from New York City's ghettos, this is clean." He did not comment on the quality of his supervisory abilities.

Each mess hall has a seating capacity of 768 — 96 rectangular steel tables for eight, aligned in orderly rows. The tables are bolted to the floor; the inmates sit on backless steel stools. Until 1971, the mess halls were filled almost to capacity at each meal, and a sergeant boasted that Green Haven could feed six or seven hundred inmates in each mess hall in thirty-five minutes. Not long after the Attica riot, the administration thought it wise to limit the number of men in the mess hall (a traditional prison trouble spot) at any one time, so different blocks on each side go to the mess hall at staggered intervals. In 1976, there were rarely more than two hundred men in each mess hall at once.

Men proceed, in companies, from their blocks to the mess hall, walk from the entrance around the sides of the mess hall to two cafeteria lines at the mess hall's kitchen end, where they pick up partitioned plastic trays, plastic bowls and cups, metal spoons and forks (but no such amenities as paper napkins), and go through the food line. They help themselves to some items and to beverages in plastic cups and mugs and are helped by kitchen workers stationed behind the counter to others. Meat, cake, milk, juice, fruit, sugar, and rolls are rationed; potatoes; rice, vegetables, and bread are not. The inmates know it is a prison rule that they must fill the tables in sequence, and that officers assigned to the mess hall will enforce the rule. Whites at Green Haven almost always want to eat with whites, blacks with blacks, and Puerto Ricans with Puerto Ricans (although the latter are somewhat less color-conscious); therefore, the inmates take considerable trouble to line up according to race before their company leaves the block for the mess hall. Each man who sits down pulls out the stool for the next man, an ancient prison courtesy. Over the entrance to each mess hall is a gas tower, where a guard is stationed at each meal, ready to release tear gas from holes in the ceiling in case of a riot. It has never yet been necessary to use gas in Green Haven's mess halls. There was only one serious mealtime incident in each mess hall at Green Haven in 1976. At breakfast on February 18, an officer in the west mess hall observed Dwight Harvey, who had recently been released from segregation, filling a plastic quart bottle with milk from the milk dispenser. The officer told Harvey he wasn't permitted to take the milk out of the mess hall. Harvey started yelling at the officer and hit him — and three other officers and two sergeants who came to his assistance — before about seventy-five inmates rushed over from the other side of the mess hall and helped subdue Harvey, who was once again taken to seg. At supper in the east mess hall on September

1, the second day of what turned out to be a four-day prison strike, an inmate was assaulted because he had gone to work. Visiting and eating were permitted by the inmates during their strike; working was not.

On a typical weekday in 1976, the Green Haven menu read as follows:

Breakfast: Hot Farina
Stewed Prunes
Jelly Filled Buns
Coffee-Milk-Sugar
Bread

Dinner: Seafood Patties W/Catsup
Boiled Potatoes
Spinach W/Vinegar
Sugar Cookies
Milk & Bread

Supper: Diced Franks & Kidney Bean Casserole
3-Bean Salad
Jello
Kool-Aid & Bread

The main topic of conversation at Green Haven's meals is often the food. No one likes it, although some prisoners thrive on it and leave Green Haven looking much fitter than when they arrived. Some of the complaints run along racial lines. Many blacks would prefer soul food, many Puerto Ricans would prefer more pork and rice and beans. In the early 1970s, in a concession to Green Haven's sizable Black Muslim population, whose religion forbids them to eat pork, the amount of pork served was sharply curtailed, and the prison's prize-winning swine herd was phased out. Pork can now be served only twice a week and must not be used to flavor soups or sauces. Some of the complaints are fairly universal. No one enjoys cutting liver with the bowl of a spoon. Just about everyone would like to be able to season his own food: there is salt on the tables at Green Haven but no pepper, because pepper is considered a dangerous weapon. Everyone bemoans the lack of choice (as people do in the army and in college dorms and everyplace else where choice is lacking). If you want coffee for dinner and Kool-Aid is on the menu, you drink Kool-Aid. Almost everyone finds the meals too high on starch and too low on fresh fruits and juices, which is easily explained by the facts that starch is cheap and fresh fruits and juices are expensive and that the food budget at Green Haven is $1.45 per inmate per day. Sometimes, the prisoners say, the original ingredients the cooks start with are all right but are ruined in the cooking process: what isn't overcooked is undercooked or miscooked. At Green Haven, the captain or a lieutenant is required to sample each meal and judge it on a printed form. Usually the sampler writes "fair" or "good" on the line next to "Quality" and "ample" on the line next to "Quantity" and leaves the space intended for comments blank, but one day in 1976 a lieutenant observed that the tea he had sipped at supper was cold. He was chagrined to learn he had been drinking coffee. On another day, the comment of a lieutenant who had tried the breakfast read, "One dead roach in roll — well done." Sometimes the original ingredients never get as far as the mess hall. If a thousand pounds of chopped meat is delivered to the kitchen to be used to make hamburgers, two hundred pounds may be stolen. The inmates claim that some of the prison's guards and civilian employees steal the meat. The civilians and guards claim that some of the kitchen inmates steal the meat. Both are right.

About the best that old-timers say about Green Haven's food is what they say about its medical care: it used to be worse. A few years ago, no fresh fruits and juices were served. In August 1971, a month before the Attica riot, New York State's correction commissioner discovered that the sixty-three cents a day budgeted for each inmate's food was not sufficient to meet the minimum dietary standards set by federal guidelines. A directive went out to spend what was necessary to meet nutritional standards. They are now being met.

A few years ago, all meals at Green Haven were mandatory. Even a man who didn't feel like eating had to go to the mess hall and sit there, if only to stare at an empty tray. In 1976, the noon meal alone was mandatory. Like so many other things at Green Haven, it wasn't as mandatory as one might have supposed. Statistics on how many men eat each meal are kept as faithfully as statistics on how many men take showers and how many cells are searched daily. One evening, on a day when the mess halls had looked sparsely populated at noon, Green Haven's captain was asked how many men had eaten the noon meal. His answer was 906 — a figure that included those who had eaten in both mess halls, in the diet mess hall (where men suffering from diabetes, ulcers, and other ailments are fed), in the blocks, on the farm, in the hospital, and in segregation. This number was just slightly higher than the number who had eaten Green Haven's nonmandatory breakfast and supper. The captain was asked what the prison count was that day. He said it was over seventeen hundred. He was then asked why the eight hundred other inmates hadn't eaten the noon meal, since it was mandatory. "The noon meal is mandatory," he said, ending the conversation.

Malinow is one of the inmates who very rarely eat the mandatory noon meal. If he goes to the mess hall at all, it is usually only once a week, for Sunday dinner, which he considers the best meal of the week. On Sundays, the menu includes "good" meat (pork chops, roast chicken, or roast beef), served with mashed potatoes; the desert is usually ice cream. Some of Malinow's friends go to the mess hall twice a week — for Sunday dinner and also for Saturday breakfast, the one morning bacon and eggs are served — but Malinow isn't much of a breakfast eater. It isn't just the uninspiring food and the fact that he can manage to eat well enough on his job and in his cell, it is also the atmosphere of the mess hall that keeps Malinow from going there. Like many experienced inmates at Green Haven, he leads a circumscribed life, avoiding crowds and cutting down on his chances of being hassled by officers and inmates he doesn't know. He dislikes the long walk to the mess hall, the waiting in line, and the possibility that he may inadvertently wind up at a table next to some inmates he describes as "the new element," by which he means young black drug addicts. "If one of the new element jumps in line ahead of me or makes a remark about honkies and he knows I've heard it, I'd have to hit him and that would get me into trouble," he said. "I don't need trouble. But I can't let such a remark go by. I'm not from a blue-blooded family, I don't have a million dollars. All I have is my image, how I'm regarded in prison, how I carry myself. Some inmates won't react — you can call their mothers or fathers anything — but from then on they're considered trash, and they're treated accordingly. They'll let a remark go by, and the next thing you know they'll be standing in the yard in front of the TV set and some guy standing behind them will say, 'Hey, creep, get out of here,' and they'll have to go."

In the back, or south, part of the prison, behind the mess halls and the storehouse and the eight large cellblocks, are a number of other buildings — the Protestant Center (attended by about thirty of Green Haven's nine hundred Protestants on a summer Sunday in 1976); the Catholic chapel (attended by about fifty of Green Haven's over seven hundred Catholics on an average Sunday); an omnibus building containing the vocational school, the state shop (which issues prison uniforms and shoes), the tailor shop (which alters prison clothes), and two mosques — one for Green Haven's Sunni Muslims, one for the followers of Wallace D. Muhammad; J block; the auditorium building, into whose basement the commissary recently moved; the laundry and the barbershop; the gymnasium; the school building (which contains the regular library and the law library); and two industrial buildings. All of Green Haven's buildings are linked by a series of tunnel-like corridors. The corridors are endless and gloomy, with only a modest number of electric light bulbs and small barred windows for illumination. Most of them are unheated. They are cold and damp in winter, hot and damp in summer. Rain and snow seep into them, making them slick and leaving long-lasting puddles. The concrete floors are dark and dusty, even though inmate porters sometimes sweep them with coffee grounds to try to hold the dust down. Guards are stationed at certain strategic places along the corridors — outside the entrances to both mess halls, for instance, and at the entrance to the school — and there are a number of locked gates and checkpoints. The entrances to the Administration Building and the Hospital-Segregation Building are particularly well secured. Inmates are always frisked before they enter the Administration Building. In 1976, inmates travelled with relative freedom through the corridors, sometimes with passes, sometimes without. A prisoner who works inside and who doesn't want to go to the yard can spend ten or fifteen years at Green Haven without going outdoors, simply by commuting from his cellblock to his job or to his place of worship. Malinow rarely goes to the yard. He no longer participates in sports, says he has outgrown idle prison conversations about past and future Cadillacs and women, and considers the yard another place to avoid the new element. He squints into the unaccustomed sunlight when he goes to the outside visiting room or to a Fay Field picnic and, like a number of other men at Green Haven, suffers from a case of prison pallor.

There are a few prison buildings outside the walls — the superintendent's house, which is no longer used by the superintendent (post-'75 superintendents were deprived of perks as well as tenure); the power plant; and the water-filtration plant. A few hundred yards outside the prison is a place Malinow thinks of on the rare days when his usually optimistic nature gives way to melancholy and he fears he will die in prison — Green Haven's cemetery. Not many men die in prison, and the bodies of most of those who do are claimed by their families. Only thirty-three men have been buried in the prison cemetery since 1949, the last two in 1974. Until 1976, the cemetery was a scruffy-looking place, overgrown with weeds. It wasn't fenced off from the nearby prison dump, and trash had drifted over and settled among the graves. Thirty-three cement headstones with nothing chiselled on them but the dead inmates' prison numbers marked the thirty-three graves. In 1976, Malinow and a number of other members of the Holy Name Society went to Green Haven's Catholic chaplain. They told him they didn't think men should be degraded in death as they were in life at Green Haven, by being reduced to numbers, and they had no trouble persuading him that the cemetery should be cleaned up. The Holy Name Society raised money to buy bronze markers to put on the graves and had the inmates' names and dates of birth and death inscribed on them. Malinow got in touch with a friend of his — the brother of a former inmate — and asked him to donate three hundred feet of chain fence to enclose the cemetery. His friend came through with the fencing. The Catholic chaplain and half a dozen inmates went to work on the cemetery. They pulled weeds, cleared rocks, put up columns to support the chain fence, made the cemetery look more respectable, and took pride in their victory over the state's indifference.

Everything about prison life is spelled out by New York State's Department of Correctional Services in memos, so it isn't surprising that memo no. 4014, dated 12/14/76, tells how to dispose of an inmate's body. According to the memo, the D.O.C.S. will provide a suit of clothes and up to three hundred and fifty dollars for transportation of the inmate's body if his family is burying him, but not a coffin or a container. If, however, an inmate is to be buried in a prison cemetery, the

D.O.C.S. will provide not only a suit of clothes but a simple wood coffin. When the D.O.C.S. assumes full responsibility for an inmate's burial, it stipulates that it will claim death benefits (such as Social Security) normally afforded the next of kin. Should these benefits fail to satisfy burial expenses, money from the inmate's account is to be applied to the funeral cost. "In prison, it even costs you money to die," Malinow says.

No matter who buries a prisoner, his life in New York State is more expensive than his death. It is costlier to keep a convicted felon in a maximum-security prison in New York than to send a young man or woman to an Ivy League college. Harvard's annual charges for room, board, tuition, and incidentals are about $8000. The state of New York spends $9768 a year to keep a man at Green Haven. Over half this sum — $5618 — is allocated to the salaries of the security staff. The state spends $475 per prisoner on food annually, $210 on fuel, and $171 on inmate wages for prison work. (It is much more expensive to keep a prisoner in a smaller, medium-security or minimum-security prison, so the average cost of keeping a man in prison in New York State is $13,713 a year.) George Malinow does not think that the taxpayers are getting good value for their money. Many of the state's taxpayers do not know precisely what they are getting for their money, but some do have a certain understanding; a victim of one of Malinow's robber friends at Green Haven said not long ago, "I sleep better knowing that that thief is behind bars."

Like most prisons, Green Haven furnishes the essentials: room (cell) and board (three starchy meals a day in the mess hall); clothes (green uniforms, a white shirt, an allotment of undergarments, outerwear, and footgear); laundry service; haircuts; and even a certain amount of entertainment and recreation — earphones in the cells, a weekly movie in the auditorium, television in the yards and in a few cellblocks, sports in the yards and the gym. Green Haven also issues some products that are necessary for keeping clean and well groomed — toilet paper, razor blades, soap (an abrasive variety made at Great Meadow, in Comstock), a toothbrush, and toothpaste — although the block officers in charge of distributing these supplies often run out of them. In addition, cigarette rolling paper and Top tobacco are made available, but Green Haven's inmates are former members of the affluent society, which is not a roll-your-own society except for marijuana smokers, and few avail themselves of the state-issued tobacco. (The rolling paper, however, is appreciated by the marijuana smokers.) There are many things not provided by the state that most prisoners regard as even more necessary than people on the outside do — for example, talcum powder and deodorant, because of the prisoners' more limited bathing facilities. Store-bought cigarettes, instant coffee, immersion coils for heating water, and between-meal snacks — especially for the fifteen-hour period between supper and breakfast — also seem necessary, and help to fill the empty spaces of prison life.

There are two ways an inmate can legitimately obtain such items at Green Haven. He can get them in the two monthly packages that a prisoner in New York State may receive from people on his approved visiting list, or he can go to the commissary every two weeks and buy up to forty-five dollars' worth of groceries, toiletries, and miscellaneous items, if he can afford to. The commissary sells several hundred items — but at prices pegged to salaries on the outside rather than to prison wages. A carton of cigarettes costs $4.70, a ten-ounce jar of instant coffee costs $3.41, a six-and-a-half-ounce can of tuna fish costs $0.68. If a man earns $2.75 a week and smokes a pack a day, he can't even keep himself in commissary-bought cigarettes unless his family has deposited money in his inmate account. The wife of one of George Malinow's friends, who knows how much it costs the state's taxpayers each year to keep her husband in prison, figured that it also cost her $2000 a year to make his life more agreeable there. That was what she spent on bus fare, packages, postage, collect phone calls, and money orders. A lot of men in prison have no families. Many of those who weren't single when they got to Green Haven are single for all practical purposes by the time they have been there a year or two, so they must provide for themselves. Others come from poor families; one of the most frequent forms of identification that visitors present to reception-room guards is a welfare card. A few prisoners sell paintings, leather handbags, and other arts and crafts through the prison hobby shop, or send their handicrafts out with visitors to be sold, but not many earn a lot of money this way. For most men, their only legitimate income is their inmate wages. To some prisoners, going to the commissary is one of the most frustrating experiences at Green Haven. They make out their "buy slips" the night before they are scheduled to go to the commissary, and they wait in line for hours to be served, only to be told that the items they have chosen are sold out. They must then see what else is in stock that they want, and hastily determine whether they can afford the substitutes. They feel the lack of purchasing power keenly — the pint of ice cream, the bag of potato chips, the box of cookies beyond their reach. The average commissary purchase at Green Haven is $15.01 every two weeks.

Most of the men at Green Haven are in prison precisely because they were not willing to go without on the street. They are no more willing to go without in prison, so they hustle to obtain what they cannot afford to buy. Some men sell special services. Inmates who want to be sure of getting their clothes back from the laundry "buy" a laundry man for a carton of cigarettes a month. In 1975, Green Haven's laundry closed for renovation. Before it closed, it had a steam presser. When it reopened, in 1976, it no longer had a steam presser, because the new prison uniforms were permanent press. The laundry's loss was the tailor shop's gain. The tailor shop had a steam presser; the tailor shop workers now charge a pack of cigarettes for each shirt or pair of pants an inmate wants to have ironed. The tailor shop employees also charge for such illegal alterations as converting straight-legged prison pants into bell-bottoms. Hustling usually involves breaking a prison rule. Some men gamble. Some sell sexual favors. In 1976, the going rate for fellatio was five packs of cigarettes. A great deal of the hustling involves appropriating state property for one's personal use, in which case it is usually called swagging.

Almost every job at Green Haven offers possibilities for swagging. In 1975, when the commissary was on the ground floor of the vocational building, a sergeant discovered that the inmates assigned to bag groceries and stock shelves were making good use of a hole in the floor. The hole had once been used for a steam pipe and had never been covered up except by the inmates, who covered it with a moveable pallet. They used the hole to toss cartons of cigarettes down to inmate friends who worked in the maintenance tunnels below the commissary. The cigarettes were later sold or traded to other inmates, with the proceeds divided between the commissary workers and the maintenance men. In 1976, the hole having been plugged up, the commissary workers found other ways to send out cigarettes. For instance, they opened up boxes of saltines, emptied the boxes, refilled them with cigarettes, reglued the boxes, and slipped them into their friends' commissary orders.

The kitchen is another first-rate place to swag. Supervision is limited, and kitchen workers can take far more food than they can eat, and sell it or swap it. One of Malinow's friends, who receives five cartons of cigarettes a month from a crime partner he didn't rat on, doesn't smoke but loves to eat. His recent purchases from a kitchen worker have included a dozen eggs (two packs of cigarettes), a pound of rice (one pack), a pound of coffee (one pack) and several steaks (three packs apiece). He also has a contract with his friend in the kitchen for a daily loaf of soft bread (one carton a month). Kitchen workers have access to the various ingredients used at Green Haven to make booze — yeast, raw dough, sugar, fruit, potatoes, cereal — and either sell the raw ingredients or make and sell the finished product.

In the fall and winter months, two or three steers are butchered each week on the Green Haven farm. The farm inmates are allowed to remove the heart, the lungs, the liver, and the tail and cook them for themselves. It is easy for them to cut off a few steaks while they are at it, some to eat, some to sell. During the summer months, when there is no butchering, the farm workers eat, and sometimes sell, pheasants. Each spring, the New York State Department of Environmental Conservation, through the Dutchess County Federation of Sportsmen, entrusts a large number of pheasant chicks to Green Haven. The birds are fed on the farm during the summer months and are released by the federation before the fall hunting season. Some do not survive to be shot at. Each week, the farm workers report that a few of the young pheasants have met with accidental deaths. The victims of these alleged drownings and other mishaps are eaten on the cellblocks after the farm inmates have plucked them and carefully buried their feathers on the farm.

The butcher shop is another logical place for inmates to steal steaks. That was what all the butcher shop inmates were caught and fired for doing in February 1976. Their replacements lost little time in following suit. Steak is rarely served in Green Haven's mess halls. Once, early in 1976, when steak was on the menu, Green Haven's food-service manager said he had taken the precaution of telling the kitchen inmates to cook eighteen hundred portions of steak to be sure of getting the sixteen hundred he figured he needed. He got only fourteen hundred. He had to make a list of the inmates who showed up at the mess hall after the kitchen had run out of steak, and feed them their steak another day.

The state shop workers will often tell an inmate they are out of certain items in his size, and so they are, the items having been peddled to their friends. The extent of their swagging became obvious as a result of the Great Frisk, in November 1976. Inmates who want pills — uppers, downers, tranquillizers — buy them from hospital workers. The porters are convenient middlemen. Sometimes the butcher shop inmates or the state shop inmates lack the mobility to deliver their products to their customers on the various blocks. The porters are always assigned to a company on the flats and they get to know the block officers, who run the block from their secure "cage" on the ground floor. The block officers ordinarily don't want to hassle their porters (and be hassled by them in return), and tend not to check them as they come and go. A lot of steaks travel around Green Haven in porters' garbage carts and feed-up wagons.

Green Haven's guards and civilian employees are not infrequently involved in the prison's barter economy and in ripping off the state. A guard who wanted an expensive fire extinguisher for his house knew an inmate whose job gave him access to some fire extinguishers. The inmate loved Italian food. He traded a fire extinguisher for three pounds of spaghetti and a pizza. Some guards often let prisoners steal steaks, because the guards are given their share.

It is the parole-clothing department's function to provide each man who is released from Green Haven with the clothes that the state says he is entitled to: a pair of slacks, a jacket, a shirt, underwear, socks, a belt, a pair of shoes, a tie, and (between November 1 and April 1 and on rainy days the rest of the year) a topcoat. Some men leaving prison don't want some — or any — of the clothes. In the records of parole clothing, however, every departing prisoner takes everything he is entitled to, which gives the department some clothes to use as it sees fit. Parole clothing also has the job of lending civilian clothes to the men who leave Green Haven temporarily for outside court appearances or on furloughs. Although these clothes are usually returned in good condition and are dry-cleaned and lent out again, some are reported damaged beyond repair. That gives the department more clothes to use at its discretion. Occasionally, it is claimed that the pipes above the racks in parole clothing have developed unfortunate leaks. The number of ruined clothes is duly recorded. Still more clothes become available to meet the needs of the parole clothing workers.

Green Haven keeps statistics on how many prisoners hold jobs as porters, how many are clerks, and how many work on the farm, but these statistics are perhaps misleading. An inmate at Green Haven was recently asked his prison occupation. He happened to be employed in the furniture shop, but his answer didn't mention his job assignment. "I hustle, I swag, same as on the street," he said.

Newspapers cover crime and punishment as they do everything else. A rape is news, a robbery is news, a murder is news. A trial (if a suspect happens to be apprehended and happens not to cop a plea) is news. A criminal's newspaper life usually stops with his prison sentence. Unless a man happens to do something very bad or very good in prison, he disappears from print, because ordinary prison life, like ordinary life outside, is seldom considered newsworthy. Early in 1977, two prisoners in New York State did something out of the ordinary. On January 4, Hector Lopez, a Green Haven inmate serving a sentence of fifteen years to life for murder, got into the newspapers for hitting two guards over the head with a steel bar, fracturing their skulls. Four days later, Winston Moseley, an Attica inmate, who in 1964 stabbed Kitty Genovese to death outside her apartment house in Queens while thirty-eight neighbors ignored her screams for help, received a bachelor's degree in sociology.

Ninety-nine percent of New York State's inmates don't assault guards. Ninety-nine percent of New York State's inmates don't get college degrees. Instead, they put most of their thoughts and energy into making their lives in prison as comfortable as possible. In the summer of 1976, George Malinow kept a diary for four days — four ordinary days spent in the pursuit of comfort at Green Haven, four ordinary days of swagging and spinning out time.

Tuesday, August 10, 1976
6:30 A.M. Bell rings very loud and long. A certain C.O. [correction officer, or guard] does this (rings bell long) whenever he comes on duty, and I and many other inmates here would like to hit him with a shoe, as he seems to do this on purpose!

God — I hate to get up, I feel so tired!! Serves me right for staying up doing glass painting till 1:55 this morning. But — get up I must and do so. Wash up, shave and get dressed in my work clothes which is green regulation issued pants and shirt and work shoes. Put on water to be boiled for my coffee. Have coffee and 2 do-nuts. Smoke a cigarette and listen to the news, via earphones.

7:15 A.M. Doors open up. I immediately rush off to the mess hall entrance area on the West Side entrance, being I'm one of the first inmates up — no one is near that area at this time of the morning. Terry, a friend of mine (inmate) who works in the kitchen, is there awaiting me. He hands me a large card board box which contains 20 dozen eggs (fresh ones), about 20 pounds of raw bacon, and about 20 pounds macaroni, 20 to 30 oranges, 2 large cans orange juice and one large can of olive oil for cooking. I immediately *rush* back to my cell, to avoid the other inmates about due to start going to the mess hall for their breakfast.

Hide all said foods items in my cell and my friend Andy's cell. Andy is just at this time up and washing. We joke together about our sudden good windfall from our friend.

7:40 A.M. Andy and I proceed to go to work, the parole clothing department located at the basement of the Administration Building. Terry stops us to ask us to please get him some shorts, 2 white shirts and black socks. We tell him that we'll give it to him next morning. We reach the check point gate of the Administration Building, get pat frisked and we sign the logbook at the desk to verify at what time we arrived to work. Also left our institutional passes at this check point with the C.O. assigned there, as must be done.

We arrive at the basement parole-clothing area where we work. C.O.s Stevens and Barton are there already. Stevens works the 7:20 to 3:20 shift. Barton does not usually arrive this early because he works the 9:45 to 5:45 shift but today he is working extra early over-time as he has been assigned to drive one of the inmates to an outside hospital for a medical appointment.

The coffee pot is ready as C.O. Stevens always plugs in this pot early as he arrives about 20 minutes to 7 each morning. So Andy, I and Stevens all have coffee and cake. C.O. Barton is busy with the checking of papers for the inmate he is due to take to the hospital so he doesn't join us. We have the radio playing and listening to the local news broadcast. Meanwhile, there are 4 men going home on parole this morning and they just arrived and are getting dressed. Andy and I both help and make certain that all these 4 inmates going home, have all their clothes and personal property packages they may own. They have cups of coffee and relax in casual and happy conversation — about the steaks, drinks and women they'll soon enjoy out there, etc.

Andy and I, both at times, have been asked by many persons — does seeing men talk like this and seeing them go home each day bother us? We don't see it that way as Andy and I, feel very glad to see as many as possible leave any prison as prison represents "hell," in all respects!!

7:50 A.M. All the men due to go home now, leave with C.O. Stevens, to go upstairs to an office where they'll all receive their $40 gate money and whatever's in their inmate account and their release papers. Then C.O. Stevens will escort them out and drive them in the prison van bus to Hopewell Jct. station where they will board a bus for N.Y. City. I sorted out all their state issued clothing they turned in to our dept. and also gathered all the earphones they brought to our dept. upon departure. Bagged all state clothes to be sent to State Shop, their final destination.

8:05 A.M. We have an extra relief C.O. to stay with us, as C.O.s Stevens & Barton are out on assignments. Said relief C.O.s name is Officer Dover (works in officers' mess from 10 A.M. onward), who is one of the best natured officers in all respects that I have ever come across. Good sense of humor, always smiling & happy go lucky. Very well mannered, fair and easy to relate with. Should be made a warden.

Andy and I, go to our kitchen room at our basement job area and have another cup of coffee and do-nuts. We relax and talk about general topics on the outside.

8:30 A.M. Another 3 inmates that work with us now arrive to work also. They are Danny, Benno, and Ned.

This morning — we have to take a full inventory of all the stock garments we have and record each item in our general inventory stock so we will know what to order, we are short of. After Danny, Ned, and Benno all have their coffee and buns, all 5 of us get ready to do the inventory.

8:50 A.M. Andy and I, start counting the jackets, slacks, socks, handkerchiefs, belts, shoes and shirts. Danny and Ned start to count the ties, topcoats and the other apparel that the men wear to go out on furloughs, death visits and to courts.

10:35 A.M. We all are caught up on our inventory and go to have coffee again and relax. During all this time of inventory taking, Benno sat at the desk to answer all phone calls of general inquiry and also, made up lists for calling men the next day — that have to be fitted out with civilian clothes for their due release dates soon.

11:05 A.M. Benno starts to prepare the foods that he will cook for our lunch as we are not going to go to the mess hall as there is only franks for lunch. Benno is making steaks, fried onions, French fried potatoes, sauce gravy and sweet green peas for our lunch meal. Benno is an exceptional cook! When he cooks, we all leave the kitchen to be out of his way and also, not to distract him then. One or more of us are available to help him — if he calls us, but most times he does it all by himself.

Of course, he cooks — so all others of us do the cleaning up and wash the pots & dishes.

11:40 A.M. We are just about ready to start eating. We all are in conversation about how good Benno cooked the steaks, the high price of food outside, etc. The radio is playing a late song hit and we all are enjoying the food and are in a good mood.

12:25 P.M. We are done eating — so Andy, Danny and I all take out the dishes, silver ware, pots to the sink area away from the kitchen and wash & dry all. Meantime, Ned swept out kitchen while Benno went to his desk to relax.

12:45 P.M. No inmates to dress this afternoon so Danny and I, re-check all the men due to go home the next morning — on our out going releases sheet. We line up all the clothing outfits and their personal packages containing personal property at the benches where they will get dressed in the morning.

1:15 P.M. We all now sit around the desks and are in conversation about many topics. The parole board's unjust decisions, rehabilitation, politics and prison mismanagement, etc.

2:05 P.M. Phone rings and we have to go to the store house to pick up 6 large cases containing jackets and slacks. Andy, Danny and I, all take a strong push wagon and check out from the check out gate at the administration area, get pat frisked and proceed to go to the store house. Along the way, we stop off at E block, on the East Side, to find out if 2 of the men locking there will be at our Jaycee's meeting tonight? They said they will. We leave for the store house.

We arrive at the store house, load our wagon with all the large cases and pick up a copy of the order-form. We arrive at the front administration check point and again are pat frisked. We start sliding the boxes, one at a time, down the stairs to the basement where we work at. We get all boxes to the rack area. We open all boxes, take out garments and count them. The total checks out correctly. C.O. Stevens signs the receipt form copy and I take it back to the store house civilian clerk. When I return, Andy, Danny, Benno, and Ned are about half way done placing the slacks on the shelfs in their respective sizes, and the jackets on the line racks, in their respective sizes.

I join them in doing this and I sort the jackets. We stop this work at 2:45 P.M. I check and pull out coffee pot plug, stove plug, radio plug and toaster plug. Meanwhile — Andy dumps out all the trash into plastic trash bags due to go out to the dump area, via truck, in the morning. Benno dumps out all water from wash pails in kitchen. Danny washes out coffee pot and prepares it for next morning's use.

2:55 P.M. All of us leave our job area in basement, get pat frisked again at check out gate, pick up our passes and proceed to our cells in C block, all except Ned as he locks in J block.

3:05 P.M. I arrive at my cell, change clothes, wash up and go to the wash room on my gallery's end, to wash out and hang up the clothes I left there to soak yesterday.

3:25 P.M. Returned to cell, put water on for my thermos bottle to make my coffee. Layed down, smoked a cigar and relaxed listening to some soft music via earphones.

4:10 P.M. Got up, made cup of coffee, had a ham and Swiss cheese sandwich. Cleaned up table, brushed teeth and started to get all the necessary materials ready to do my glass painting. Worked on glass painting until lock in.

5:05 P.M. Bell rings — lock in time. Doors close and 2 C.O.s walk by & check the doors & count as they walk past my cell. I continue on working on the glass pictures.

5:25 P.M. C.O. stops at my cell and hands me 8 letters (personal), 2 more business letters and 1 magazine on real estate. C.O. continues on handing out mail to other cells.

Read 3 of these letters which come from the Philippines. One from my sweetheart, one from her sister & the 3rd from her mother. Finish reading all mail and lay down to catch the prison phone bulletin announcements on prison news.

5:55 P.M. Get up, wash up, brush teeth and get all my papers and materials ready for my Jaycees meeting due tonight at the school class building at J block, from 6 to 8:30 P.M.

6:00 P.M. Doors open up. I proceed to block door exit where many other men are waiting to go to different night classes and program classes. The block C.O. checks each one of us out on his master sheet.

I arrive at my Jaycee class room and start writing out on the black board the agenda for tonight's meeting. An outside male Jaycee coordinator arrives and our Jaycee meeting starts. We discuss various project possibilities. One project involves bringing boys from the high schools within a few miles of Green Haven to the prison to see what it is like so that they will never want to commit crimes and will never wind up in prison. We also form committees for each project. Meeting ends at 8:25 P.M. and all of us leave to return to our blocks.

8:35 P.M. Returned to cell. Wash and make cup of coffee & smoke 2 cigarettes. Start to work again on my glass pictures and continue until 10 P.M. I stop to eat a salami & cheese with lettuce & tomatoe sandwich. Smoke 2 cigarettes and relax on my bed.

I start to think of my sweetheart in the Philippines. What's she doing, etc.? That's rather silly cause since it is a 12 hour difference in time from N.Y. City, it goes without saying it has to be about 10 A.M. there so of course, she can't be sleeping.

10:20 P.M. I start working on my glass pictures again. I

accidently spill over the bottle of drawing paint all over my glass and I am angry as hell at myself for my carelessness! Finally get that particular portion on my glass cleaned and I have to re-draw that part of the picture again.

10:55 P.M. The bell rings and that means it's time to lock in for the night. Doors close and the 2 C.O.s again check the doors & take the count. I continue on working on the glass pictures. I feel very tired tonight so I stop working on these pictures at 11:40 P.M. I clean up all paint brushes, table and put away to a safe area, the glass paintings to dry during the night. Have a fast cup of coffee, then wash up, brush teeth and get undressed.

11:55 P.M. Put on only small night lamp, put on phones to catch midnight news. Light up cigarette and listen to the news on phones. Music (Western songs) comes on by some local Poughkeepsie disc jockey and I listen to it until 12:30 A.M.

12:35 A.M. I put out light, pull out phone plug and go to sleep.

Wednesday, August 11, 1976

6:05 A.M. Woke up and put water on for coffee. Smoked a cigarette and listened to the news over earphones. Water ready and I make my cup of coffee and wash up, brush teeth and get dressed in work clothes.

6:30 A.M. Bell rings to get up, for the block inmates. I count out 3 dozen fresh eggs that I had hidden in my cell previously into a small box. I put this box in the bottom of a large metal bucket that I use to soak clothes. Next, I also put several pounds raw bacon into a plastic bag & also place this in the pail with the eggs.

I sort out 3 dress shirts and 2 pants to take to my job section so I can neatly press these clothes for myself. Check myself to make sure I haven't forgotten anything — my institutional pass, locker keys, lighter, cigarettes and pens. Lay on bed, relax and smoke a cigarette, while listening to radio music.

7:20 A.M. Doors open up. I go to Andy's cell (2 cells away) and check to see if he is ready to go to work. He is — so we proceed to walk through the corridor hall. Near the mess hall — our friend — Terry is there waiting for us. He hands us a package of chop meat — about 15 pounds in weight. Andy carries this — as I am loaded carrying my pail and clothes to press.

We explain to Terry, that we didn't forget him — with regard to the clothing items he asked for the other day, as we couldn't bring it out yesterday. We assure Terry that he'll receive it tomorrow morning.

We are early — so along the way to work, the companies are now moving to the mess hall from A blk. Many men we know shout out their usual greetings to Andy and me.

Andy & I arrive at the administration check point gate. We hand in our passes and sign the inmates logbook, indicating we checked in to work & at what time. We got pat frisked. The two C.O.s at this post, smile & ask — "what's in the pail & bag?" I tell them — "food for us and our bosses." They laugh & tell us to go on. No doubt due to all the years I've been in G.H.; and these 2 C.O.s know me from all said years, they don't wish to bother me & give me a break.

We reach the basement locked barred door & holler — "Hey — open up, hard workers here!" C.O. Stevens comes & let's us in. We go to the kitchen & put the eggs, chop meat and bacon in the refrigerator. I put my clothes to be pressed near the ironing board for pressing later on.

7:45 A.M. Ned, Benno, and Danny arrive to work in the basement, in addition some inmates due to go home on parole release. Andy & I attend the men getting dressed and place all their property packages near them. Ned, Benno, Danny, Andy, I and some of the men going home, are in the kitchen having coffee. C.O. Stevens is busy at desk getting in order, all the release papers for the men going home now.

7:55 A.M. The men going home leave together with C.O. Stevens. C.O. Dover is the extra relief officer left with us.

We check list to see how many inmates who still have to be

measured & fitted out with their going home clothes for call out today. We obtained cell locations, names & have C.O. Dover phone all blocks in which said men lock at, to have them sent to parole clothing dept. at 1 o'clock P.M.

All of us — stray off to attend to our personal needs — washing clothes, pressing clothes, reading, etc. I go and press all my clothes I brought down this morning.

9:35 A.M. We are sitting near the desk, talking when C.O. Dover answers the phone. He informs us that the Chief Clerk said that the Nassau County Sheriff's Office have 2 transportation officers on the way and they ought to arrive at G.H. about 10:30 A.M., to pick up 2 inmates that will be taken back to Nassau County Court for their legal proceedings.

C.O. Dover phoned the blocks where these 2 inmates lock that are due to go to Nassau Court, and informed the block officer to tell these 2 inmates they are due to go to Court right away & to bring their toilet articles & cigarettes with them.

9:55 A.M. The 2 Nassau County Sheriff officers arrive & are waiting at our work area for the 2 inmates they came for. Both sheriff officers have coffee with us in kitchen. They tell us and C.O. Dover about the latest news events regarding the Nassau County Jail, etc.

10:20 A.M. The 2 inmates due to be taken to court arrive with their personal property.

Andy & I, both take one man each, to dress him out in civilian attire. Next, Andy & I, pack their personal property in large shopping type paper bags & mark their names & numbers on each bag.

Said 2 inmates are searched by the Nassau Officers & they are then hand cuffed and they all leave our basement area.

Andy and I both have coffee & do-nuts. C.O. Stevens returns to our area. C.O. Barton still hasn't arrived but he phones from B block, to tell us that he is assigned there till 12 noon, as the sgt's chart room is short officers.

11:05 A.M. Andy and I leave to return to our block (C blk.), to rest and do our personal tasks in our cells. Meanwhile, Benno and Ned are preparing the lunch time meal which will be hot roast beef, mashed potatoes, corn niblets and ice cream (pints from commissary, stored in our refrigerator from commissary buy).

Andy and I both arrive at our C blk. without meeting anyone along the way. Andy goes to his cell and turns on his cassette player and lays on his bed to relax & listen to the music.

I put on water for coffee & gather all my socks and handkerchiefs that need washing. I soak these in 2 separate pails, intending to wash them later on at night.

I prepare to shave & take a hot shower. Having done so — I have my coffee and smoke. I dress up in clean work clothes and lay down to rest, listening to the radio music.

I fall asleep & Andy wakes me up and asks if I'm ready to go back to work? I check time & it's now 12:35 P.M. I tell him in about 15 more minutes. I brush teeth & take measurements of one large glass picture so I can make a large enough card board box to put it in (glass picture) so that when my visitor comes to see me on Saturday, he will be able to carry it easily & safely to his car to take home.

12:55 P.M. Andy and I take one case of canned cola soda with us from Andy's cell to go to our refrigerator at where we work at. We walk through corridor & are stopped by several inmates we know who ask us if we have any black paint — about a quart as they wish to paint their yard weight boxes (box to hold weight lifter's weight iron). We tell them we have and we'll bring the paint out in the yard at 3:30 in the afternoon to their location.

We reach the administration check point gate, get pat frisked and go to our job area in the basement.

Andy puts 15 cans of soda in the refrigerator & the rest in storage locker in kitchen.

1:20 P.M. The men who were called for to be dressed for going home in a few weeks have arrived to our work area.

Andy, Ned and I, take one man each to dress out for measurements. There are 12 men to dress & measure. We are done soon and the escorting C.O. takes all the men out and leaves.

2:15 P.M. Andy & I still haven't had time to eat our meal that Benno and Ned prepared for lunch but all rest have already eaten. Andy & I eat, help to wash up and put away dishes, silver ware, etc. We sweep and mop up entire kitchen floor.

2:45 P.M. Ned prepares coffee pot for morning's coffee tomorrow. I pull out all electrical plugs (toaster, coffee pot, radio and fans). Dump out water pails from kitchen. Andy bags up all trash in plastic bags for the garbage truck collection in the morning. C.O. Stevens and the rest of us all leave as we are done working for the day. We all get pat frisked again at the gate check point & pick up our institutional passes.

The corridors are crowded as most men are returning from their jobs to the yard and cellblocks. We are busy discussing some law and we don't stop to speak to anybody along the way to C block.

2:55 P.M. Andy went out to yard on some errand. I go to wash room and finish washing & hanging up my clothes on line in wash room.

Go back to cell — change clothes and wash up, brush teeth, sit down and relax listening to the music on the tape recorder being played next cell to mine.

3:20 P.M. I make cup of coffee, have do-nut and one apple. Clean table and prepare to continue doing my glass paintings. I am working on this while at the same time I have my earphones on, listening to Spanish music. I just remembered now that we forgot to pick up the gal. of black paint for our friends. We'll have to apologize & obtain it tomorrow.

Danny just came to my cell with a large paper bag containing the clothing items Andy & I, both forgot to pick up for our friend in the kitchen — Terry. I thank Danny — he's a life-saver!

4:55 P.M. Bell rings — lock in time. Doors close & the 2

block C.O.s check doors & take count. I continue working on glass pictures.

5:25 P.M. The C.O. stops at cell — it's mail delivery time, and he gives me 3 personal letters, 2 catalogues and 4 business letters. I clean up paint brushes. Lay on bed, put on phones to listen to radio news & also, the prison bulletin events broadcast, while I open and read my mail.

6:08 P.M. Doors open and I go out to Benno's cell on gallery back of mine, in my block. I ask Benno what does he want me to bring down relative to food items in the morning to our shop kitchen for tomorrow's lunch meal? He wants more macaroni, cans of sauce and garlic. I discuss some other misc. topics and leave to go back to my cell.

7:25 P.M. A C.O. stops by at my cell to look at my glass pictures. He asks if I sell my pictures and I tell him I don't. I only make them as gifts for my friends.

I make a cup of coffee and have a kielbasa sandwich. Smoke 2 cigarettes and lay on bed to relax. I recall I must reply to 3 letters tonight, so I put away all the glass pictures, clean off table and start letter writing.

8:55 P.M. Feel tired. Make cup of coffee and smoke another cigarette. I am thinking of the family I've become close to via correspondence located at Illinois. Lay down to relax and fall asleep! Wake up and notice it's now 9:45 P.M. I go out to see what program is on the T.V. at the end of the gallery. It happens to be an old war movie, "Back to Bataan," so I stay to watch it and relax.

10:05 P.M. I returned to cell area and got into discussion about the conditions in this prison; how some C.O.s are pressing the inmates into provoking trouble by their aggressive attitude, etc.

10:45 P.M. I returned to my cell and washed up, brushed teeth and got undressed. Put on water for coffee. Checked to see that I have everything ready to take out in the morning with me to work. I put the sauce and macaroni in a bag to take to our kitchen in the basement in morning. Layed down on bed to relax and smoked cigarette.

11:00 P.M. Bell rings for lock in time. The 2 C.O.s pass by check door to see it's closed and count. Started to write my usual very long type of letter to my sweetheart in the Philippines — Liwayway. Completed 20 pages (both sides) and set it aside for tomorrow to complete it to a possible 20 more pages. I always write such long letters to Liwayway, cause she has to wait approximately 10 to 14 days from the time I mail it via "air-mail." The loss in time takes place after it reaches one of the main air ports in the Philippines. Further, inasmuch as she has to wait 14 days for my letter — I feel it is only right that my letter contains much to read, so she can enjoy reading all I say to her and be happy. Such a heavy type letter usually costs me 4 to 6 dollars, depending on the weight. Must bear in mind — I usually include many photos, newspaper clippings, etc.

12:05 A.M. I am tired. I turn off lights & go to sleep.

Friday, August 13, 1976

6:30 A.M. Bell rang — time to get up. Brushed teeth, washed up and got dressed in my work clothes. Made cup of coffee and smoked a cigarette. Put phones on to listen to latest news.

Straightened out cell, swept floor and made up bed.

7:20 A.M. Cell doors open up and I go to see if Andy is up yet? He is just getting out of bed. I tell him — I'll go & check with Terry, at the mess hall — if we have any food items due? I reach mess hall corridor door. Terry is waiting for me. He hands me about 5 pounds of oleo in a paper bag & one 30 pounds of macaroni in a box. I take all this and head for my cell in C blk. I reach my cell without meeting any C.O.s.

I tell Andy what we just received. We obtain a small push cart wagon — load the macaroni, oleo & 2 boxes of canned sodas we previously bought from the commissary. We also find some clean empty boxes (about 7) at the end of our gallery. We also take these boxes as we can use them to pack the personal property of men going home.

We are early arriving at the check point gate of the Administration Building. The steady old time C.O. is on duty there who knows Andy & me — well! We sign the logbook & hand in our passes. We tell the C.O. that we have boxes for packing. He waves us on & doesn't bother to check the boxes — only pat frisks us.

We reach our basement work area okay. I put the box of macaroni away in the storage cabinet & the oleo into the refrigerator. We put all the other empty card board boxes away in the bin for that purpose.

7:40 A.M. The men due to go home this morning (8 men) have arrived to get dressed, as have also, Benno, Ned & Danny, to work. The men are all dressed. Andy & I make certain that they all have their personal property packages to take out with them. They have coffee and sign all the necessary papers for their releases with C.O. Stevens.

7:55 A.M. C.O. Stevens takes the men upstairs who are going home. We say our "good byes" to them. We have the relief officer, Mr. Dover, with us until C.O. Barton arrives which will be about 9:15 A.M. We all have coffee & do-nuts, the radio is playing and we are discussing football games and professional football. I favor the N.Y. Giants but I have to take a lot of teasing as the N.Y. Giants did badly last season. Oh well — we can't always be winners!

8:35 A.M. Ned goes to his own desk at the back of the basement parole clothing dept. and he starts stamping out the "time cards" for the personnel of Green Haven. Andy goes to his sewing machine to do some work on some pants and shirts of his own & several of his friends. Danny starts typing out some forms for inventory and also, the lists of all men due to go out on furloughs. Benno is re-stocking all the shelfs with the various garment items for parole release. C.O. Dover loves the sport of basketball and he is telling Danny about his son's playing on a school team, etc. I go over to the bench area & start to bag up all the prison issued clothing that the men left that went home this morning.

9:05 A.M. Five men come down to our area with their personal property, as they are due to all go home next week. I and Andy pack up their property in individual boxes and mark their numbers & names on each package, plus the date they will go home.

9:35 A.M. C.O. Barton arrives & C.O. Dover leaves. We all stop whatever we're doing and have our coffee and do-nuts. C.O. Barton tells us of a fire that happened during the other night — where 2 children died in the house fire. It was allegedly due to some faulty wiring in the house.

10:15 A.M. We all decide since it's Friday and I expect a visit tomorrow that we won't dress any more inmates during the afternoon today. Instead — we'll sweep and mop up the *entire* basement area & do a general clean up — which we usually do on Saturday morning — as we also work on Saturdays & Sundays if there's work to do and get paid for Saturdays & Sundays even if there isn't. Benno goes into the kitchen to prepare for our lunch meal.

11:35 A.M. Phone rings and C.O. Barton tells us that we have to go to the store house to pick up 6 large crate boxes which contain slacks. Andy & I leave together to go to the store house with a large push wagon.

We reach the store house & load all the boxes on the wagon. A friend of ours meets Andy & me. He asks us if we can use some coffee, sugar and canned milk. We say yes. He works upstairs in the food supply area. He comes down on the freight elevator and loads onto our wagon 50 pounds of sugar, 30 large cans of milk, 30 five pound type bags of grind coffee and 3 large cans of Tuna Fish. We leave. We move fast and stop to speak to no one along the way.

We get all the boxes down to the basement area, open all

boxes and take a count of the slacks, etc. All checks out accurately.

1:20 P.M. We eat late — our lunch but there won't be any men to dress this noon so we aren't pressed for time.

2:05 P.M. We clean up the kitchen. Then we all put away the slacks into their proper sizes into the bins set for this purpose.

2:35 P.M. All of us now sweep and mop up entire basement, empty water pails, pull electric plugs out, check doors to be sure all are closed. We all leave as it is now 3:00 P.M. We pass thru the corridor halls and as usual — we stop to speak with several men Andy & I both know. Andy hands the shorts he altered to the person he promised it for.

3:15 P.M. I arrive at my cell room. I feel a very severe type of headache and I go to the block officer and obtain 6 aspirins off him. I take all 6 at one time and I decide to lay down on my bed. I take off my work clothes and get under the blanket. I fall asleep and don't wake up until I notice it's 7:45 o'clock.

7:45 P.M. The headache seems to have gone but for some reason, I still feel sorta dizzy. I wash up — have a cold soda and smoke a cigarette. I lay back down on my bed and relax. I am thinking when will that day arrive when I'll be going home? It seems like I've been born in prison I've spent so many of my years in them.

8:40 P.M. I just noticed 2 letters laying on my cell door. I open them and both are nice long type of letters from 2 male friends of mine.

8:55 P.M. I take the 2 glass pictures that I was working on & are finished, and insert them into the 2 frames I had made for them. I place them into a card board box and take them upstairs to the top gallery in C blk. and give them to my friend who I made them for. They are going to his old mother. He thanks me and knows that I won't accept any sort of payment for making them.

9:25 P.M. I go to Andy's cell room and he has about one gallon of strong homemade brew. I feel a bit depressed —

so I decide to put "one on" and Andy, his friend Baron and I all start drinking together. We discuss old times on the streets, people we knew, have some good laughs and finish off drinking the entire gallon. I feel quite mellow! Not very drunk — but enough so that I feel just great! I leave and go to my cell room as it's close to the 10 P.M. count. The bell rings — so I stand by my door as the C.O. walks by taking his count.

10:05 P.M. I lay down on my bed — put the phones on — listening to some soft music. I light a cigarette & pull out the last lengthy type letter from Liwayway. I re-read it slowly and start thinking about her. What she's doing — how hard she has to work for a mere few dollars to support herself & her mother as her father passed away. I can't wait to go out free so I can help out Liwayway & her mother financially as one American Dollar equals 7 Philippine pesos. So $100 (U.S. money) would give them $700 in Philippine money.

10:40 P.M. I get up and have a cup of coffee and a piece of peach pie. Still feel good from the brew Andy gave me. I feel rather sentimental and I start thinking about my son — Arthur, what he's doing? How tall has he grown? Does he hate me for not being at home with him during his young years when he needed a father the most? I shake off my thoughts now about Arthur, as I don't want to become depressed tonight!

11:05 P.M. The bell just rang and it's time for all the men in C block to lock in their cell rooms. Andy rushes over to my cell, before the doors close & hands me a brown paper bag. He laughs & says — "enjoy it!"

He rushes back to his cell. The doors close. I look in the bag & there's a quart more of homemade brew! Boy — Andy is really something! I put it away till after the C.O.s take the count. They walk by now. I put out all the lights in my cell and lay on my bed. I pour a large glass of brew and I sip it slowly! I finish it & pour all the rest into my glass. I finish this off fast & lay back to relax and think. I wonder when it will be when they finally let me go free?

Saturday, August 14, 1976

9:30 A.M. I just woke up and overslept. I expect my visit which will be outside the walls as weekend visits for me are approved for such outside visits, at 10 A.M. today. I shave and take a shower. Surprisingly, I have no hangover headache from my drinking last night.

9:45 A.M. I am all dressed & ready for my visit. I have 2 glass pictures that I will give to my partner — Patrick on my visit.

10:15 A.M. I walk all the long distance by myself to the rear gate exit. It happens to be a very beautiful warm, sunny day today. The large bar gates open up for me. I enter the compound & the C.O. there pat frisks me, hands me my outside pass with my photo & description on it so I in turn can turn it over to the outside area C.O. there. The C.O. also checks out my 2 glass pictures & reads my approval slip for taking out said 2 pictures. The C.O. shouts up to the tower guard "okay — let him out — he checks out okay!" The large solid steel door slides open & I walk outside the walls. It's a funny feeling as I can actually run away if I so desired! But I'm not about to do something that stupid — so I smile to myself. I wait there & the small prison van bus comes to me — and drives me to the back of the prison where the outside visitors' area is. I get off the bus with my pictures, thank the inmate driver — I know & check in with the visiting office C.O. there. I turn my outside visiting pass to him & also give him my approval slip to permit my visitor to take home the 2 glass pictures I brought with me. I walk over to my 2 visitors, Patrick and old Carl Terra, two old time, very dear friends of mine. I show them the glass pictures and they both state how beautiful the pictures look, etc. We discuss many topics — of old times and present general problems on the outside these days.

11:45 A.M. It's near lunch time and Patrick brought up cold cuts, sodas, cake and fruits so we all eat and relax during lunch. We all then go out doors to the yard area and we walk around for about 1/2 an hour just discussing my chances of coming home, etc. We then go back inside the small building and a friend takes several photos of us all together and singularly. I introduce my friend to Patrick & Carl Terra.

2:05 P.M. We have a soda again and Patrick tells me that he also left me a large food package for when I return to go back. Patrick and Carl both contributed & left me $50. I thank the both of them for all this.

2:30 P.M. It's time for Patrick and Carl to go home as they both want to arrive home early before the heavy traffic takes place going to N.Y. City. I bid them both good bye. I obtain my outside pass back from the C.O. & he gives me the receipt for the $50 left for me. I get on the van bus & ride back to the rear gate. The door opens & I go inside. I hand back my pass & enter a small room in the building there & get a strip frisk. I get my regular institutional pass back & head for the package room to pick up my food package. It is a large card board box and it's quite heavy. It consists of 4 separate large cakes, 5 pound Polish canned ham, 5 rings of Polish kielbasa, 2 jars of Horse Radish (one white, one red), 1 loaf of white bread, 1 rye bread & 1 black bread, 2 packages Swiss Cheese, 2 packages of tomatoes, 2 heads of lettuce, apples, oranges, pears, box of chocolate candy, 2 large jars instant coffee, 2 large jars Coffee Mate Cream, 2 boxes cubed sugar, 4 large cans fruit cocktail, 1 large jar Tang, 1 jar peanut butter, 3 cartons of Pall Malls & 1 box of 50 cigars. I arrive at my cell room at C blk. & put away all the food items.

3:05 P.M. I start to write two separate letters of "thank you," to Carl Terra & Patrick for visiting me, leaving me money & the food package. I immediately put the 2 letters into the mail box so I won't forget to do so later on.

3:40 P.M. I change off into my clean sweat shirt & pants. I make up a small bag with some of the meats, etc., and go to give it to a friend in A block. He is happy to receive it. We spent about 1/2 hour discussing some glass pictures, patterns & frames he is to make for me. I leave & return to my cell room.

4:25 P.M. I start to make up sandwiches, coffee and cut into sections 2 of the large cakes. I deliver some of this to Andy and Baron at Andy's cell. We eat, have coffee and talk about my visitors, etc.

4:50 P.M. It is close to lock in time & the count so I return to my cell room. I lay on my bed — put on earphones and get ready to listen to the radio news. The bell rings so it's count time. The cell doors close & the 2 C.O.s take count. I listen to the news and smoke a cigarette. The prison news comes on now & I listen.

5:25 P.M. The C.O. comes around with the mail. I receive 3 personal letters. One from my adopted niece — Jane in Long Island, one from my adopted sister in Illinois & one from a Puerto Rican young lady, from Brooklyn. I read the letters and feel sleepy from the out doors hours spent on my visit. I close my eyes and fall asleep listening to the soft music over the earphones. I wake up and see that the cell door is already opened. I look at the clock and the time is now 7:35 P.M. I have a cup of coffee and smoke a cigarette.

7:50 P.M. I don't feel like doing anything tonight but just relaxing as I have to get up early to attend Mass in the morning. I go to the T.V. set to see what movie may come on. It is a World War II war picture which I am fond of so I sit and watch it. This movie started at 8 P.M. and ended at 10 P.M. I really enjoyed it!

10 P.M. We have to go to our cell doors for the 10 o'clock count. The count is over and I make myself a heavy kielbasa sandwich and have a cup of coffee. I clean up the table, brush my teeth and wash my face. I then lay down to relax & listen to some soft music on phones.

10:25 P.M. I go over to Andy's cell and we talk about a certain court decision that came down recently from the N.Y. Court of Appeals. It has to do with Andy's case and a parole revocation hearing that Andy was supposed to receive but was never granted to him, in his case.

10:55 P.M. It's close to lock in time so I return to my cell room. The bell rings and it's count time & lock in time for C blk.

11:00 P.M. I leave on only the small lamp light & I get into bed. I put on phones to listen to some Western music. It's not the type I like — so I change to listen to Latin music. I don't understand the words but the music is nice & soft so I listen to it. I light up a cigar.

12:35 A.M. The cigar is about finished. I put it out, turn off lights & pull out phone plug & go to sleep.

There is, of course, no typical day in the life of an inmate at Green Haven, because there is no typical inmate. There are about eighteen hundred and fifty-five inmates at Green Haven on a given day, and about eighteen hundred and fifty-five ways of doing time. In some respects, Malinow seems unique. He probably writes the longest letters to the most distant country, and he justifies their length with the most idiosyncratic logic. He is more experienced at swagging, more likely to get away with it, and consequently better off than most of the younger men at Green Haven. He was once one of the younger men, and can remember many years when he had to go to the mess hall to eat because he had no friends to visit him and bring or send him packages — years when he was not as well connected as he is now, and had less desirable jobs.

What is interesting about Malinow's special and relatively easy life at Green Haven in 1976 is how much it still has in common with, say, the life of a young black inmate assigned to the optical shop rather than to parole clothing, who spends his free time playing basketball instead of painting on glass, writes no letters, and smokes marijuana whenever he can get it, in addition to drinking homemade booze. To begin with, one thing that almost all of Green Haven's inmates share is a short workday. Because there are more guards and civilians on the 7:20

A.M. to 3:20 P.M. shift than on any other, the prisoners' workdays are circumscribed by these hours. Three of these eight hours are usually spent eating meals and traveling the prison's long corridors between the cellblocks and the mess halls and the mess halls and the job areas. The workday usually lasts four or five hours: roughly from 8:30 or 9:00 A.M. to 11:00 A.M. and from 12:00 or 12:30 P.M. to 2:30 P.M. In the three workdays Malinow chronicles in his diary, more of the time he put in at parole clothing was spent drinking coffee, chatting, eating, washing dishes, and doing personal chores than dressing inmates, fetching clothes from the storehouse, and taking inventory. Malinow almost never works more than two hours a day, simply because there is almost never more than two hours of work for him to do.

On the three workdays he describes, Malinow was actually on the parole-clothing premises during his so-called working hours. Most other prison activities are also scheduled during the 7:20 A.M. to 3:20 P.M. shift's hours, however, and inmates are often absent from their work assignments to take care of personal business. Malinow might not have been at parole clothing if he had felt ill and wanted to go to sick call; if he had had a toothache and had managed to get an appointment with a prison dentist; if it had been one of the two days a month that his block was scheduled to go to the commissary; if he had had legal work to do and wanted to look up something in the law library; or if he had wanted to go to the barbershop for a haircut. If he had had weekday visitors, as Benno and Danny often did, he could have spent from 8:00 A.M. to 3:30 P.M. in one of Green Haven's two inside visiting rooms. If he had been coming up for parole, he might have had an interview with his parole officer or his Service Unit counselor, or made a trip to Green Haven's Pre-Release Center, which tries to help men with their post-prison plans. If he had received a package in the mail, he would have had to go to the package room to fetch it. If he had run out of paint, he might have made a trip to the hobby shop to replenish his supplies. If Malinow had been caught drinking booze or transporting illicit eggs or oleo, he might have had to appear before the Adjustment Committee and he might have been keeplocked. The work-absenteeism rate at Green Haven is high. In October 1976, school attendance was 55 percent.

Parole clothing is an oasis at Green Haven. Craig Stevens, the C.O. in charge of parole clothing, chooses the inmates who work for him carefully. He doesn't accept any troublemakers — a category in which he places drug addicts, homosexuals, militants, child molesters, and drunks. The men do willingly whatever work there is to be done; they recognize a good job and an easy boss when they see one. When a member of the parole board asks a prisoner, "What have you done for yourself in prison?" — a favorite parole board question — the board doesn't seem pleased to hear that a man has worked in parole clothing. Most of the Board's twelve members seem happier to be told that a man has gone to school. In recent years, school has been considered more rehabilitative than a pursuit like industry, which was considered rehabilitative by earlier generations of prison administrators and parole board members because industry was supposed to teach good work habits, which would keep a man straight on the outside. If the parole board were to visit the prison school, it might wonder whether school was more rehabilitative for the ordinary prisoner than any other activity at Green Haven.

On Thursday morning, May 6, 1976, twelve of the seventeen men who were enrolled in the beginning-reading class were sitting in a well-furnished, well-lighted classroom at Green Haven. Between 9:00 (when the class was scheduled to begin) and 9:15, the teacher took attendance. The men discussed the five absentees at some length. One had been transferred to Great Meadow — unjustly, they felt. One was upset because another inmate, who had committed a crime that was more serious than his, had received a much shorter sentence, and was brooding about it in his cell. A third was in court, with a case they thought he might win on a technicality. Between 9:15 and 9:30, a man stumbled through a one-page text called "Buying Groceries." At 9:30, another man was asked to read the next page in the book, a text entitled "At the Bank." "Don't feel like reading," he said. The teacher called on another man, who sighed and began to read. As he read, two men filed each other's nails, one combed his hair, one wrote a love letter to his girl, and four or five stared into space (one of them smelled of alcohol, two appeared high). The text read:

> Mary and I keep our money in the bank.
> Henry and Elizabeth keep their money in the bank, too.
> It is not safe to keep much money in the house.
> I know a man who kept his money in the house. One day a burglar got his money. After that he kept his money in the bank, too.
> It pays to keep one's money in the bank. Money in the bank is safe.

It took the reader, a young man who had played hooky during his elementary-school years, ten minutes to get that far. There were a few more sentences on the page, but he stopped, wearier from the exertion of reading eight sentences than a long-distance runner might be after going twenty miles. He also looked puzzled. He scratched his head and laughed. "Mr. Kotter," he said. (The teacher's name happens to be Lamarbella, but his students call him Kotter, because Lamarbella is too hard a name for them to remember, and because they think he resembles the actor who plays the schoolteacher in "Welcome Back, Kotter," a television show they like.) "I ain't too sure 'bout dat book," he continued. "Willie here is a bank robber. If'n I put my money in a bank and Willie robs that bank, it don't be so safe." Willie beamed with pleasure.

The 9:45 buzzer sounded, signaling the end of class. The men in the beginning-reading group were supposed to attend three forty-five-minute classes a morning. That was their entire work-day. The next class on their schedule was beginning arithmetic. One of the nail-filers said he was going to skip arithmetic, because he had more important things to do. He was going to make his way to Fay Field to dig up some money that his woman had brought in on a picnic a while back. Fearing a cell search, he had buried it there for safekeeping. He wanted it that afternoon to buy some grass that had been smuggled in to one of his friends the previous day. "I don't mess with no arithmetic nohow," he said. "Counting money was never no problem for me. On the street, I worked for a dry cleaner. Each piece of clothes had a ticket. Some tickets said 'Clean,' some said 'Press,' and some said 'Clean and press.' My trouble was I couldn't read the tickets, so to be on the safe side I cleaned and pressed everything. When the boss man found out, he fired me. Can't say as I wanted the job. I just had to have some kind of legit job to keep the parole officer off my back. Hell, there's much more money in stealing than in dry-cleaning."

Lamarbella had once taught fourth grade and sixth grade in a small town a few miles from Green Haven. He had been laid off several years earlier, when the town's elementary-school enrollment declined, and had come to Green Haven because it was the only teaching job he could get. He preferred teaching children, because they learned much faster, but he had nothing against inmates. "I'm lucky to get an hour's work out of them a week," he said. "One day, a guy will be feeling bad about a Dear John letter he got from a girl; another will be feeling bad about being hit by the parole board. I don't push them. I take what I can get from them. Friends ask me if it's scary working in a maximum-security prison. It isn't. I imagine working here is like working in a dynamite factory. After the first month or two, you don't even think of it. I've never been hit by an inmate, and I don't know of any other teacher who has been. The only thing that really bothers me about this place is the lethargy that hangs over it. When I first came to Green Haven, I brought a book to read during my lunch hour. I soon stopped reading. Now I'm always yawning, just like the inmates, and I sit around at lunchtime doing nothing."

On May 18, 1976, the ten students who showed up at a high-school English class were more attentive than the beginning readers but also more exasperated with the lesson of the day, which happened to be grammar. The students were scheduled to take the high-school-equivalency examination in June, and were reviewing the possessive, objective, and nominative cases. The possessive case was immediately disposed of: everyone understood mine, yours, his, and hers. The class clown said, "Most of us are at Green Haven for taking what wasn't ours." The teacher went on to the nominative case: any pronoun that followed the verb "to be" had to go in the nominative case. "So," he explained, "if you say 'Knock, knock' and someone asks 'Who's there?' and you're alone, the correct answer is 'It is I.' If you're with a friend, the correct answer is 'It is we.' " The students argued that that sounded ridiculous. "If my buddy and me knocked and said 'It's we' instead of 'It's us,' the people wouldn't open the door," one said. "They'd think we was nutty as a fruitcake." "My buddy and *I*, we *were* nutty as a fruitcake," the teacher said automatically. The students all began talking and laughing at once, agreeing that "It's me" was a much better answer than "It's I." When the noise had subsided, the teacher said, "It's perfectly all right to say 'It's me,' but not in English class and not on the high-school-equivalency exam." "Man, you know the high-school-equivalency's a farce," a student said. "College graduates and Ph.D.s can't get jobs. What good's a high-school-equivalency going to do any of us?" The teacher looked down, cleared his throat, and went on to the objective case. Later, the teacher gave an example of the objective case to a colleague. Discussing Green Haven's school, he said, "You can lead a man to water, but you can't make him drink."

Malinow is among those who took the high-school-equivalency test. He passed it without studying for it, and considers it useless. "I'm not interested in an education, I'm interested in making money," he says. The classification sergeant says it is harder to get inmates at Green Haven to go to school than to be porters. "They just aren't interested," he says. The supervisor of Green Haven's academic school, who has been at the prison for nine years, says that in 1968 the school had eight paid civilian teachers, a number of inmate teachers, and a supplies budget of $3200. In October 1976, the prison's educational program had forty-three paid employees, twenty-five volunteers, abundant supplies, and a budget of several hundred thousand dollars. "It's questionable whether we're getting that much more out of the extra salaries and the extra thousands of dollars, but the inmates sure are getting a lot more textbooks to steal," the supervisor says.

One might think there would be greater enthusiasm at Green Haven for learning a vocational skill than for learning reading, arithmetic, or grammar. There is not. In the fall of 1976, Green Haven's vocational school offered eleven trades. On October 12, enrollment in the vocational school, which had a capacity of 180, was down to 138. A week earlier, the civilian vocational supervisor had made an announcement over the prison earphones for three days in a row, inviting all inmates interested in the vocational area to drop him a note. Only eight inmates had responded. On October 12, there was no one in the vocational school's auto shop, because it was closed; the civilian auto instructor had had to go to Albany for the week, and no substitutes may be hired for such eventualities. Only four of eleven men who were supposed to be in the sewing-machine repair shop were there; two were playing basketball in the gym, one was refereeing the game, one was at the prison's Protestant Center, one was at the Sunni's mosque, one was keeplocked, and one was at a Reality House meeting. (Three staff members from Reality House, a drug-treatment center on 125th Street in Manhattan, drive up to Green Haven twice a week. They spend about three and a half hours on Monday and about an hour and a half on Tuesday rapping with no more than fifty inmates. The Reality House sessions are Green Haven's only drug program.) Printing, building maintenance, electronics, welding, motorcycle repair, carpentry, and major appliances were also suffering from low attendance on October 12. The electronics instructor was still saddened by the recent defection of a student who had shown some promise in electronics. He had noticed that the man often came in, stayed for a while, and then left. He asked around, and learned that the man was in the vocational-school bathroom, washing his clothes in the sink. The instructor told him that electronics students were not permitted to spend their time washing clothes. The man wasted no time in transferring to the major-appliance shop, where inmates learn to repair washing machines, refrigerators, dryers, and stoves; washing clothes is one of that shop's fringe benefits.

There were seven men and over a hundred thousand dollars' worth of machines in the machine shop on October 12. "Years ago, we said our problem was that we had obsolete machines and that we were made to use them just to do prison-maintenance work," the machine-shop instructor said. "Now, thanks to federal grants, I've got a $35,000 turret lathe, an $8000 engine lathe, a $7000 engine lathe — everything you need for surface grinding and milling. This is really a better-than-average-equipped job shop, and we're free to train the men just to use the machines. Now it seems our problem is that we can't get the men down here and that the workday is too short to teach the men who do come. We're competing with industry, which pays better."

Welding was popular with the inmates when it was first introduced at Green Haven, in 1970, but it proved to be a passing fancy. Although a man can be employable after six months of studying welding — mastering the machines in the machine shop takes much longer — the inmates found welding dull. "Welding's a repetitive type of skill," the vocational supervisor has explained. "Learning the three basic positions of welding, which you must do, is boring. Most places want heli-arc welders, who can weld stainless steel and aluminum, but most of our men dropped out before they got that far. The others didn't do very well. We had the Department of Transportation come and give a test. Only one inmate was qualified to take the test. He failed. We have three heli-arc machines sitting here. What a waste."

In 1974, Green Haven's vocational supervisor set up a motorcycle repair shop, since repairing motorcycles was an up-and-coming trade on the outside. The inmates received their initial training on small engines; the idea was that they would progress to motorcycles. Three Hondas had been bought. Two months went by, the men hadn't mastered the small engines, and soon half of them dropped out for lack of motivation or were transferred to other prisons. "They wanted instant gratification," the vocational supervisor said not long ago, with a certain sadness. "They never got to the point where they could work on the Hondas."

Enrollment in the carpentry shop had recently plummeted from twenty to nine after the instructor cracked down on stealing wood. Once the inmates could no longer make jewelry boxes and picture frames to sell to their friends, they lost interest in carpentry.

On January 1, 1976, federal and state money that would enable eighteen inmates to take a ten-month course in drafting became available. The inmates could get a one-year certificate in mechanical drafting from Dutchess Community College. The drafting instructor thought he would easily be able to enroll 1 percent of Green Haven's population — eighteen students — simply by announcing the course. He got twelve prospective students. He then went, accompanied by the vocational supervisor, to H block to recruit new arrivals on the reception companies, and got two more. He spent two days helping them fill out the grant forms. By October 12, a number of the original students had dropped out. Six eventually completed the course.

About the only thing that seems to differentiate Green Haven's four industrial shops from Green Haven's academic and vocational schools is that industry pays better. The idleness is the same. On November 3, 1976, the optical shop wasn't open, because its civilian foreman was ill. In the upholstery shop, men were sitting around doing nothing. The foam rubber and plastic they needed to make and repair chairs for the Department of Correctional Services and other state agencies had failed to arrive. The few men who were in the furniture shop complained that their work was boring. In the knit shop, which makes underwear for men, women, and children in the state's prisons and mental institutions, the foreman said his workers were stealing him blind. "Last Friday, one man must have finished off ten dozen men's long-sleeved T-shirts," he said. "I got half a dozen of them. Nine and a half dozen were stolen. The guards down here used to know the men and tell them to work. Now they pay no attention. Winter's coming. Every state agency wants long-sleeved T-shirts, but the inmates do, too. I can't fill my orders."

The New York State Special Commission on Attica, which studied the riot of September 1971, noted that, according to the D.O.C.S., the official purpose of prison industry is "to teach inmates occupations and skills and to develop good work habits comparable to and employable in free industry." The commission took cognizance of the fact that during the day work was all too frequently interrupted by call-outs. Attica, in 1971, had a night shift in its metal shop. The commission approved of the metal-shop night shift as "an attempt to make better use of the institution's facilities and offer a more normal working situation to selected inmates," and seemed sorry to report that the night metal shop had been closed down after the riot. In 1976, Green Haven had a night knit shop, whose normal working situation the members of the Attica Commission might have found disheartening.

At seven o'clock on Monday evening, August 16, 1976, thirty men — all of them black and Puerto Rican — were supposedly in the knit shop, assembling T-shirts and acquiring good work habits. About twenty men were actually there. Some of the absentees had been punched in on the knit shop's time clock by their friends; that way, they wouldn't lose their earnings, which averaged twenty-one cents an hour. Two guards stood at one end of the big room, talking. At the other end, the knit shop's night civilian industrial-training foreman sat at his desk, in an office surrounded by a chain-link fence; earlier in the year, he and one of the guards hadn't spoken for several months. When the foreman stood up, he could see what the workers seated between him and the guards were doing at their sewing machines. One man was resting; he had broken his machine "accidentally on purpose." One man was turning an ordinary prison-regulation T-shirt into a T-shirt with a plunging neckline. "It's for his lover," the foreman explained. Another was altering pants. "I look the other way if they do their own work," the foreman said. Half a dozen men were working at a snail's pace. The others were working at a moderate pace. "I expect them to take it easy and to goof off," the foreman said. "I couldn't see working for these wages myself. Until 1974, the men were paid according to how many pieces they produced. When the state replaced the piecework rates, which were relatively high, with low hourly 'work-incentive allowances,' that effectively took away all their incentive. I came here to help the inmates, to instill the Protestant work ethic in them, but I've failed. It's a continuous adversary proceeding, and I've given up." The night knit shop's hours are 3:30 P.M. to 10:30 P.M., with a short break allowed for sandwiches. (Each inmate gets two sandwiches, one of the night knit shop's fringe benefits.) At eight o'clock, all the sewing machines stopped. The guards, the foreman, and the inmates had made an agreement to work from 3:30 P.M. to 8 P.M. and call it a night. The inmates ate their sandwiches and then either talked or took naps or read magazines. At 9:30 P.M., the phone rang. It was the guard in Tower 6 calling to say that the lieutenant on the 3:20 P.M. to 11:20 P.M. shift was out making his nightly inspection round and would probably reach the knit shop in a few minutes. "Show time!" the foreman called, and he blew a whistle. The men scurried back to their machines. The lieutenant came into the room, looked around, and left. The men stopped work five minutes later and loafed until quitting time. Each man took two T-shirts when he left — another, unwritten fringe benefit of the night knit shop. One man helped himself to half a dozen, because he needed them to give to a man in the machine shop who had spent the day fixing the knit-shop man's watch and tape player with the machine shop's tools.

The Attica Commission deplored the amount of cell time spent by most inmates. Instead of being locked in at 5 P.M. for the night, men should be out enjoying recreation and other programs, the commission said. Green Haven's evening programs did serve the purpose of getting the men out of their cells, but it was doubtful whether they accomplished anything else. An evening Alcoholics Anonymous meeting at Green Haven is often as ferocious as an Erhard Seminars Training session, and many of those in attendance seem to be drunk. Groups like the Jaycees hold meeting after meeting, but often, because of conflicts among inmates or between inmates and the head of Green Haven's Department of Volunteer Services, the meetings bring no results. Despite the many Jaycee meetings attended by Malinow and others, no high-school students ever came to Green Haven to see the evils of prison. The evening ceramics class often lacked clay in 1976, and its expensive kilns were rarely functioning. On August 4, a few of the men in the ceramics class were sitting around talking about an inmate who had recently been released from prison after serving thirteen years. Just before leaving, he had become so upset because he couldn't fire any of the dozens of pots he had made that, in frustration, he smashed them all.

The conversation of confined men, whether the confinement is that of a mine, a ship, or a prison, tends to be specialized. The men who spend their days or evenings sitting around in Green Haven's parole-clothing department, in its knit shop, and in its ceramics class — or on the blocks, in the yards, or on the farm — tend to talk about crime and punishment. When they discuss their past crimes, they rarely express contrition. They are not sorry that they robbed; they are sorry that they got caught robbing. Not infrequently, they claim that the so-called honest citizens they robbed are no better than they are. "This one store I held up, I took $52 from the cash register and the guy claims I took $320," one of Malinow's robber friends says. Sometimes the prisoners plan future crimes and offer instruction to others in their own specialties. Green Haven is a good place to learn about safecracking, obtaining weapons, and fencing stolen merchandise. A number of men meet their future crime partners in prison. Malinow committed the third and fourth crimes for which he was convicted with men he had met at Clinton. Occasionally, a man succeeds in committing a new crime while he is still behind the wall of Green Haven. One man was recently indicted for filing a false income-tax return for 1975 and collecting a rebate from the Internal Revenue Service, though he had been imprisoned the entire year.

Green Haven's prisoners enjoy comparing Green Haven with other prisons where they or their acquaintances have served time, especially when such comparisons are unfavorable to Green Haven. The inmates don't see why they can't have television sets in their cells, as the men at San Quentin can; why they aren't allowed to have cash, as the men at Brushy Mountain State Prison, in Tennessee, are; or why they can't be paid the going rate for the work they do, as some prisoners in Connecticut, Minnesota, and Illinois are.

The inmates sometimes amuse themselves by telling apocryphal tales — the one about the old-timer who caught a sparrow in the yard, painted it yellow, and sold it to a new arrival as a canary — and sometimes by telling true stories that only sound apocryphal; for example, the one about the inmates who got into Green Haven's hobby shop on October 12, 1976, and stole $1107.75 worth of camel's-hair and red-sable brushes, cerulean-blue and burnt-sienna oil paints, soft charcoal and hard carbon pencils, linseed oil and varnish, and pastel sets and palette knives, none of which were ever recovered. The inmates occasionally take pleasure in passing around copies of Albany's memorandums which they have swiped from their bosses' desks; for instance, the one dated November 15, 1976, according to which the term *facility hospital* was to be replaced with the term *inpatient component,* and the term *sick call* was to be replaced with the term *inmate health encounters.* At Green Haven, it often seems that 1984 has already arrived.

Among the prisoners' favorite topics of conversation are the sins of their keepers. In 1976, the inmates at Green Haven were still talking about Chester Tompkins, an inmate who had gone into a violent frenzy in April 1975 and had died in the prison after being teargassed. Then, there were accounts of the half dozen guards and civilians who slugged each other in the prison in 1975 and 1976; most of the fights were not serious, but one resulted in a guard's retiring on a disability pension. The prisoners especially enjoyed talking about the lieutenant who had tried, early in 1976, to use an inmate to set up a Service Unit counselor he suspected of committing homosexual acts with prisoners. The lieutenant had asked the inmate to entice the counselor into a homosexual act. The plan had backfired when the inmate told other inmates and the counselor himself about the proposal. The matter had been brought to the attention of outside civil-liberties organizations by the inmates and the counselor, and finally came to the attention of Albany. Green Haven's superintendent, deputy superintendents of programs and security, captain, and senior Service Unit counselor had been summoned to Albany and reprimanded. The lieutenant hadn't been reprimanded — the superintendent had longed to catch the Service Unit counselor — but he was one of the men involved in the death of Chester Tompkins, and later that month he had to pay a lawyer whose help he had sought when Albany wouldn't supply him with legal aid in that matter.

The prisoners also like to talk about the numerous officers and supervisors who turn up for work drunk or hung over; about the various officers who are up on charges for abusing their sick leave; and about the officers and civilians who have been suspended, fired, or permitted to resign for stealing state property or bringing liquor into Green Haven, or who have been caught smuggling marijuana into the prison. The prisoners also enjoy talking about the various officer cliques — who is "in" and who is "out" — and about the officers' petty resentments. In 1976, an officer who felt that two other officers were given overtime trips they shouldn't have been given went home with high blood pressure and stayed home for over a week. The prisoners also delight in gossiping about the private lives of the prison's officers, supervisors, and officials: about the married sergeant who is having an affair with another sergeant's secretary; about the married guard in his thirties who drives to work every morning with a clerk still in her teens; and about the married supervisor who has made homosexual advances to several inmates and has been seen at a gay bar in Poughkeepsie.

In his diary, George Malinow writes that prison is "hell," and proceeds to describe a life that many people would judge fairly comfortable for a convicted felon. Malinow insists that a person who hasn't been imprisoned for a considerable length of time cannot understand how hard it is to lose one's freedom in general and how hard it is to endure the daily humiliations of prison life (the constant searches, for example) in particular, but he admits that everything is relative, and that conditions in

New York State's maximum-security prisons have improved in the three and a half decades he has spent in them. "O.K., so maybe prison is moving in the direction of purgatory," he says. Had Malinow kept a diary five or ten years ago, it would have been a very different document. He wouldn't have been able to engage in many of the activities he has recently enjoyed most. He couldn't have carried on such a lengthy correspondence with Liwayway; received outside visits from Patrick Halloran and Carl Terra; spent his evenings at Jaycee meetings; or stayed up until 1:55 in the morning painting. A few of the changes that made these activities possible were being introduced shortly before the Attica uprising occurred, but there have been more changes at New York State's maximum-security prisons in the last five years than in the preceding thirty. Most of them were made in 1972, a few months after the Attica riot. Just as in Christianity there is B.C. and A.D., in New York State penology there is B.A. and A.A. — Before Attica and After Attica.

Before Attica, prisoners were far more cut off from the outside world than they are today. Visiting a prison, for example, was much more difficult five years ago. Before Attica, members of a prisoner's immediate family — which was defined as his father, mother, sisters, brothers, wife, and children — could visit him once a week. Other relatives and all friends and former convicts had to apply in writing to the warden ten days ahead each time they wanted to visit, and were allowed to visit once a month if they were approved. A wife had to produce a marriage certificate at the time of her first visit; common-law wives were not approved for visits, although about twenty per cent of the black and Puerto Rican inmates had common-law marriages. Until 1972, visitors to Green Haven were fingerprinted at the time of their first visit. Only the old visiting room existed at Green Haven until 1974, when an outside one was opened, and inmates and their visitors sat across from each other at a long M-shaped table separated by a thick mesh screen. The screens came down on June 15, 1972.

Correspondence was also much more limited. Until 1972, incoming and outgoing mail was censored and was also restricted in volume. Inmates could write only four letters a week, each no longer than two pages — the front and back of a standard lined form. An inmate was warned that his letter would be returned if he went beyond any of fourteen regulations printed at the top of the form. Three of them read "It contains Criminal or Prison News," "Begging for packages or money not allowed," "You did not stick to your subject." Malinow, a long-winded man who finds it difficult to write a letter of fewer than six pages even to a casual friend, and who loves to go rambling around subjects, remembers writing to a friend and saying, "Give my regards to my nephew Barry," and getting the letter back with the query "Who is Barry?" Many of his incoming letters had words inked out or snipped out.

Before 1973, prisoners at Green Haven couldn't place phone calls to their family and friends regularly. Until then, they could place a call only in an emergency. Malinow made one phone call during his first thirty-four years in prison — in 1949, to make arrangements to visit his mother during her final illness. Now prisoners can call their families and friends collect twice a month.

Prisoners at Green Haven spent much more time confined to their cells before 1972 and had much less to do there. Almost everyone locked in at 5 P.M. and stayed in until 7:15 the next morning. There was no Jaycee chapter and few outside volunteers. One of Green Haven's former wardens was fond of saying, "Prison walls are to keep the public out as well as the prisoners in." In the years before 1972, no talking was allowed after 7:30 P.M., lights went out at 10:00 P.M., there was nothing to listen to on the earphones after midnight. A man could read in his cell before lights-out, but such magazines as *Playboy* were banned. A prisoner couldn't have a typewriter or a tape player until 1972. The nine hours he spent out of his cell each day were also more strictly regimented. Meals were mandatory —

really mandatory — and inmates were marched to the mess hall in pairs; a guard banged on the wall with his stick when he wanted them to stop or go or quiet down. Everyone was locked in for a daily count that was taken at noon. Dress codes were stricter: an inmate could wear his prison uniform and a white shirt but no colored shirts. Haircuts had to be short and neat. No beards were permitted. Life was considerably less comfortable: most men got showers only once a week, in an odoriferous bathhouse, and there was no indoor physical recreation until 1973, when Green Haven's gym was opened. There was more religious freedom for some prisoners than for others: New York State was very slow to recognize the Black Muslims as a bonafide religious group, because it found them threatening; it took years — and many court cases — for the Muslims to get mosques, permission to wear prayer caps, and facilities for fasting during the holy month of Ramadan. Legal work was harder to do: Green Haven got its law library, as a result of a federal grant, in 1972. If a man had a complaint about prison life, it could take him years of fighting in court to correct the wrong. In January 1972, Green Haven got an Inmate Liaison Committee, which enabled elected prisoner representatives to meet with the superintendent to discuss policy and procedure. In May 1972, the Department of Correctional Services introduced the Inspector General Program, to insure that prisons were operating in compliance with the law and with the correction commissioner's directives. In August 1975, Green Haven became the first prison in the state to have an Inmate Grievance Program giving inmates "an orderly and expeditious method of presenting grievances." A grievance committee composed of two elected inmates, two staff members (usually a sergeant and an officer), and a nonvoting chairman (a civilian, an officer, or an inmate) started dealing with inmate complaints and grievances. A complaint or a grievance is defined as "a specific allegation against a person or persons, or institutional and / or departmental rules, regulations or policies, or the absence of a rule, regulation or policy that the grievant has reason to believe is arbitrary, capricious, coercive, oppressive, discriminatory, or inconsistent with the department's posture on rehabilitation." Grievances that are not settled to an inmate's satisfaction at the prison level may be appealed to Albany. In 1976, grievances filed at Green Haven and at other prisons in the state (which now all have grievance committees) continued to bring change. The Sunni Muslims, for example, claimed that their religion required them to wear beards. Albany at first denied their grievance, then did some research, found out that their claim was true, and allowed the Muslims to wear beards. Once the Muslims were permitted to wear beards, all the other prisoners got to wear them, too. In early 1976, the state was taking 10 percent of all sales inmates made through the hobby shop; it stopped taking the 10 percent after a grievance was filed on the matter. In 1976, an A-block officer on the 3:20 P.M. to 11:20 P.M. shift said that after five o'clock he would not hand out supplies kept in his cage. A prisoner filed a grievance, and Albany ruled that the officer would distribute supplies after five. The officer then told the prisoner, "I don't give a damn what Albany says. I'm not handing out supplies after five."

Prisoners like George Malinow weren't the only ones at Green Haven who said in 1976 that prison was hell. To the guards, not only was the prison hell but instead of moving in the direction of purgatory it seemed to be heading toward one of Dante's inner circles of hell. As much as the inmates welcomed the After Attica changes, the guards resented them. The guards longed for the days Before Attica, when, as some of them put it, "prisons were prisons, and not country clubs," "the animals were all locked up in their cages at five o'clock," "clubs were trump," "we ran the prison instead of having Albany and the prisoners run it," "there were fewer niggers in prison and no militant niggers, and practically no nigger guards," and "prisoners knew their places."

The men who came to work as guards at Green Haven in the 1950s and 1960s fell into two groups. One group consisted of local residents, who decided that a job as a prison guard was preferable to, say, working for the telephone company or in construction or for a computer firm, because it offered civil-service security and the promise of a pension after twenty-five years. There were many well-paying jobs in Dutchess County, however, and so there were never enough men in the small unincorporated hamlets and townships near the prison to fill all the jobs as guards. The second group consisted of men from the upstate areas in which New York's other maximum-security prisons are situated. In a place like Dannemora, being a guard at Clinton is by far the best-paying job a high-school graduate can get; the salary has always been a few thousand dollars above the average wage in Clinton County, where the cost of living is relatively low, and a guard and his family can live like royalty. In 1976, a prison guard's pay started at $11,410. All of the state's other maximum-security prisons are older than Green Haven, which opened as a state prison in 1949. Auburn, the first, opened in 1817. Attica, the newest before Green Haven, opened in 1931. By the 1950s, there were many young men in these upstate towns who were eager to follow in their fathers' footsteps — and, in some cases, in their grandfathers' footsteps — and become prison guards. The jobs, however, were invariably filled — sometimes by these very forebears. If a young man from Auburn wanted to be a prison guard and met the qualifications (he was required to have a high-school diploma, be legally eligible to carry firearms, be between the ages of twenty-one and thirty-seven, and meet certain height, weight, hearing, and vision requirements), and passed the civil-service exam, he usually had to start out by working at Green Haven, where there were vacancies. The day he arrived, he put his name on the transfer list to go back home. He usually spent two or three years at Green Haven before there was an opening upstate. Once back home, he stayed until he retired. Thus, Green Haven always had fewer permanent, experienced guards than the other maximum-security prisons. In October 1976, there were only three officers at Green Haven who had come to work in 1949; seven from 1950; one each from 1951, 1952, and 1953; three from 1954; two from 1955; fifteen from 1956; fourteen from 1957; and so on. Indeed, only 200 of the 479 officers at Green Haven in 1976 had come in 1971 or earlier. The others had come in 1972 or later. At Clinton, a guard with fifteen years on the job is referred to as "a new mick."

The local men who came to work at Green Haven and the few upstaters who married local girls and stayed on in Dutchess County found the prison a pleasant enough place to work in the fifties and sixties. There was always some swagging and some booze-making, but it was kept within reasonable bounds. In those years, there were few inmate deaths, few escapes, and few assaults on officers. There were also very few inmate rights. The guards didn't worry about inmate rights. They believed that the convicts were in Green Haven for punishment, and that imprisoned men forfeited most of their rights when they came to prison. Until the sixties, when blacks came to constitute the majority of the prison population, the prisoners themselves, like Malinow, accepted the status to which the guards and society in general had relegated them. The racial change in the prison population coincided with the social upheaval and rebellion first of the civil-rights movement and then of the protest against the Vietnam war. Many black convicts became politicized and militant, and saw themselves not as criminals but as political prisoners of a white society that had put them on the path to prison from their childhood by depriving them of the rights and benefits enjoyed by whites. There were volunteer civil-liberties lawyers available to argue their suits for them, and the courts, under the libertarian influence of the Warren Court, were willing to listen. The courts began to hand down decisions that said, in effect, that a convict was to be deprived of the minimum, not the maximum, rights of an ordinary citizen. The social dissidence of the sixties and the hope of an improved status that the courts began holding out exacerbated the natural racial tension of a prison system where a black majority was guarded almost exclusively by rural whites. The result was the Attica riot of September 1971 and the turning topsy-turvy of the world that the white guards had known. The changes that the courts had begun to mandate flowed from the Department of Correctional Services, in Albany, under Russell G. Oswald, who took over as commissioner at the beginning of 1971 with the intention of reforming the prisons. After Attica, the aim of the D.O.C.S. was to avoid another uprising by liberalizing prison conditions. Above all, the governor, the legislature, and the commissioner and his senior assistants in the department did not want another riot and its unseemly publicity of state-police sharpshooters and corpses. Attica "hangs over the department like original sin," one observer has noted.

The liberalization proceeded on the rationale that more humane prison conditions would ease tensions and that better-designed rehabilitation programs would truly rehabilitate. Albany's memo of May 17, 1972, announcing the forthcoming change in visiting rules was typical of the directives that started to come down in the After Attica environment:

> Departmental objectives include the resocialization of inmates and assistance in the solution of their personal and legal problems. Accordingly, visits with family members, friends, former business associates, former and prospective employers, governmental officials and counsel may contribute to the good morale and treatment of inmates, and future good adjustment in the facility and community . . . You are encouraged to maintain contact by visits with your family, friends and others. We want to help you to do so . . . without screened barriers.

The superintendent at Green Haven in 1971 was a man who had always lived in the old prison world. When he learned, toward the end of the year, of the kind of changes that Albany was planning, including the removal of the screens in the visiting room, he told a few friends, "I won't be here when the screens come down," and he wasn't. He retired, took a year off, and later became the director of purchasing and personnel at a small college upstate.

The guards did not like the sight, as Malinow did, of prisoners embracing their loved ones in the visiting room when the screens came down, in June 1972. The guards did not think that inmates were entitled to such privileges. Their unhappiness grew when the prisoners and some of their visitors began to perform more intimate acts and when a number of the visitors were caught passing their husbands and boyfriends marijuana in balloons during kisses. The guards also objected to the prisoners' being allowed to have visitors of all types, rather than just their families and girlfriends.

To the guards, the various people who come to Green Haven in behalf of the prisoners have their sympathies in the wrong place. The guards sympathize with the victims of the prisoners' crimes and think that everyone else should, too. They are repelled by female volunteers who come to Green Haven from Bard and other nearby colleges, braless and with REMEMBER ATTICA buttons pinned to their blouses. The guards refer to these young women as "the liberal bitches from Bard." If one of these volunteers falls in love with a prisoner and is seen embracing him in the visiting room, as sometimes happens, the repugnance of the guards is intensified — particularly if the volunteer is white and the prisoner is black. A favorite form of needling practiced by the guards in 1977 was to ask visitors, "What's the name of the man who was executed by firing squad in Utah?" The visitors would almost always answer, "Gary Gilmore." The guards would then ask, "What are the names of the two college students Gilmore killed?" The visitors almost never knew.

The guards also feel a special antagonism toward journalists, who have been given slightly freer rein to visit Green Haven and to interview prisoners there, as a result of a court case in the early seventies, and toward Legal Aid lawyers, who come to help the prisoners get out. The journalists, the guards feel, portray them as sadists and brutes and the prisoners as good guys and victims, and this angers and confuses the guards. They point out that no guard is a convicted rapist, murderer, or robber. The guards mention that while the Legal Aid lawyers seem to thrive, the one society in Manhattan dedicated to assisting the victims of crime almost went bankrupt in 1977. In the guards' lineup room at Green Haven is a bulletin board that is used for routine announcements. The newspaper clippings thumbtacked to the bulletin board show what is on the guards' minds. One of the first newspaper clippings to appear on the board in 1976 was an article about the arrest, in February, of Dennis Belle on charges of kidnapping a thirteen-year-old newsboy and forcibly sodomizing him repeatedly over a period of seven and a half hours. Belle had previously served twenty-seven years in prison for hanging an eight-year-old boy — a crime he committed when he was fourteen years old. The law under which Belle had been sentenced was changed eight months after he went to prison. With the assistance of a Legal Aid lawyer, Belle won his release from Green Haven in January 1974. The guards felt that the consequences of the lawyer's intervention were paid by the newsboy. There were many similar clippings on the bulletin board in 1976. In April, four men, three of whom had served time at Green Haven, held up and killed two security guards in a Times Square movie theater; all four were out on parole; one had been paroled in March. In May, a newspaper clipping showed a photograph of Walter Flanigan holding a pistol to a young woman's head. He had kidnapped the woman — whom he had formerly dated — and held her at gunpoint for five hours before surrendering to his parole officer. Flanigan had been paroled from Green Haven in November 1975, after serving twelve years of a twenty-to-life sentence for killing his father-in-law with a rifle in September 1963. An August newspaper clipping was about Lester Morton, who had injured five New York City policemen by throwing lye at them, searing their eyes; Morton had been released from Green Haven in December 1975.

All these men, the guards note, had enjoyed the After Attica changes to more liberal prison conditions and theoretically more rehabilitative rehabilitation programs. The guards believe that it is a mistake to treat convicts as if they were law-abiding citizens — that such courtesies and privileges only make them cocky and cause trouble. A guard never uses the term *mister* in addressing an inmate, although an inmate is supposed to use the term *officer* in addressing a guard. The guards call the inmates by their first or last names and resent hearing visitors address them as mister. The guards do not believe prisoners should be permitted the privacy of incoming and outgoing mail. All mail should be censored, as it was Before Attica, they say.

The After Attica changes meant a lot more work for the guards, without a compensatory increase in the guard force. In the old days, the guards did not have to process nearly as many visitors, nor were they cursed, screamed at, and occasionally hit by prisoners' wives or girlfriends. Watching over a visiting room where the visitors are separated from the prisoners is one thing; watching over a visiting room without screens is another. The settled routine, to which the guards were accustomed, became completely unsettled. The guards' self-esteem was lowered when they were deprived of their all-blue police-type uniforms, in August 1972, and made to wear navy blazers and Cambridge-gray slacks, which, they complain, make them look like motel clerks or movie ushers. They had liked looking like police officers. The guards also contend that the After Attica liberalization of prison conditions raised tensions and caused more trouble at Green Haven, instead of reducing problems. As an example, they cite the trouble between Tony Pagano and Scott Besson. Had visiting been restricted as it formerly was,

Besson would not have been able to copulate with a white woman in the ladies' room of the outside visiting room; Pagano's visitor would not have been insulted; Pagano would not have been honor bound to punch Besson; Pagano would not have suffered serious head injuries in a piping; steps would not have had to be taken to avoid a racial clash between whites and blacks. Furthermore, the guards say, they are the ones who are blamed by their superiors or by Albany for the troubles that Albany has brought on with its liberalization of prison conditions. The superintendent at Green Haven is required to report all "unusual incidents," like the Pagano-Besson affair, to the commissioner. The superintendent of Green Haven at the time this incident occurred, on May 30, 1976, reported that it might not have taken place if the two guards in the outside visiting room "had been more alert." The guards defended themselves by saying they were so busy checking packages and processing visitors that they could not possibly have seen Besson enter the ladies' room. The lieutenant who investigated the incident concluded that the guards were right, and that a third guard was needed to watch the outside-visiting-room bathrooms if the inmates were to be prevented from using them for purposes for which they were not intended. "I add that if we are to allow this type of program we must be ready to accept the problems that occur," the lieutenant commented. "Freedom of movement makes way for freedom of action." The loose visiting conditions also make it impossible to prevent sizable amounts of drugs and other contraband from being smuggled into the prison, the guards say. When they did catch a visitor mailing in drugs — seventy-seven marijuana cigarettes — in the spring of 1976 and suspended her visiting rights, Albany undercut their authority by reinstating her as a visitor.

The discontent of the guards in the post-Attica environment led to a drastic change in the amount of experience the guards in actual contact with inmates had. Until 1970, the deputy warden, still colloquially known as the principal keeper, had the authority to assign all officers to their jobs. The disadvantage of this system was that the P.K. played favorites. The advantage of the system was that the P.K. could use his authority to give men who had demonstrated a talent for handling inmates jobs as block officers and those who tended to irritate inmates jobs where they would have little to do with them. In the fifties and sixties, many of the guards working with the inmate population at Green Haven had considerable seniority. Night duty was something that junior officers had to accept. Tower duty was considered a punishment — a mini-Siberia to which a guard who had bollixed up the count might be exiled. The towers are so boring that on one occasion a guard in one tower straddled the top of the wall and worked his way over to the guard in the neighboring tower to ask him for a match. In 1970, the guards' union, the American Federation of State, County, and Municipal Employees, negotiated an agreement whereby guards could bid for jobs by seniority. Once a man had bid for and obtained a job, it was his for as long as he wanted it. Most experienced guards lacked the time in service to retire, as Green Haven's superintendent had done in 1972 to avoid seeing the visiting-room screens come down, but they could remove themselves as much as possible from the prisoners, and they began to do so. The towers became desirable posts, filled by senior men. Other senior officers switched to the evening or night shifts, when most or all of the inmates were locked up. If they wanted to stay on the day shift, they bid for jobs that gave them as little inmate contact as possible, or gave them contact on terms that they considered favorable. They selected positions as construction or transportation officers. Construction officers, like the men in the towers, have no inmate contact. Something at Green Haven is always being built or rebuilt, and the task of the construction officers is simply to escort the civilian construction workers and see that they don't leave tools lying around that can be used as weapons. Transportation officers ride buses transferring inmates to other prisons or from other prisons to Green Haven.

The prisoners are always handcuffed and shackled. Transportation duty also has the advantage of paying a great deal of overtime. A busload of prisoners can't stop between Clinton and Green Haven just because an officer's eight-hour shift is up. In 1976, a sergeant assigned to transportation earned about as much as Green Haven's superintendent. Other senior officers took jobs working with a few selected inmates in such places as parole clothing and the officers' mess. By 1976, only three of Green Haven's seventy most senior officers were still working on the blocks. The prison was handling the inmates with its least qualified newcomers.

Attica and the changes it set in train have also created a cultural and racial confrontation within the guard force itself. The state of New York does not keep the voluminous statistics on its officers that it does on its inmates. By their own account, however, most of the older guards at Green Haven are men from lower-middle-class rural backgrounds, often hard-drinking men, who enjoy hunting, fishing, camping, and golf. One can see their tastes reflected in Green Haven's vacation schedule. A guard with seven years' seniority is entitled to twenty vacation days a year. By properly combining his vacation days and his regular days off, such a guard can manage a two-week vacation in the first eighteen weeks of the year and a second two-week vacation in the next eighteen weeks of the year. By working the state's eleven annual legal holidays — among them Washington's Birthday and Veterans' Day — a guard can take a third two weeks off during the last sixteen weeks of the year. Vacations are bid for according to seniority. Vacation no. 6, in the third period, the two weeks in late November that encompass the deer-hunting season in Dutchess County, is always taken before the second most popular vacation time, also in the third period, no. 8, which includes Christmas. These older guards are conservative politically. They usually register Republican, and they voted for Gerald Ford in 1976. They believe in "my country right or wrong," they supported the war in

Vietnam, and they think that Lieutenant William L. Calley, Jr., was made a scapegoat for the My Lai massacre. They admit to being male chauvinists; they were unhappy when Green Haven got its first three female guards, in 1973, and were unhappier still when the total went to eleven female guards by 1977. They don't mind working wives as long as the wives don't become career women. They pride themselves on their masculinity. Statistically, it would seem inevitable that a few of the guards are homosexual, but if they are they stay deep in their closets and profess their dislike for "homos." Most of these men also think that "nigger" is a proper synonym for "black." This racism did not cause a problem in the guard force in the fifties and sixties, because there were practically no blacks for it to rasp against. In the fifties, there were two black officers at Green Haven. In the sixties, there were six. These blacks were accepted because they were residents of the local community and reflected its mores, and because there were so few of them. Green Haven's white supervisors and older white officers are so unselfconsciously racist that they pay these few blacks from the Before Attica decades what they regard as the highest compliment: "He thinks just like a white man."

At the time of the riot, in September 1971, there was not a single black guard at Attica. The Attica Commission took note of the extent to which the racism of rural white guards had grated on the black majority in the prison population and on the growing number of Puerto Ricans, and of how the resulting tension had contributed to the outbreak, and Commissioner Oswald had agreed, during the unsuccessful negotiations to arrange a peaceful settlement of the uprising, to begin a program to recruit "a significant number of black and Spanish-speaking officers." Under the pre-Attica system, anyone who took the civil-service examination for a guard's position competed on a statewide basis. Blacks and Puerto Ricans had not scored high enough to obtain jobs in meaningful numbers. The program instituted by Albany in 1972 made it easier for blacks and Puerto Ricans to become guards. Albany divided the state into seven prison regions. Green Haven fell into Region 7, which included New York City. Clinton was placed in Region 4. The new rules specified that a candidate could take the examination only in the region in which he or she resided, and then solely for prisons within that region. A young man at Dannemora might score ninety-five when he took the examination, but if there were no openings at Clinton or any of the smaller prisons in Region 4 he could not become a guard. The time-honored custom of working at Green Haven for several years until a transfer to Clinton came through was ended. And if a black or Puerto Rican resident of New York City scored seventy-five on the examination and there were sufficient vacancies at Green Haven and other prisons within Region 7 to admit candidates with such low scores, he could become a guard. Since there have always been openings at Green Haven and elsewhere in Region 7, blacks began to enter the guard force in considerable numbers for the first time, and Puerto Ricans to a lesser extent. The physical standards were also changed, to permit the shorter Puerto Rican men to pass.

Most of the white guards at Green Haven were hostile to the new black arrivals. There was a cultural as well as a racial antipathy between the two groups. The jivers who liked long sedans and city night clubs had little in common with the deerslayers in their pickup trucks. The blacks did not move up to Dutchess County, because they did not want to leave New York City. Following the pattern of their white predecessors, as soon as they arrived at Green Haven they put their names on transfer lists for the new prisons opening in the city. (Twenty-eight of the seventy-six men who came to work at Green Haven in 1974 have already transferred elsewhere.) The older white guards were repelled by the Afro and corn-row hairdos that some of the black guards wore, and got more upset when a few of them returned the clenched-fist black-power salute of the black inmates and called these inmates "brother."

A handful of the new black guards also had relatives or childhood friends serving time at Green Haven. The whites wondered whose side they would be on if there was trouble. A number of the new black officers also tended to be easier on the prisoners. They did not get angry if they were accused of maternal incest. Black prisoners said they preferred having more black guards because it was nice to see black faces among those in authority and on the payroll. Many of the white prisoners, including Malinow, also liked the black guards, for their more relaxed attitude. The white officers continued to keeplock prisoners who cursed them, and felt that the blacks' contrasting leniency made them look unfairly mean. Some of the new black officers did not have good work habits. Their car pools from the city were chronically late or did not show up at all, and a number of the black officers first hired were terminated for being absent without leave too often. Time did not lessen the antagonism. In 1976, the white and black officers at Green Haven practiced self-segregation, just as the inmates did. They usually sat at separate tables in the officers' mess, and they did not socialize after work or on occasions like the annual union picnic. When one white sergeant was asked why the officers' mess was so obviously segregated, he replied, "We don't rap the same."

A dispute over who would get promoted, inevitable once larger numbers of blacks had begun entering the guard force, heightened the racial antagonism. Until 1972, the examination for sergeant had been administered on a statewide basis. Two black officers who failed the October 1972 test filed suit, charging that the examination was arbitrary and biassed against black and Spanish-speaking officers. A total of 1264 white officers had taken the test, of whom 30.9 percent passed; of 119 Spanish-speaking and black officers, 12.5 percent of the Hispanic and 7.7 percent of the black officers passed. The passing score was seventy. In April 1974, a federal district judge found in favor of the two black officers who had failed, ruling that the state Department of Civil Service and the D.O.C.S. had not proved that the test questions related to the content of the job. Since the judge's ruling, there have been no civil-service examinations for sergeant. Appointments to provisional sergeant were made at the individual prisons. The white officers contended that the appointments were unfair, with blacks being favored because Albany wants more blacks in supervisory positions. The whites also complained that they were being further penalized because those who took the 1972 sergeant's examination and passed it could, if they had been appointed sergeants, have taken the next lieutenant's examination, and, after the mandatory three years in grade, advanced another step in their careers.

In 1976, morale among the white officers at Green Haven, who were still in the majority, was bad. By October, there were seventy-five black and twenty Hispanic officers at Green Haven. There were still only four black and eight Hispanic officers at Clinton. While many officers had found it necessary to take part-time second jobs, because the small annual raises they received during the 1970s had not kept pace with inflation, they saw all sorts of money being spent on the inmates. They did not believe that it was necessary or desirable to spend a million and a half dollars renovating old cellblocks into new honor blocks for inmates. Prisons should not be made more comfortable, they said. Comfort would only make prisons less unpleasant places for prisoners to return to, and too many were returning already. They didn't see why inmates should be given free college educations at Dutchess Community College, where they themselves had to pay to send their children.

The new honor blocks and a second innovative housing system that permitted inmates relatively free daytime movement within the prison, combined with the After Attica flight of experienced officers to jobs with little or no inmate contact, began to cause a breakdown of control at Green Haven in 1976. The honor blocks disrupted the traditional pattern of movement within the prison. Previously, all men had locked according to the jobs they held. The officers had escorted the men to and from their jobs. It had been relatively easy for an officer to accomplish this when, for example, all the furniture-shop workers were housed on the same block. Once C and D blocks had been renovated and men had been assigned to these blocks as a reward for good behavior, the old system of controlled movement was destroyed. Furniture-shop men, who had always locked on F block, might now be locking on C and D blocks as well. There was no practical way for a guard to round all of them up. In late 1976, the superintendent decided that new arrivals could be housed wherever there were empty cells, regardless of what jobs they were assigned. The result was free movement for most inmates, except when they were locked in their cells for the 5:30 P.M. count, and at night. This brought confusion and occasional chaos. The number of assaults on officers began to rise. In 1976, there were thirty-five assaults, with forty-eight officers, supervisors, and civilians injured, including those who had come to the assistance of the first person attacked.

In 1977 things got worse. At the beginning of January, a thirty-year-old black prisoner named Hector Lopez, who was serving his fifteen-year-to-life sentence for stabbing and shooting a man to death in 1971 in the Bronx with a knife and a shotgun while robbing the victim of twelve hundred dollars, fractured the skulls of two guards by bludgeoning them with a steel ratchet bar used to work a ventilating panel in a cell-block window. Lopez had been boated to Green Haven from Attica in August 1976 for fighting with inmates there. His record showed nineteen prior incidents of disobeying prison rules, general belligerence, using threatening and abusive language to officers, and brawling. In December, one of the officers on B block, Bennett Krieger, who had a reputation for running a tight ship and was not popular with inmates, had written Lopez up for threatening him. Lopez had received two weeks in keeplock from the Adjustment Committee in December and had sworn revenge on Krieger. On January 4, 1977, at 3:20 P.M., as the guard shifts were changing, a number of inmates who were not authorized to be on B block got there, because of the new free-movement policy. Krieger, his fellow officer Dale Lambert, and Jasper Kane, one of the officers who were relieving them, rounded these inmates up and ordered them out the block door. In doing this, Krieger spotted Lopez and yelled at him that he was going to be keeplocked again for not returning to the block on time. To leave the block, Krieger and Lambert had to walk through a group of inmates who were loitering in front of the door — some of them the inmates who had earlier been chased off the block. Lambert went out first, and Krieger stayed behind to leave some instructions with Kane. Lambert got about ten feet from the door and saw Lopez in the crowd holding a sixteen-inch steel bar over his head as if he were about to hit someone with it. When Lambert tried to disarm him, Lopez bludgeoned him several times, fracturing his skull and lacerating his head with the sharp edges of the bar. Lambert staggered down the corridor, semiconscious and bleeding severely from a large, gaping wound at the back of his head. Krieger, unaware of what had happened, because none of the inmates had helped Lambert or warned Krieger and Kane, walked out of the block door and into the gathering of prisoners a couple of minutes later. Lopez rushed at him out of the group, shouting, "You want to lock me up, motherfucker, I'll give you something to lock me up for!" Swinging the bar, he knocked Krieger back inside the block door and down, stunned, on one knee. Kane dived forward and tackled Lopez around the waist, but just as he did so Lopez brought the bar down and smashed it into the top of Krieger's head. An officer who had joined Kane on relief grabbed Lopez around the neck, and together they wrestled him down, and held him until he stopped struggling and could be locked in his cell.

Lambert was fortunate enough to encounter a twenty-six-year-old black inmate named Brian Parks in the corridor, who picked him up and rushed him to the prison hospital, despite yelled threats from other prisoners that they would kill him later for "helping a pig." Lambert has credited Parks with saving his life. Parks subsequently had to be put in segregation to protect him from other inmates, but he was later rewarded with a transfer to a medium-security prison. Lambert and Krieger were taken by ambulance to hospitals in Poughkeepsie. Lopez's weapon was not found until the following day, behind a toilet in a prison yard, where inmates had concealed it. Lambert recovered and resigned. Krieger recovered and recently went back to work at Green Haven. Lopez was convicted of assaulting one of the officers, received a fifteen-to-life concurrent sentence, and was transferred to another maximum-security prison.

Benjamin Ward, the first black commissioner of the Department of Correctional Services, visited Green Haven the day after the two officers had been assaulted. The guards expected him to say something sympathetic about what had happened to Lambert and Krieger. Instead, he gave a talk criticizing the guards' performance in general, and made other remarks that the guards interpreted as sympathetic to the inmates. Commissioner Ward had always been regarded as pro-inmate by the older white guards. His talk convinced them that they were right in routinely referring to him as "that goddam nigger commissioner in Albany." After his visit, the guards posted a clipping from the Poughkeepsie *Journal* on the lineup-room bulletin board containing a statement by their union vice-president calling on Governor Carey to fire Ward for "pro-prisoner" attitudes. The union vice-president also accused Ward of lacking any understanding of prison life.

In early January 1977, a black officer named Justin Phillips was arrested and suspended on charges of smuggling marijuana into the prison, after an investigation that had included the assistance of a black inmate informant. In April, three more black guards were caught bringing in marijuana. They, too, were apprehended with the help of black inmate informants, some of whom were rigged with tape recorders to obtain evidence. At the same time, the assaults on guards — in almost all cases, white guards — continued at a high rate through the winter and spring. There were more assaults than there had been at any time in Green Haven's history except 1972, when a great deal of turmoil accompanied the introduction of the After Attica changes. From the refuge of a tower, one of the old-timers commented with a hyperbole that accurately conveyed his attitude and that of his white colleagues: "It seems that all the black guards are going out in handcuffs and the white guards on stretchers."

Suddenly, in the summer of 1977, the state of New York began to officially disavow the ideal of rehabilitating criminals into law-abiding citizens — a goal that it had set for itself more than a century and a half earlier, with the opening, in 1817, of Auburn State Prison. The rise of towns and cities after the Revolution had made it impossible to keep criminals within bounds by the Colonial methods of the stocks, the pillory, the whipping post, the branding iron, banishment from the community, and an occasional hanging. American society developed the armed police force and the state prison. Attitudes toward human nature also underwent a change. In Colonial times, the Calvinist notion that man's nature was flawed by original sin had prevailed. Crime had been viewed as sin to be punished. By the early nineteenth century, the contrary view of Montesquieu, Voltaire, and the other thinkers of the eighteenth-century Enlightenment — that man was a creature of reason, innocent in his natural state and amenable to change — had taken hold in America.

The concept of applying this new view of man's nature to criminal behavior and transforming criminals into decent citizens through a proper regimen originated among Quaker reformers in Pennsylvania. It quickly caught on in New York as well. Pennsylvania called its penal institutions penitentiaries, because prison was supposed to be a place where a criminal did penance until he was reformed. The Pennsylvania system was one of complete solitary confinement. The inmate was to be reformed by being isolated from contact with any evil influence. He was led blindfolded into a cell with an exercise area and, after an initial period of solitude to reflect on his crimes, was given a Bible to read and handicraft work to do. From the Bible he would learn charity and faith in God; the handicrafts would teach the virtue of work; and the solitary confinement would inculcate abstemious habits. By the time the prisoner was blindfolded again, at the end of his term, and led back into the outside world, he would be a different man. New York tried the solitary-confinement system at Auburn but quickly abandoned it. Eighty inmates were confined in the experiment. More than half of the deaths at Auburn in 1823 were from among the eighty prisoners in solitary, several others went insane, and the governor pardoned most of the survivors after two years. The New York proponents of solitary confinement were thoroughly discredited when one of the pardoned criminals committed a burglary on the very night of his release and twelve others were eventually reconvicted.

New York instead adopted what became known as the Auburn system of reform through work and silence, and called its penal institutions prisons rather than penitentiaries. If the convicts were put to work rather than confined in isolation, small individual cells would do for them, and they could help pay the costs of their confinement through prison industries. Under the Auburn system, it was possible to build cells at an average cost of $91 each, compared to $1650 each for the much larger cells (including exercise areas) devised by the Pennsylvania reformers. The Auburn system thus commended itself to legislators, who could, perhaps, understand economy more easily than the reformation of convicts. The economy motive led to the subsequent adoption of the Auburn system by most other states. The convicts were dressed in black-and-white striped uniforms to make them look grotesque and to help break their lawless spirits through humiliation; they were permitted no visitors, no correspondence, no knowledge of events in the outside world, and no reading material other than a Bible and in some cases a prayer book; and they were subjected to a deliberately robot-like daily routine of work in harshly enforced silence to prevent them from communicating with one another. They got up at 5:15 A.M. in summer and at sunrise when the days were shorter, and were marched to and from their cells in an Auburn invention called the lockstep. It was a single file in which each convict placed his right hand on the shoulder of the man in front of him and kept his head turned toward the escorting guards. The guards watched the faces for any movement of the lips or any use of the facial muscles that might be construed as a signal. When not marching, the convicts had to keep their heads lowered and their eyes on the ground.

In the various shops for weaving, tailoring, and the making of shoes, tools, barrels, and furniture, the prisoners labored in silence. They ate in silence, and they were locked in at night to keep silent until they were permitted to go to sleep in their cells. They were forbidden to sit or lie down on their sleeping mats or in their hammocks until the signal was given to take off their striped uniforms, at lights-out. Guards patrolled the galleries in stocking feet to detect the slightest whisper. Sunday was one of the most dreaded days, because the men were locked in their cells after the morning service — at which the chaplain preached — and were not let out until dawn on Monday. They also could not sit or lie down until lights-out on Sunday night, and were forced to stand or to pace back and forth until then. There was not much room for pacing, because the cells measured only three and a half feet wide (approximately half the width of a present-day Green Haven cell), seven feet long, and seven feet high. They could read their Bibles, but the reading had to be done while they were standing or pacing. The illiterates and some of the semiliterates were fortunate. They were taken out of their cells on Sunday morning for schooling before the service and again in the afternoon. Any infraction of this unchanging and remorseless discipline was punished by flogging.

The man who ran Auburn in 1826, a profoundly religious prison reformer named Gershom Powers, gave a lecture to each arrival. He assured the new prisoner that the experience he was about to undergo would provide "the most favorable means . . . for repentance and reformation, by forming regular, temperate and industrious habits, learning a useful trade, yielding obedience to laws, subduing evil passions, and by receiving moral and religious instruction." The convict would return to the world at the end of his sentence "with correct views and good resolutions," Powers further assured him, and would "become a blessing to [his] friends and to society, and exemplify the power of deep repentance and thorough reform." Powers died in 1831, before he could be disappointed. The dehumanizing regimentation did not terrify and the evangelism and the schooling did not keep criminals from returning to crime. Crime continued to flourish, and by 1825 the legislature had authorized the construction of another prison, adjacent to the village of Sing Sing, on the east bank of the Hudson, thirty-three miles north of New York City. The site was chosen because it would be easy to transport convicts, supplies, and the products of prison industries by riverboat, and because of the marble deposits there, which made it possible for the state to use convicts to build their own prison. For the next three years, prisoners from Auburn labored under the lash quarrying the marble and cutting it into blocks, and fabricating the iron doors and bars, to erect Sing Sing's first grim cellblock, for eight hundred convicts, where George Malinow was confined when he was first sent to Sing Sing, in 1938. The prison was initially given the pastoral name of Mount Pleasant. The legislature enlarged Sing

Sing and Auburn in the early 1830s. Population growth and the beginning waves of immigration brought more crime. In 1844, the legislature authorized the construction of Clinton. In 1911 came Great Meadow, and in the spring of 1930 Auburn inmates were transported to Attica to labor at constructing a state prison there.

Periods of corruption and abuse within the prisons alternated with periods of reform, when different and supposedly better methods of rehabilitation were attempted. In the 1840s, there was a short-lived attempt at rehabilitation through kindness and an appeal to the better instincts by easing discipline, improving prison living conditions, allowing family visits and limited family correspondence, providing some opportunity for education, and granting the unheard-of indulgence of a ration of chewing tobacco for the convicts at the new Clinton prison. The attempt to rehabilitate through kindness ended with a return to harshness, but gradually, over the years, the most egregious legal cruelties were abolished. Flogging was forbidden by the legislature in 1847, and solitary confinement on short rations was substituted as the official punishment. The great frequency with which flogging occurred shows that many convicts refused to be broken by the forced labor and the regimentation. Sing Sing was called a "Cat-ocracy," because of the unremitting use of the cat-o'-nine-tails there. The guards got around the abolition of flogging by dispensing unauthorized beatings and other tortures. The reformers never gave up, however, on their ideal of rehabilitation. In the 1870s, they succeeded in bringing about another major change. The new concept was proposed at the 1870 founding meeting of the National Prison Association, in Cincinnati. Better rehabilitation programs and more humane prison conditions would make it possible for competent prison administrators to judge when an inmate had been rehabilitated into a law-abiding citizen and could be safely released back into society under some form of supervision, the congress asserted. One of its resolutions read,

"With men of ability and experience at the head of our penal establishments, holding their offices during good behavior, we believe that it will be little, if at all, more difficult to judge correctly as to the moral cure of a criminal, than it is of the mental cure of a lunatic." The legislature was persuaded to adopt the concept, and in the 1870s and 1880s it passed a series of statutes creating the structure of indeterminate sentences, a state parole board, and parole officers to supervise convicts after release which still prevails in New York.

The trouble was that neither the cruelties of prison nor these various methods of rehabilitation — from Gershom Powers' humiliation and moral regeneration to indeterminate sentencing and parole — achieved any appreciable reduction in the number of convicts who returned to prison or in the level of crime. Auburn quickly degenerated into a place where society warehoused criminals. So did Sing Sing and every prison built thereafter. Some criminals were undoubtedly rehabilitated by the different methods tried, and some were undoubtedly deterred from future crime by fear of the cruelties, but the behavior of most criminals was unaffected. The worst of the remaining legal cruelties, with the exception of indefinite solitary confinement, were abolished in the early twentieth century. The lockstep was ended in 1900; the striped uniforms were done away with in 1904; and the imposition of silence was finally lifted just before the First World War. The idea of rehabilitation refused to die as easily, however. Another cycle of corruption, abuse, and overcrowding in the 1920s culminated in prison riots. At Clinton, in July 1929, sixteen hundred inmates rioted, and three of them were killed during the suppression of the uprising. There was a worse outbreak at Auburn six days later, when a trusty threw acid in a guard's face and grabbed the keys to the arsenal. The convicts passed out the guns, killed the assistant warden, burned six shops, and wrecked most of the rest of the prison before they, too, were put down. By then, Attica, which, at a cost of nine million dollars, was to be the ultimate in prison security, comfortable living conditions, and rehabilitation, was already under way. Shortly before the prison opened, in 1931, the *New York Times* predicted in an article that it would be a "Convicts' Paradise" for the two thousand inmates it was designed to house.

The fact that Attica turned out to be the most grim and fortresslike of New York's warehouses for criminals did not deter Governor Nelson Rockefeller from appointing another commission, in 1965, called the Special Committee on Criminal Offenders, to discover how to transform the state's prisons into genuinely rehabilitative institutions. One of its co-chairmen was Russell Oswald, then chairman of New York State's Board of Parole. After three years of research and study, the committee issued a report urging the state to abandon "the ancient concepts of prison and reformatory, and to start working with a new concept: the correctional institution," and stating, "Only then will we be able to break out of the conceptual bondage that results in what amounts to maximum security for almost all inmates of all ages." The first fruit of the committee's report was the outbreak of renomenclaturing in 1970, under which guards became "correction officers," prisons metamorphosed into "correctional facilities," and other euphemisms banished other unpleasantnesses. The Department of Correction and the Division of Parole were merged, on January 1, 1971, into the new Department of Correctional Services.

Oswald, who had headed the parole board for twelve years, was appointed by Governor Rockefeller to be the first Commissioner of Correctional Services. He had just started his program to transform the prisons when the Attica riot in September and its forty-three deaths permitted him to push forward full-scale, with the federal government providing a great deal of the money. After Oswald left, Peter Preiser and then Benjamin Ward carried on. The modest school and vocational activities, the pint-size Dale Carnegie courses, and the Gamblers Anonymous meetings of the 1950s and 1960s gave way to the enormously expanded school program, motorcycle repair, the machine shop, the drafting course, photography, black studies, Italian culture, ceramics, Bard College volunteers, Jaycees, the gymnasium, and all the new privileges, like picnics and the relaxation of former discipline. What information was available indicated that the programs were again failing to achieve any measurable reduction in the number of criminals returning to prison or in the level of crime. "Prisons are so rehabilitative that 60 percent of us here at Green Haven have already had the benefit of the rehabilitative experience several times," Malinow says.

The penologists currently in fashion agree with Malinow and think that Calvin had a point about human nature. They have been saying for quite a few years now that virtually every study reaches the same conclusion: prisons cannot rehabilitate enough of the criminals in them to make any difference; no matter what methods of rehabilitation are attempted, they do not work. Human nature is too complicated and too intractable to be amenable to the degree of change necessary to rehabilitate the criminal personality. These penologists say the best that society can hope to do is to protect itself as much as possible within the limits of justice and humanity. It can put criminals in humane prisons for periods of time commensurate with the crimes committed. Some of these penologists want to abandon rehabilitation except for programs that are small and entirely voluntary on the part of the prisoner. They wish to abolish the entire structure of indeterminate sentencing and parole that New York State and the rest of the country adopted in the years following the meeting of the National Prison Association in 1870, precisely because the concept assumes that criminals can be rehabilitated and released under supervision. In its place, the penologists would establish a body of explicit standards that would require the sentencer to impose a definite sentence. The code would prescribe minimum and maximum sentences for each crime, to give the judge some freedom to adjust the length of the sentence to the circumstances of the crime and the previous record of the convicted defendant. The minimum and maximum limits would be sufficiently close, however, to deprive a judge of the great latitude he now has in sentencing. One recent study on the subject argues that the system would also be fairer, because it would eliminate the current wide disparity in sentencing and make the judge focus on the crime committed, rather than let him base his sentence on his opinion of the character and social worth of the individual, or the extent to which he thinks that the individual might be rehabilitated. In 1976, California became the first state in the country to adopt a penal code of rigorous definite sentences which largely eliminates the discretion of the judge to set particular prison terms. Governor Jerry Brown praised it as the greatest reform of criminal justice in the state in half a century.

Whatever the opinion of the penologists and Governor Brown, the Department of Correctional Services in Albany could not seem to bring itself to concede that rehabilitation did not work. As recently as May 1976, the lead story in the D.O.C.S. monthly newspaper was devoted to a defense of the rehabilitative worth of stamping out license plates at Auburn. The headline read, "Inmates Acquire Marketable Skills in Stigmatized License Plate Shop." The article did acknowledge that an inmate would be unable to find a job in a license-plate shop in New York after his release, since the only one that exists is at Auburn prison. Nevertheless, there once more were those "marketable skills" that "can be used in private industry." One hundred fifty years later, the ghost of Gershom Powers was speaking from the license-plate shop. Once embodied in a bureaucracy and in public buildings of stone and metal, an idea acquires a kind of immunity against reality.

When the immunity finally does start to wear off, great change does not occur rapidly. The bureaucracy, the buildings, and the ingrained attitudes are all still there to impede it. The announcement that change is beginning can come suddenly, however, and that is what happened in the summer of 1977. Commissioner Ward had given a hint six months earlier, in a talk to a group of editors and reporters over lunch at the *Times*. He said he favored the abolition of indeterminate sentencing and its replacement by the new code being advocated by penologists. "We should have a system . . . in which a person knows that if you commit this crime, this is what you will get," he said. He did not, however, want to see the parole system entirely abolished. Rather, he said, participation by the former inmate should be made voluntary. The parole officer should exist to try to help the ex-convict adjust to society, instead of attempting to control him. The change would ease the case load of the state's 325 field parole officers, who, he noted, are theoretically supervising fourteen thousand parolees.

On June 16, 1977, Ward sent an odd-sounding memorandum to all prison superintendents in the state. The D.O.C.S. budget for fiscal 1977–78 was $240 million, and Ward said that it was his "firm intention to reduce the cost of correction in the 1978–79 fiscal year." He instructed the superintendents to consider for elimination all full-time academic and vocational schooling, and all volunteer programs, which "have, in many cases, become very expensive because of necessary security coverage, limited inmate involvement, and 'call-outs' from other programs." The superintendents should instead concentrate on expanding "industrial programs" to help support the prison system and further reduce costs, he said. Then came an interesting sentence: "The alleged rehabilitative worth of such industrial programs should not be a prime consideration unless there is clear, documentable evidence of its nature." As Ward must have known when he wrote the memorandum, there was no danger that such evidence would appear, because it had never existed.

Four days later, on June 20, 1977, in a speech before a meeting of the National Institute on Crime and Delinquency in Salt Lake City, Mark D. Corrigan, the D.O.C.S. deputy commissioner for administrative services, said that state penal administrations across the country should "declare a moratorium on the seemingly endless consideration of correctional rehabilitation," and went on, "All we have discovered about rehabilitation is that we are not doing it . . . Let us begin to focus on cost." Four days after that, Lewis L. Douglass, executive deputy commissioner of the D.O.C.S., discussed the department's altered philosophy in a newspaper interview in Albany. "It is time to take a look at some areas previously viewed as sacred cows in running a liberal prison system," he said. Along with slaughtering the sacred cow of rehabilitation, there was going to be a new "get tough" policy on prison discipline. The trend toward ever-increasing liberalization begun by Commissioner Oswald and carried forward by his successors was being halted.

On June 26, 1977, two days after Douglass's press conference, the superintendent of Green Haven shut the prison down. All inmates were locked in their cells and were put through what became known as the Great Reshuffle. Fourteen hundred of the eighteen hundred men in the prison packed up their belongings and were moved to different cells. The prison returned to the pre-1976 system of having all inmates lock on a specific company and cellblock according to their jobs. The innovation of relatively free movement during the daytime, brought about by the new honor blocks and by the superintendent's decision in late 1976 to let an inmate lock in any empty cell regardless of his job, was rescinded. The honor-block system itself was abolished, since granting an inmate the privilege of locking on an honor block as a reward for good behavior interfered with controlled movement by jobs. C, D, and J blocks, with their cell-and-a-half "houses" and tiny rooms and coveted television sets, were given back to the inmates who worked in the kitchen, at the farm and on other outside jobs, and in the Administration Building. The blocks were no longer called honor blocks. They were referred to as "privileged blocks," but the privileges were curtailed. The privileged were allowed to watch television or otherwise relax outside their cells until 8:30 P.M. — not until II P.M., as before. On the other, ordinary blocks, the prisoners continued to lock in at 5 P.M., as usual, unless they were participating in some authorized evening activity. The noon meal became really mandatory, even if some of the inmates simply sat in the mess halls and did not eat; and the men were moved to and from the mess halls by companies. In the most retrogressive step of all, the prison went back to the pre-1972 system of having the inmates lock in for a noon count. The guards were happy about this retrogression and hoped it would endure, because it permitted them to sit down in the officers' mess for a slightly more leisurely lunch.

The Great Reshuffle sent the morale of the guards soaring. They felt that they had better control of the prison, and the overtime during the first five days was marvelous. It ran to more than forty-five thousand dollars and was useful for summer vacations. At the end of June, Commissioner Ward requested and received the resignation of the superintendent he had appointed in September 1976. The deputy superintendent of security at Great Meadow was offered the post. He spent four days at Green Haven and then returned to Great Meadow, saying he did not want the job. Green Haven's deputy of security was appointed the new superintendent — the seventh in seven years. A new deputy of security was brought down from Albany. The prisoners were upset by the changes, but neither they nor the guards believed that the tightening up meant a return to the strict discipline of the past. Too much had been given to the prisoners by the era of liberalization that Commissioner Oswald and Attica had initiated, and by the various decisions of the courts on prisoners' rights, to be taken away now. The atmosphere was more one of uncertainty and disarray. The department did not seem to know quite where it was going or precisely what it wanted to do. The classification sergeant, who had functioned as Green Haven's one-man C.I.A., went into a holding pattern by transferring to the kitchen. With the prison administration in such confusion, it was unclear whether he would be backed up if one of his intelligence capers went awry. He decided to suspend them until some recognizable line of authority emerged. Whatever additional changes came after the Great Reshuffle of 1977, he was certain of only one thing, as he had been after the Great Frisk of 1976. No amount of tinkering would alter the predilections of criminals or solve the problems of running places to house them. "It's all like taking aspirin for cancer," the classification sergeant said. "It just lessens the pain for a few minutes. It doesn't do anything to the disease."

George Malinow was born in a frame tenement house in the Greenpoint section of Brooklyn on September 10, 1920. His father, Paul Malinow, a Polish immigrant, died when George was about two. Malinow has no memories of his father and little knowledge of him. He doesn't know when his father came to the United States, or how he earned a living, or whether the family's name may have been Malinowski or Malinowicz in the old country. His mother, Helena, was already married when she came to the United States. Her maiden name was Huss. Malinow knows as little about the Husses as he does about the Malinows. "It wasn't the custom in a working-class family to hold dem frivolous types of discussions with the children," he says. "There were too many practical matters to worry about."

George Malinow was by far the youngest of Paul and Helena Malinow's three children. His brother, Nicholas, was born around 1907. Nicholas returned to Poland as a child to live with one of his grandmothers, married and settled down there, and went back to Brooklyn only once, on a brief visit. Malinow hasn't seen him since 1927. When Malinow was last out of prison, in 1966, he heard that his brother was back in this country. He intended to try to find him but didn't get around to it during his seven weeks at liberty. Malinow's sister, Marianne, was born in 1911 or perhaps 1912. "She must of been eight or nine years older than me, because when I was still a little kid she was already working and keeping company," he says. Marianne married a heavy-drinking man of German ancestry, Franz Muller, and became a heavy drinker herself. The Mullers had two sons and two daughters and any number of turbulent fights before they went their separate ways; the four Muller children were raised in Catholic orphanages and foster homes. A couple of years ago, while Malinow was checking a list of inmates who had just been transferred from Clinton to Green Haven, to see if there were any old-timers on it, he spotted the name William Muller. That was the name of one of his sister's sons. Malinow had last seen that nephew in 1943, when Malinow was in the Army and the nephew was a child. He sent a friend over to ask this William Muller a few questions about his family; his answers proved that he was Marianne Muller's son. Malinow was as pleased to see William Muller in prison as a doctor might be to go to a medical convention and meet up with a long-lost nephew who had become a physician. "He's a good kid," Malinow says. "He makes great money as a bridge painter when he's out. He owns a 127-foot boat. He's here only because he had a little misunderstanding with a girl he was living with and beat her up. He broke her jaw. He told me he didn't really mean to hit her so hard. The girl's mother liked Billy and didn't want her daughter to prosecute him, but the girl was mad because he'd hurt her face. She asked him why he hadn't broken her arm instead, and made a big thing of it." It is characteristic of Malinow to minimize the crimes of people he likes. Muller is serving a seven-year sentence for assault, his third serious crime. At the age of forty, he has spent seventeen years in prison. Muller had heard he had an uncle who was "away." He, too, was glad to find a relative in prison. He is proud of his uncle's good reputation ("He's never turned state's evidence"), and has made him some frames for his glass paintings, and, when Malinow was pressed for time, has even ghost-painted some pictures that Malinow wanted to give to friends. Both Muller and Malinow lost track of Marianne Muller many years ago.

When Malinow was about five, his mother remarried. Her second husband, Thomas Kanfer, was also a Polish immigrant. As a child, Malinow was told that Kanfer was not his real father, but he didn't let that bother him. He called Kanfer "Pop" or "Papa" and regarded him as his real father. "I would never have thought of using the word 'stepfather,' " he says. "I couldn't have had a more devoted or loving father. My mother slapped me occasionally. My father never hit me in his life, and there were God knows how many times when I deserved a good walloping."

Helena Huss Malinow Kanfer was described by a parole officer who visited the family several times between 1940 and 1942, when Malinow was being considered for release from his first prison sentence, as "haglike," "excitable," and "inclined to dominate the household." William Muller remembers her as "a tough old Polack." Malinow prefers to remember her as a kindhearted, unfortunate woman. He recalls that when he was a little boy, accompanying his mother on her neighborhood errands, and she saw a stray kitten in the snow, she was apt to pick it up, put it in her black leather shopping bag, and take it home; there were usually three or four cats and a dog in the Kanfer household. Helena Kanfer, a short, slight woman, suffered from asthma, but she worked at night cleaning office buildings. Malinow is bitter about the hard work she had to do, and claims that the low-paying drudgery shortened her life by fifteen years. His mother died in 1949, at the age of sixty-five. Her death was ascribed to high blood pressure.

When Kanfer first came into Malinow's life, he was a chef at a hotel in Manhattan. It was a good job to have in the mid-twenties, when food purchases took a large portion of a poor family's income. On holidays, Kanfer's boss sent him home in a big car with baked chickens or turkeys for the family.

Sometime around 1928, Kanfer fell down a flight of stairs at the hotel while carrying an armful of crockery. He never fully recovered from his accident and was never again able to work as a chef. He went to work for a display-fixture company in Brooklyn as a night watchman, a low-paying job that he kept until he retired, in 1941. His salary throughout the 1930s was eighteen or twenty dollars a week. Once Kanfer became a night watchman, the family ate less well. Breakfast consisted of milk and toast; lunch consisted of bologna or liverwurst sandwiches and soup; dinner — day after day, year in and year out — was goulash or another kind of stew. "We never went hungry, but we didn't have the food we wanted," Malinow says. "The only good meals I remember were at Christmas and Easter. Then we had kielbasa and ham — a real feast — and we looked forward to coloring eggs from one Easter to the next." Malinow remembers Kanfer, who died in 1952, at the age of eighty, as a gentle person. When his wife got angry and started to shout, Kanfer left the house and stayed away a few hours, until her anger subsided, on the theory that the presence of two people was required for an argument to take place. Kanfer would sometimes take young George on outings — to the Brooklyn Botanic Garden, to Coney Island, to parades. "My mother never became an American citizen, but my father did," Malinow says. "He loved this country. He was very patriotic. He insisted on flying a flag from our window staff on every American holiday. He was a quiet man, but once in a while, when he had a glass of Polish vodka, he became moody and sentimental and spoke to me like a grownup. He had once been a chef on ocean liners. He would take out a suitcase and show me packets of letters tied up in ribbons — the envelopes were beautiful colors and the stamps were from many foreign countries — and he would tell me how good it was to travel and what a good chef he had been."

Malinow's childhood was spent in a series of modest four-room apartments in Greenpoint. The kitchen of each of these railroad flats, which were all within an area of a few blocks, contained a sink, an old-fashioned wood-and-coal stove, a tub — in which George took a bath every Saturday evening — and an icebox. George's chores included emptying the pan into which the ice dripped. One of the apartments had a toilet in the hall outside and gas lamps; the others had electricity, which was turned off when the family couldn't afford to pay the electric bills. Sometimes George had a bedroom of his own, sometimes he slept on a foldaway bed in the living room. "The nicest object my parents owned was their brass bed," Malinow says. "It gleamed. It made me think of golden castles." Malinow's early wardrobe for everyday wear was limited to a pair of plain pants, a couple of shirts, and a pair of sneakers or old shoes. Twice a year — before Easter and again before Christmas — he got a new dress suit, or a jacket and a pair of good pants, and a pair of new shoes. He wore his dress outfit to church on Sunday morning — if he went to church. The Kanfers were regular churchgoers, and Malinow made his First Communion, but he seldom attended church. "I've never had a religious nature," he says.

Most of the people in Greenpoint were working-class poor, but some of the men had better-paying jobs than Kanfer and enjoyed more worldly goods. When Malinow saw boys who were better dressed than he was, and visited homes where steaks and chops and roasts appeared frequently on the table, he didn't like the contrast. "I wondered why some families had so much and some so little," he says. "It didn't seem right that some kids had three pairs of pants, including white flannels, and white shoes." When he was about ten, he and a group of neighborhood boys started stealing. They all knew older kids who stole. "In our neighborhood, crime wasn't a novelty," he says. The boys stole wood from a nearby lumberyard, lead pipe and brass knobs from condemned houses, and coal from the barges that docked along the Greenpoint waterfront. "Some places had watchmen, but there's a limit to the amount of watching a watchman can do," Malinow says. "We got away with a lot without getting caught. That made me get in the habit of stealing." Once in a while, neighborhood policemen did catch the boys stealing. "The cops would form a double line and offer us a choice," he says. "Either we could go through the line and take a beating or we could go with them to the station house. I always took the beating. It was better than facing the family in court."

The boys sold the stolen goods and split the proceeds, occasionally netting as much as forty-five dollars apiece for a day's stealing. Malinow usually spent some of the money on himself — he bought himself clothes, he went to the movies — and some on food for his family: "cakes and hams that would last us a whole weekend." He often brought cash home for his parents. He knew they wouldn't condone his stealing, so he kept his source of revenue to himself. When he put twenty dollars on the kitchen table and his mother asked him where he had got the money, he sometimes told her he had earned it working on the docks, and he sometimes (for the sake of variety) told her he had won it betting on a dice game. She had forbidden him to gamble, and reprimanded him for having disobeyed her, but whenever he asked her if she wanted him to return the money he'd won, she said no, leave it there, just don't do it again. During his thirty-six years in prison, Malinow has periodically been asked why he stole as a child. He considers the question tiresome, because the answer is perfectly obvious to him and he thinks it ought to be equally obvious to others. "I stole because stealing was the only means available to me to obtain what I needed and what my family needed at home," he says. "I would not have stolen if I had come from a middle-class family rather than from a poor family." When it is pointed out to him that many poor people don't steal, he is not flustered by this idea. "Why is it that some people see a burning building in which women and children are trapped and just watch the flames, while others see the building and risk their lives to dash in and try to rescue the women and children?" he says. "Everyone reacts differently. Some fathers can see their children eating bread for supper. Others can't, and go out to steal so their children can eat better. But I'm not condemning my father for not stealing. He was a righteous, religious, law-abiding man. Whenever I think of him, I think of his high morals. He was outstanding. But he had the immigrant mentality — "We've always been peasants, we'll always be peasants.' There was no point in asking him about better food; he would have said we were doing our best. That wasn't good enough for me. I'm not saying stealing is right. I'm saying what drove me to it."

Malinow liked school until he had to study algebra. To dodge this hateful subject, he started playing hooky and running away from home for a few days at a time. In the spring of 1935, he ran away to New Jersey with three friends. One of them, a boy called Pete, despised his mother. Before the boys left New York City, Pete wrote his mother a letter telling her in profane language what he thought of her. Pete's handwriting was not good. Malinow's handwriting was as legible when he was a teen-ager as it is today, so when Pete asked him to address the envelope, he did. The four runaways hitchhiked to New Jersey on the back of a truck. They were picked up by the police in a small town near Hackensack a couple of days later and were sent back to Brooklyn. Pete's mother had turned the letter over to the police and had signed a complaint against her son. The four boys were taken to children's court. A handwriting expert asked them for samples of their handwriting. The expert ruled that Malinow had written part of the letter as well as the address. The judge, ignoring George's protestations of innocence and his parents' pleas to let him stay at home, sentenced him and Pete to three months in the Catholic protectory in the Bronx, a place for juvenile delinquents. The two other boys were allowed to go home. At the Catholic protectory, George and Pete had to study their regular school lessons during the day, and received religious instruction in the evening. There was only an hour or two in the afternoon for recreation. Malinow loathed the rigid supervision. "The brothers killed us with prayers," he says. "They had us praying coming and going. What kid likes to say his prayers when he doesn't have to? The brothers were much more brutal than the neighborhood cops. If you laughed or giggled when you weren't supposed to, they hit you across the face with a ruler or beat you with a leather strap. That three months in the Catholic protectory — it seemed like ten years to me — was a bad turn in the road. It made me very bitter. I returned home hating authority. I'd been punished for something I knew I hadn't done. I didn't come out thinking of behaving better. I came out thinking of getting even."

As teen-agers, Malinow and his friends had branched out into stealing assorted goods from empty factories and warehouses and from sealed freight cars in Long Island City's railroad yards. His first arrest as a juvenile came six months before his stay in the Catholic protectory, when he was fourteen and was caught breaking into a restaurant. He was given probation. He didn't like having probation officers come to his home and school to check up on him, he didn't like having to travel by trolley to downtown Brooklyn to make his probation reports, and he didn't like the sternness of the probation officers or their custom of keeping him waiting "in an unfriendly atmosphere" for half an hour to see them, but probation never prevented him from stealing. He got away with his crimes more often than not, although he was brought into court a number of times for violating probation. "Whenever I got into trouble, my mother smacked me and my father explained why what I'd done was wrong," Malinow says. He didn't mind the smacks, but he dreaded his father's use of psychology, so for a day or two he would resolve not to steal again. After a few days, however, he would feel a need for something that he or the household lacked, and he would find himself out doing exactly what he'd planned not to do. "I don't believe any parent could have kept a child like me from running away or stealing," he says. "I was a stubborn Polish kid."

When Malinow was next arrested — in July 1937, for breaking into a vacant house with a neighborhood pal named Fred Giritski — he had completed his first probation sentence, dropped out of school, and quit his first regular job. He had finished the eighth grade at the age of fifteen, in June 1936, after being left back several times for absenteeism. He spent the summer of 1936 alternately working as a delivery boy for a delicatessen and stealing coal. In the fall of 1936, he enrolled at a vocational high school. He had applied for working papers, which came through in September, very shortly after his sixteenth birthday, and he then dropped out of high school. "I had a mental block against school," he says. "My mind was on financial matters." In the fall of 1936, he got a job as a shipping clerk, at eleven dollars a week, at the display-fixture company where his father was a night watchman, a block or two from home. He soon found the job boring, and felt that it had no future. He had no desire to subject himself to the sort of life his father was leading, no wish to wind up a poor old man. Stealing was easier and more lucrative, so after a few months he quit. In July 1937, he and Giritski were indicted for burglary in the third degree and grand larceny in the second for breaking into the vacant house but were allowed to plead guilty to petit larceny. They received suspended sentences and two years' probation. Eleven months later, Malinow got into his first serious trouble with the law.

It had rained during the day, and there were puddles on the streets of Queens on the evening of Sunday, June 12, 1938. At half-past ten, Michael Dillard, twenty-two, and his fiancée, Evelyn Scott, also twenty-two, were sitting in Dillard's father's new Buick sedan, which was parked outside the house of Miss Scott's aunt and uncle, in Astoria. The young couple were going to be married in August and were happily making wedding plans. The evening was muggy, and the car windows were open. Miss Scott's home was in Sag Harbor, farther out on the island, where she had just been given a bridal shower, but she was working as a secretary for a department store in Brooklyn and was living temporarily with her aunt and uncle. A number of shower gifts — sheets, towels, glasses, and kitchen utensils — and some of Miss Scott's summer dresses were stacked on the back seat of the car. Dillard, a pharmacist, was about to drop his fiancée off and drive on to his home, in Nyack, where the couple planned to live after their marriage. His parents would store the gifts and the dresses for the next two months.

Dillard and Miss Scott were saying good night when an object that unpleasantly resembled a gun appeared in the car's left front window. The left back door opened, and four young men scrambled in, seating themselves on top of the dresses and shower gifts. The intruders told Dillard to start driving and not to try anything funny. Dillard and Miss Scott both felt metal objects in their backs. There was a tavern on the corner, and Miss Scott assumed that the four had held it up and were simply using the sedan as a getaway car. At first, she was not terribly frightened. She had the presence of mind to slip off her diamond engagement ring and put it in her mouth as they rode along; the streets were dark, and she figured that the four young men wouldn't see what she was doing. She also removed a dollar bill from her handbag and slid it into her sandal. She was reaching into Dillard's pocket to extricate his wallet when one of the boys saw that she was moving, warned her to keep her hands up, and pushed the gun harder into her back. The prospective bridegroom was ordered to drive from Astoria to Jackson Heights to Long Island City. After about half an hour, he was ordered to stop in a lonely spot directly under the Queensboro Bridge. Two of the boys pulled Dillard out of the driver's side of the car, and two pulled Miss Scott out of the passenger side. At that point, she began to fear for her life. In the shadows of the bridge, the boys frisked Dillard and relieved him of his watch, his class ring, and his wallet, which contained his driver's license and his father's car registration as well as twelve dollars. He asked the boys if he could have his license back. They handed him the wallet minus the cash. Meanwhile, Miss Scott was robbed of her watch and her handbag. The boys tried to take a ruby ring she was wearing, but they succeeded only in scratching her finger; the ring was tight, and they couldn't get it off. As Miss Scott was wondering what the four would do next, someone in a nearby apartment turned on a light. The light seemed to startle the boys, who clambered back into the car and sped off.

Miss Scott and Dillard started to climb a stairway in one of the bridge towers to the trolley platform overhead. Miss Scott was so shaky and the stairway was so long that she didn't think she could make it, and said as much to her fiancé. He said he would not leave her there alone, and urged her upward. On the platform, a trolley car stopped for them. When they told the driver what had happened, he refused to take their nickel fares out of the dollar bill that Miss Scott had preserved, telling her she might need it. He let them off at the precinct station house across the bridge. The police there told the couple they couldn't help them; according to police regulations, the couple would have to report the crime to the precinct closest to the spot in Astoria where it had begun — but they were persuaded to send out an alarm for the stolen car, and they did drive Dillard and Miss Scott to Astoria. At the Astoria station house, Miss Scott and Dillard said that the four robbers looked and sounded as if they were from the slums — their faces were hard, their manners rough. The couple had scarcely finished their account of the robbery when they learned that the car had been found, wrapped around a light pole just a few blocks from where they had been let off. They were driven back to Long Island City to identify it. Some of the shower gifts had been thrown from the car as the boys fled, and lay in the muddy street. Miss Scott's clothes hadn't been touched, but whatever shower gifts hadn't been discarded were gone; in their place was a black imitation revolver that police described to reporters as "an exact replica of the real thing." It was five o'clock on Monday morning before Miss Scott got back to her aunt and uncle's house.

A few hours later, the story of the robbery was front-page news in several newspapers. NYACK YOUTH, GIRL ABDUCTED AND ROBBED; THUGS GET GIFTS OF ENGAGED PAIR; FIANCEE KIDNAPPED, OUTWITS BANDITS, the headlines said. Miss Scott became more and more apprehensive as she read the newspaper accounts of the crime. She was afraid that the thieves would be furious at reading about the diamond ring that had eluded them, and would return to claim it. (The papers had also provided her aunt and uncle's address.) She went back to work a day or two later, escorted by her cousin, her cousin's boyfriend, the boyfriend's brother, and the police, but she suffered from nervous indigestion. A week later, her uncle called her at work with some good news. The four young men who had robbed her had attempted to hold up a car in Jackson Heights. The driver, who turned out to be an off-duty policeman, had chased them off after they robbed him. Later that night, as they were loitering on a corner in Jackson Heights, they aroused the suspicions of two radio-car patrolmen, who stopped them for questioning. One of the four leaped over a wall and ran away across a cemetery; the three others were taken into custody. They were armed with cap pistols that looked like real guns. After some questioning, the three boys — Fred Giritski, seventeen; Louis Stokowski, eighteen; and Charles Preniszni, eighteen — all from Greenpoint, admitted the "shower holdup" and several other holdups of couples in parked cars. Giritski betrayed the name of the fourth robber: George Malinow, seventeen, who was arrested a few hours later at his parents' apartment, where he was sleeping soundly. He, too, confessed to the Dillard-Scott crime and to some other robberies. It was the first but by no means the last time Malinow was informed on. He later took what comfort he could from the fact that Giritski, who had been promised preferential treatment for giving him up, received the same sentence he and the two others got.

The four boys — all but Stokowski were on probation at the time of their arrests — were held without bail. In late June, they were indicted for first-degree robbery, first-degree grand larceny, and second-degree assault. On July 13, they were allowed to plead guilty to second-degree robbery. On July 15, they were sentenced to five to ten years in state prison. Miss Scott and Dillard went to court for the arraignment and the sentencing. The boys' parents were also in court, and looked "as if they would have killed you if they could have got hold of you," Miss Scott said later. "They seemed as poor, as shabbily dressed, and as tough as their sons." Miss Scott thought at the time that five to ten years in prison wasn't long enough for the fright she and her fiancé had experienced, but primarily she was relieved that the boys were being taken out of circulation, so that they couldn't come back to bother them or anyone else. Miss Scott and Dillard were married on August 21, 1938; she felt glad to get out of Queens. The Dillards eventually had five children, and the family lived quietly in Nyack, where Dillard owned a drugstore, until his death, in 1962. Mrs. Dillard still lives in Nyack with her youngest child. She has never again been the victim of a crime.

Dillard's father carried adequate insurance on his eight-hundred-dollar 1937 Buick, which was almost totally demolished, and was able to replace it with another new Buick at little or no cost. The Dillards never got any of their cash, shower gifts, or jewelry back. Their watches and his class ring had been pawned. The pawn tickets had been redeemed a day before the four boys were arrested. These financial losses were small and were quickly forgotten, but it was ten years before Mrs. Dillard stopped suffering from nervous indigestion; today, looking over her yellowed newspaper clippings and talking about the thirty-nine-year-old crime brings back unpleasant memories. She suspects, however, that she was luckier than most 1977 robbery victims. "The boys weren't drunk or high on drugs, and the guns weren't real," she says. "Still, the robbery was a nightmare. About the best thing I can say about it is that we didn't wind up in the river. I sometimes wonder what would have happened if that apartment light near the bridge hadn't suddenly gone on."

Malinow's recollections of the 1938 crime are much hazier than Mrs. Dillard's, and he says he has forgotten many of the details that the newspapers of the day printed. He doesn't remember that Miss Scott saved her diamond ring by putting it in her mouth, he doesn't remember touching the shower gifts or pawning the jewelry, and he doesn't remember admitting that he had robbed any other couples in parked cars. "That was our first and only parked-car couple," he says. It is characteristic of Malinow to minimize the crimes for which he has been arrested. He does remember that Miss Scott and Dillard were "an average couple in an average car, nothing outstanding." He says that he stole the car for excitement, because it was summertime and he wanted to go joy-riding, and that he and his friends only robbed Miss Scott and Dillard on the spur of the moment. The explanation he gives for the crime in 1977 is at variance with the explanations he gave while doing time for it, between 1938 and 1942. In those years, he told prison officials and parole investigators that he had committed it because he was out of work, couldn't find a job, and needed the money. "I thought it would be better to say I did something for money than for excitement," he says now of these earlier explanations. When he is asked about the robbery of the off-duty cop (whose money was taken but not his car, and who was hit over the head by one of Malinow's companions), he has trouble at first remembering the crime at all. When he finally does recall it, he admits that the motive for that crime, which took place a week after the Dillard-Scott robbery, was money rather than excitement. "By that time, we did have urgent needs," he says. "We had to pay for some clothes we had at the dry cleaner's, and we had an urgent need to go to a tailor shop and get some trousers pressed, and we had a need to buy dress shoes. We all wore out shoes like crazy on the docks. But the couple in the car — that was just childish skylarking. That one I do regret." Even more than Mrs. Dillard, Malinow chooses to look back on the positive rather than the negative aspects of the crime. "We didn't rape the girl or injure the fellow, as kids do today," he says. "We only got a few dollars and some nonsense jewelry. It wasn't even worth the effort. We didn't consider the consequences." On July 18, 1938, three days after they were sentenced, Malinow and his three associates were sent to Sing Sing to begin facing the consequences. He believes to this day that the punishment was too severe for the crime. "We should have been sent to a reformatory or a state training school for a short time," he says. "We weren't given that type of consideration, simply because our parents were poor. None of us had money to pay a lawyer. If my people had had five hundred dollars, I'd have gone to a children's reformatory for six months. If they had had twenty-five hundred dollars, I'd have walked home with a suspended sentence. We had nothing, so we were sentenced to five to ten years in state prison."

The earliest photograph that Malinow has of himself was taken upon his arrival at Sing Sing in the summer of 1938. The photograph shows a boy with light eyes, set far apart, thick eyebrows, and ears that stick out — a boy who looks younger than his almost eighteen years. His hair, thick and dark, is cut in the working-class style of the day, long on top, short on the sides; a few strands fall willfully over his forehead. He is wearing a suit jacket and a white shirt. His tie hangs loosely at the collar; the knot looks as if it had been made by someone unaccustomed to dealing with ties. There is a what-next expression on his face. "I was very frightened when that photo was taken," Malinow says. In 1938, what prior knowledge Malinow had of Sing Sing came from a few James Cagney movies he'd stolen the money to see and from a few older men in Greenpoint who had done time there. Actually being in Sing Sing was worse than the Cagney films or the Greenpoint Sing Sing alumni had suggested. Shortly after his arrival, Malinow was assigned a number. The number troubled him. "I wasn't used to hearing, 'Hey, Nine-five-three-oh-six, get over here,' " he says. "It took me a while to listen for the number to be called and a while to know the number was me. I was used to being called Georgie." He quickly memorized his Sing Sing number, and now he can recite from memory most of the ten prison numbers he has had over the past thirty-nine years. He got a social-security number in 1936, when he went to work, but he does not know it by heart, perhaps because he has had little occasion to use it.

In 1938, Sing Sing, then a maximum-security prison, was divided into two parts. The old cellblock, which had been constructed in the 1820s, was down near the Hudson River. The new cellblock, built a century later, was farther up the hill. Like all new arrivals, Malinow was assigned to the old cellblock. He remained there for seven months and three weeks — a period of time he remembers with such precision because the average time spent down the hill was six months. He resented every extra day beyond that. The old cellblock had small, narrow cells that he thought were like dungeons. The stone cell walls were damp. The cell doors were made of latticed metal with small openings. The cells had no windows and only one bare bulb for illumination. They lacked toilets. Each inmate had a bucket. He carried out his wastes each day, emptied and rinsed the bucket, and brought it back. The cells stank. They were filthy. Rats and mice, bugs and lice thrived in the dank and the gloom. The bed had a hard mattress. The bedding was a ragged blanket with a sour odor; a lumpy pillow; and one or two tattered sheets. (The cells up the hill were relatively spacious and bright, and were furnished with such amenities as toilets.) The food provided at Sing Sing was little better than the cell. Two or three pieces of potato or a carrot, a pea, and a bean floating in what tasted like dishwater were the only clues to whether the dishwatery substance purported to be potato soup or vegetable soup. In retrospect, the food at home wasn't so bad. If it was plain, it was at least well flavored, plentiful, and served, Malinow says now, "in a colorful European atmosphere."

Malinow was kept busy during his first few weeks at Sing Sing. While going through the reception process, he was given various physical and psychiatric tests. The doctors found him to be in good health. His I.Q. was average — exactly a hundred. The psychiatrist diagnosed him as having a "psychopathic personality." While he was still on the reception block, confined for twenty-four hours a day except to go to the mess hall, to church, or to the hospital or the school building for the various tests, some Greenpoint acquaintances called on him. These men, inmates who had already been at Sing Sing for some time, left him a few magazines to help him pass the time in reception. They gave him a knife and some advice for the future. Once he was out of reception, he was to wear the knife strapped to his arm at all times. He was to use it the first time an older man made sexual advances toward him, or he would be branded a "punk" and taken advantage of for the rest of his stay in prison. With the help of these neighborhood acquaintances, Malinow got a desirable job as an apprentice in the prison printshop, which printed letterheads, forms, and reports for the Department of Correction and other state agencies.

The confinement of the reception block was followed by the tension of being out in the general population. Soon after Malinow went to work in the printshop, where he was broken in on a hand-fed press and went on to learn how to handle an automatic press, a sexual pass was made at him. He used his knife to fend it off. He was not sexually accosted again, but he wore the knife strapped to his arm for the balance of his stay at Sing Sing. "In 1938 and 1939, Sing Sing was a wide-open prison," Malinow says. "There was much more booze, money, and gambling then than there is today, and there were frequent stabbings. The prison was overcrowded. It had twenty-six hundred or twenty-seven hundred inmates. You had old-time inmates doing big time, and they had to do something. The guards knew what was going on and didn't interfere too much. They got a share of the money. There was nothing normal about life there. You never knew when you got up in the morning if there was going to be a knife fight. Everything was in doubt. The only place you could relax was your cell. I hated the constant harassment and surveillance. We were counted, frisked, marched from one place to another, and made to show our passes and identification cards from one end of the day to the other. A few weeks in state prison, experiencing that type of tension and harassment, might have done me some good. They should have made my stay very harsh and very brief. If I could have left after a few weeks, when I was still afraid I couldn't endure it, I might never have come back. After you're there longer, you not only see that you can make it, you also come into contact with older, experienced criminals who teach you things that increase your chances of returning."

Every criminal's life story seems to include the line "I learned everything I know about crime at ———," the sentence being finished with the name of the first prison to which that particular criminal was sent, so it isn't any wonder that the line appeared recently in a Woody Allen parody of a burglar's autobiography. Unlike Woody Allen readers, Malinow sees no humor in the line. When he says he learned everything he knows about crime at Sing Sing, he is speaking in absolute earnest about his own experience. If the line is a cliché, and therefore ready-made for the parodist to mock — well, many things become clichés because they're true. While poverty serves as Malinow's rationale for his childhood stealing, Sing Sing serves as his rationale for becoming a professional criminal, and no one can persuade him otherwise. At Sing Sing, his new prison friends convinced him that it was foolish to be sent to state prison for stealing a few dollars with a toy gun when armed payroll robberies were so much more lucrative. They offered him lessons in payroll robbery. They taught him how to obtain a gun, how to hold a gun steady for five minutes, where the members of a holdup team should position themselves, how to knock out a watchman or a guard with one's bare hands, how to determine which payrolls were worth taking, and other useful professional skills. "When I first went to Sing Sing and I listened to those guys, I thought to myself, Who do they think I am — John Dillinger? But by the time I left I felt capable of taking an armored car single-handedly," Malinow says. He was to put this knowledge to use fourteen years after he acquired it.

The guards and the civilian supervisor in the Sing Sing printshop were pleased with Malinow's work and attitude. He was a fast learner, he was dependable, and he behaved well. They were ready to teach him how to operate a Linotype machine, predicted a good future for him as a printer, and offered to help him find a job when he got out. Payroll robberies captured Malinow's imagination more than Linotype machines and hand-fed presses. He liked the printshop well enough, but he didn't like being at Sing Sing at all, and thought he could improve his lot by transferring to Wallkill, a small, experimental medium-security prison in Ulster County for first offenders, which offered a diversity of vocational training. He wanted to try living in the "country," and Wallkill was regarded as an easy place from which to make parole on your first try. Malinow succeeded in getting himself transferred to Wallkill in December 1939.

He was immediately happier as no. 2232 at Wallkill than he had ever been as no. 95,306 at Sing Sing. "Going from Sing Sing to Wallkill was like coming out of a desert into a lush rain forest," he says. To Malinow, Wallkill's buildings looked "just like Oxford University" (he has never seen Oxford or a photograph of it), and he liked his small room in one of the Gothic buildings. Sing Sing was the dirtiest of the prisons in New York State and one of the oldest. Wallkill was immaculate, and just seven years old. At Sing Sing, many of the inmates were hardened old-timers with long sentences. Most of Wallkill's five hundred inmates were young men serving short sentences; Malinow never felt it necessary to carry a knife there. The inmates at Sing Sing wore coarse, drab gray uniforms. The inmates at Wallkill wore snappy-looking dark-blue shirts and pencil-striped poplin trousers that held a sharp crease. Sing Sing's guards were mostly stern men who wore blue uniforms, as the police did. The Wallkill guards dressed in khaki in summer and forest green in winter and looked more like soldiers. Their courtesy almost made Malinow forget they were prison guards. "If one of them was handing me a letter and accidentally dropped it, he'd apologize," he says. "They didn't have to say, 'George, I'm sorry,' but they did. They were trained with a different outlook. They said 'please' and 'thank you,' and they didn't call you by your last name or your number. They listened to your problems and complaints." In the summer, Malinow swam in Wallkill's pool. He had ample time to frequent the hobby shop, play volleyball and basketball, stretch out on the grass, and even acquire his first case of poison ivy. He and three of his friends cooked on an outdoor barbecue and grew vegetables, flowers, and melons on a small piece of land they were permitted to cultivate. He studied for and received his Roman Catholic confirmation at Wallkill. Thomas Kanfer traveled to Wallkill by bus several times during his son's two years and two months there, and deposited a dollar or two in his account on each visit. Malinow says he dissuaded his mother from visiting, because she was too emotional. Helena Kanfer, who spoke broken English and could write only in Polish, dictated an occasional letter to a bilingual neighborhood friend; letters had to be in English so the prison censors could read them. A number of men at Green Haven attribute their crimes to the fact that their parents didn't love them. Malinow is not one of those. "My parents loved me as much as anyone else's" he says. "They hoped I wouldn't go to prison, but they knew people in the neighborhood sometimes did go to prison and they accepted it. They stood by me when I was sent away, to the best of their ability. My father believed in his country right or wrong and in his son right or wrong. My parents never said we had hope and you disappointed us. They were sorry about what happened, but they didn't make an issue of it with me."

Wallkill offered its inmates a choice of trades, among them carpentry, barbering, masonry, blacksmithing, welding, and auto mechanics. Malinow couldn't foresee any of these trades as a long-range career, but he could foresee being a car owner, so he wanted to take up auto mechanics. Some of the men in Greenpoint owned cars and didn't know how to repair them. He had heard them complain about the high cost of mechanics' work. He didn't want anyone to charge him thirty dollars to fix a broken generator that might or might not have been broken. His second choice of trades was welding; he was curious to learn how to use an acetylene torch — a skill that would come in handy if he should decide to have a go at safecracking when he got out. After the obligatory six months' work on the prison farm then required of all new Wallkill inmates, Malinow was assigned to the auto shop.

Malinow studied auto mechanics from June 1940 until his release from Wallkill, in early 1942. The courses were taught by well-qualified civilian instructors, who used up-to-date equipment. He also took academic subjects of his choice. His grades in these subjects ranged from straight A's in English to straight B's in mathematics and business law to a mixture of B's and C's in blueprint reading and science. He also received B's and C's in auto mechanics. By the time he was released, he had completed over two thousand hours in motors, brakes, carburetors, electrical units, and the like. Every three months, the instructors entered his grades and their appraisals of him on his record. A few of his quarterly reports in auto mechanics describe him as an average student with just a fair ability to reason, and a person who was somewhat easily led by others, but as a rule the adjectives applied to him are favorable: "respectful," "industrious," "self-reliant," "neat," "well liked," and "cooperative" are the most frequent. Since he didn't lose any good time in prison, he became eligible for release on parole in November 1941, after serving three years and four months in prison, two-thirds of the five-year minimum sentence. He was scheduled to appear before the parole board in October 1941, and it often took several weeks for a man to be released after the board granted him parole.

In the months preceding an inmate's appearance before the parole board, prison personnel prepare a pre-parole summary for the parole commissioners to scan when they call the inmate in for his brief parole hearing. Malinow's physical condition was noted on his pre-parole summary as good except for a little nearsightedness in his left eye. The description that the Wallkill prison personnel gave of Malinow in 1941 was almost identical to the description they had given of him when he came to Wallkill two years earlier. "Inmate is a short, thin, boyish-appearing youth with pale complexion," his record reads. "He is a weak, ineffectual person, who very obviously has not developed emotionally or intellectually, insofar as judgment is concerned. It is noteworthy that this inmate came to prison when he was but seventeen years of age, and apparently confinement has not had too much effect upon him in the sense that it has not given him any more insight into the nature of his conflicts with the law and the reasons therefor." The prison personnel observed that Malinow would have to serve six years and eight months — that is, until the maximum expiration date of his five-to-ten-year sentence — under parole supervision, and doubted whether "a man of his makeup and background" would be capable of satisfactorily completing such a long period of parole supervision. In his favor, however, they said he had completed vocational training at Wallkill which might make it possible for him to get a better job than he had been qualified for in the past. Also in his favor, they added, was the fact that he had adjusted well to Wallkill and had profited from its programs, in contrast to his co-defendants. Fred Giritski had been sent from Sing Sing directly to Attica, but Malinow's two other co-defendants, Charles Preniszni and Louis Stokowski, had also been sent from Sing Sing to Wallkill. Preniszni and Stokowski had behaved so badly at Wallkill that they had been transferred to Great Meadow, a maximum-security prison. (All of Malinow's co-defendants got out of prison in late 1941 or early 1942. None of them ever got into trouble with the law again.)

In 1941, before a man could be released on parole he had to submit a residence and a job to his prison parole officer, which had to be investigated and approved by his parole officer on the street. Malinow said he intended to live at home, so a parole officer in Brooklyn visited his parents' apartment several times before his release. Although Malinow had told one of his pre-parole interviewers that his mother planned to settle in Hempstead, Long Island, after his release, "to remove him from the influences which exist in his former neighborhood," it was obvious to the investigating parole officer that Helena and Thomas Kanfer didn't have the slightest intention or possibility of moving. Shortly after Malinow was sent to Sing Sing, the Kanfers had moved to yet another four-room railroad flat in the heart of Greenpoint. One bedroom was used to store old shoes and raglike clothes. The furniture in the second bedroom consisted of a double bed with a soiled mattress and a double mattress on the floor. (The remembered brass bed of George's childhood had been discarded several moves earlier.) The rent for the apartment was thirteen dollars a month. Kanfer had recently retired from his twenty-dollar-a-week night watchman's job. The Kanfers were living on his twenty-five-dollar-a-month allowance from the Home Relief Bureau. The Kanfers' son-in-law, Franz Muller, was temporarily in a mental hospital. His wife, Marianne, and the Muller children — whom she was about to commit to a Catholic home — were often at the Kanfers'. Helena Kanfer and her daughter argued constantly; the parole officer observed that Kanfer, whom he described as a quiet, well-dressed, but ineffectual man, had the wisdom to stand on the sidelines, seemingly inured to their pointless bickering. Mrs. Kanfer made it clear to the parole officer that she was eager for her son's release and that whatever money he earned would be helpful to the family. The parole officer reluctantly approved the filthy Kanfer apartment as Malinow's residence — although it was "decidedly substandard" — because it was the only one available to him and because his financial assistance was needed there. He doubted whether any "cooperative supervision" by the parents could be expected.

In September 1941, Thomas Kanfer tried to help his son get a job as an auto mechanic, but the prospective employer didn't send the requisite letter formally offering him a job, so Malinow appeared before the parole board a month later without a definite job offer. The board decided that Malinow deserved parole, because of his good record at Wallkill; he would be released as soon as he had an approved job. In December 1941, Malinow spotted an ad in the Brooklyn *Eagle* for a job as an auto mechanic at Famous Frank's, a small firm in the Bay Ridge section of Brooklyn, and wrote to apply for it. The firm's owner, Frank Perino, sent him a letter offering him the job, at fifteen dollars a week. The parole officer who went to check on Famous Frank's reported that the firm appeared to be reputable, the job offer sincere. Malinow went back to the parole board with the approved job in early February and was granted parole. On February 24, 1942, he was registered for the selective service. On February 26, 1942, he was paroled from Wallkill. His automechanics instructor's final entry on his record reads, "Has good chance of becoming a mechanic."

Malinow left Wallkill with $56.30 in his pocket, $36.30 from his prison earnings and twenty dollars' "gate money" from New York State. He had been paid ten cents a day to attend auto-mechanics courses and had been allowed to spend only half of his pay in prison. The rest had been set aside to be given to him upon his release. He took a bus to New York City and a subway to the parole office, in lower Manhattan, where he made his mandatory arrival report, and then took the subway home. He was both joyful to be out of prison and dismayed to see how much his mother had aged and how poor her health had become during the three and a half years he had been away. He was as eager to help his parents financially as they were to be helped. Malinow reported for work at Famous Frank's, but his job lasted just a few weeks. His "good chance of becoming a mechanic" was undermined by the curtailed gasoline shipments and the gasoline rationing that followed Pearl Harbor. "There weren't many cars on the road for mechanics to work on in early '42," Malinow says. "It was bad timing." Before Famous Frank's went out of business, Perino helped him get a job with an auto-wrecking firm right next door. The work proved to be dull and didn't make use of Malinow's Wallkill skills. He disliked the long trip from Greenpoint to Bay Ridge, and often fell asleep going home on the subway at night. While working for the auto-wrecking firm, he ran into a boyhood friend who was working at a laundry closer to Greenpoint, and got a job there, for slightly more money.

Malinow soon decided he would rather join the merchant marine, which offered an even better salary, a bonus for going into dangerous war zones, and a chance to make additional money playing dice or betting on shipboard dice games and selling cigarettes, bought cheaply aboard ship, for a good price in Europe. By then, he had already decided that his presence wasn't helpful to his aging parents. "What could I do by being around but give them aspirins or Alka-Seltzer?" he says. "I could send them money from wherever I happened to be." The United States government was then recruiting seamen, and Malinow hoped that he would be accepted. He applied, and was turned down because he couldn't read enough of the eye chart with his left eye. He decided to look into the possibility of shipping out with a private line, and in late April he obtained his papers as ordinary seaman, wiper, cabin steward, messman, and utility man. He went to lower Manhattan in search of a freighter to ship out on. He couldn't get a job aboard a freighter; the only opportunities to ship out at that particular moment were aboard tankers. The photographs of flaming tankers he saw on the walls of the Standard Oil of New Jersey office on State Street and the conversations he overheard at the union hiring hall about the certain death that awaited seamen on tankers that were torpedoed ("When she gets hit, everyone is done for. Even the water catches fire") dissuaded him from signing aboard a tanker. "I wasn't suicidally inclined," he says.

Malinow quit the laundry job over a difference of opinion with the foreman and got a job as a molder at an electric company in Greenpoint. He found the machines he had to work with noisy and the gauge-reading he had to do repetitious. He worked the night shift and was paid twenty-five dollars a week. By the spring of 1942, many of the boys he had grown up with were in the service. People were boasting of their sons in the service, and Malinow imagined that they were staring at him and wondering why he wasn't doing his part. He began to feel out of place at home. He volunteered for the army in May, arranged to have his parole reports suspended in early July, was inducted into the army on July 22, and entered active duty in early August, at Camp Upton, New York. Whenever Malinow talks about his state of mind during his first few months out of Wallkill, he always insists that the twenty-six good months at Wallkill didn't undo the damage that had been done him during the seventeen bad months at Sing Sing, and he curses the judge who sent him to Sing Sing instead of to a boys' reformatory. He also says that Wallkill was the best prison he has ever been in. "Many young men who were sent there benefitted from it and never went back to prison," he says. "There should be twenty constructive prisons like it, but today there isn't even one.

Wallkill is now just another medium-security prison and doesn't segregate first offenders or offer any exceptional training. Wallkill had the effect of partially redirecting me and lessening some of my bitterness. I could have worked at the electric company at night, to fulfill my parole requirements, and gone out stealing during the day, but I didn't. Instead, I volunteered for the army."

Private George Malinow, no. 32410969, was sent to the quartermaster-corps training center at Camp Lee, Virginia, for basic training and motor training. He was in fine physical condition and didn't mind the long, hot marches on the drill field as much as some of the other recruits did; only the sight of the M.P.s and the authority they represented angered him. He was sent from Camp Lee to an army air-forces unit at Brooks Field, on the outskirts of San Antonio, where he was put to work repairing jeeps and trucks. He enjoyed the great variety of people he met in the army, and found the southwestern drawls and twangs appealing. He was unaware of having an accent himself until his new friends expressed their pleasure at his "dem"s and "dese"s and "dose"s and began calling him Brooklyn Georgie. After a few months in San Antonio, Malinow and a few other soldiers were sent to the Atlanta motor base for several months of advanced motor training. In Atlanta, Malinow met a pretty blue-eyed blonde. He was able to spend every weekend with her and to do well in his classes with little studying, as a result of his Wallkill training. When he got back to Brooks, he was granted his first furlough. He went home to see his parents, who admired his uniform, and then he stopped off on the way back to Brooks to see his girl in Atlanta. He returned to Brooks a day and a half late but talked his way out of a penalty. He decided that he wanted to go back to his girl in Atlanta and that he wanted to go overseas. The only way to accomplish both objectives was to apply for the paratroopers, who had their training center at Fort Benning, Georgia. To his chagrin, the paratroopers didn't accept him, because of his left eye. While waiting to learn whether he would be accepted by the paratroopers, Malinow says, he passed up a few chances to be sent from Brooks Field to North Africa or the Mediterranean, but after his rejection by the paratroopers there were no other immediate opportunities for overseas service available to him there. "My mental attitude started to deteriorate," he says. "I lost complete interest in everything." On July 22, 1943, precisely a year after he was inducted into the army, Pfc. George Malinow was given another furlough. He was supposed to return to Brooks Field at the end of eighteen days.

Malinow went home to Brooklyn, where he found a shortage of able-bodied young men on hand to fill an abundance of jobs. He went to work on the docks, loading trucks and ships. The pay was adequate. There was also a shortage of able-bodied young men for young girls to date, and his social life flourished. He didn't go to Atlanta to see the blue-eyed blonde. He didn't reapply to the paratroopers, although he had heard that they had lowered their physical requirements. He didn't return to Brooks Field when his eighteen-day leave was up. Instead, he stayed in Brooklyn. He stayed there even after the army sent letters to his parents' home warning him that the penalty for desertion could be death. He stayed there even after the M.P.s came around looking for him. He intended to turn himself in and pay the price for having overstayed his leave — someday. All the time he was A.W.O.L., he wore civilian clothes but never removed his dog tags. He thought that this technicality would help to keep him from being charged with desertion. He had heard that the penalty for being A.W.O.L. a few days was the same as for being A.W.O.L. several months — a period of time in the stockade — so he kept postponing his return to the army. August sailed by, and then September and half of October.

On the night of Friday, October 15, 1943, Malinow went out partying with a group of young men and women. A certain amount of drinking was done by all. The group proceeded from house to house, dropping one party-goer off here, picking up another party-goer there. Malinow didn't know or care who owned the 1942 Studebaker that served as their means of transportation. He felt like staying out after the others had called it a night, and took the wheel of the car. The last two people in the Studebaker were Malinow and a girl. He let the girl off at her house in Brooklyn in the early hours of Saturday, October 16, and then fell asleep in the car. When he woke up, he started the car. It was drizzling, the roads were slick, and he says that the visibility was as limited as his sobriety. (Whenever he is in a melodramatic mood, Malinow says he got drunk on weekends while A.W.O.L. because he faced the terrible possibility of dying overseas upon his return to the army.) The Studebaker skidded and collided with a police radio car. The sound of the crash sobered Malinow up. He had no driver's license or car registration, and figured his best bet would be to take off as quickly as possible. In the accident, the car's right front fender was crushed against the right front tire. The tire wouldn't turn. By the time he realized that a quick getaway was not possible, one of the two policemen in the other car was standing alongside the Studebaker, ordering him out. Believing himself to be in only minor trouble for being unable to produce the driver's license and the car registration the policeman asked for — "some traffic type of offense I could talk my way out of" — Malinow got out of the car. The policeman found a .38-calibre pistol on the floor of the car, near the driver's seat. Malinow hadn't seen the gun earlier; he suspected that it had been put under the car seat by one of the guys he had partied with, and that it had slid out from under the seat as a result of the collision. He knew he was now in for a lot of trouble. He was taken to the station house for further questioning. Malinow's memory of what happened after he got to the station house is vague. The one thing he insists he remembers is that he was alternately beaten and cajoled by the cops as they unsuccessfully attempted to elicit information from him. Malinow's record, however, preserves what he claims not to remember.

When the police asked Malinow to account for his presence in the Studebaker, his first explanation was that he had borrowed it from his brother-in-law. A little later, he said that a person known to him only as Whitey, whom he had met at a grill, had asked him to drive the car to a certain place and leave it there with the keys in it. He couldn't supply Whitey's last name, his address, or any other information about him. The police had learned that the car had been stolen three days earlier. At 7:00 P.M. on October 13, a man named Harry Eisen had parked his Studebaker outside his home, in Long Island City, had gone inside to change his overalls, and had come back fifteen minutes later to find his car missing. The license plate on the car when Malinow crashed into the police radio car wasn't Eisen's; the plate on the Studebaker on October 16 had been stolen from another car. Malinow persistently disclaimed any knowledge of the car or the gun, which proved to be an unregistered, unloaded, inoperable American Bull Dog pistol.

Malinow was taken from the Brooklyn station house where he had been questioned to Queens, the borough in which the car had been stolen. He was held without bail in the Queens County jail as a parole violator. He was indicted by the Queens County grand jury for grand larceny in the first degree. (The Studebaker's value was seven hundred dollars.) His accomplice was listed on the indictment as John Doe. On December 13, he pleaded guilty to attempted grand larceny in the second degree. Four days later, he was sentenced, as a second-felony offender, to two and a half to five years in state prison. On December 22, he was sent from Queens to Sing Sing. A warrant charging him with violation of section 1897 of the penal code (the gun law) was placed in his file.

Malinow was declared a parole violator as of February 26, 1942, the date he left Wallkill. When he was released from Wallkill, he owed the parole board six years, three months, and twenty-seven days — until June 23, 1948, the maximum expiration date on his original five-to-ten-year sentence. He would now have to serve that six years, three months, and twenty-seven days in prison, starting on December 22, 1943, the day he was returned to Sing Sing. Only after he finished doing that time — on April 19, 1950 — could he begin to serve his new sentence. He would have to serve at least twenty months of the new sentence — two-thirds of the two-and-a-half-year minimum — before he would first become eligible for parole. The earliest he could hope to get out of prison again was the end of 1951.

When Malinow was arrested in 1943, he simply insisted that he hadn't stolen the car and knew nothing about the gun. When he was asked about the crime upon his return to Sing Sing, he first gave a long-winded justification for being A.W.O.L. — a catalogue of frustrations that included having been turned down by the government as a merchant-marine recruit, not having been able to advance himself in the army, and not getting to fight overseas. He then said he had committed the crime to get money to spend on his furlough and to get back to his army base. He now says he thought that money would be the best motive from his point of view in 1943, just as it was in 1938. "They weren't looking for logic, they just wanted something on paper," he says of his Sing Sing interrogators. "So they wouldn't worry about the fact that someone who had allegedly stolen a car for money would still be riding around in it three days later." His 1951 Clinton pre-parole report shows that he was still making the same excuses for being A.W.O.L. that he made in 1943 — that, indeed, he does in 1977. As for the theft of the car, he said in 1951 that he had come over the bridge from Greenpoint to Queens, was drinking heavily in Long Island City, and took the car to get home in a hurry. "I thought this was the best thing to say in 1951, because the one thing the parole board doesn't want to hear is that you're innocent," he says. "I'd only have hurt myself if I'd said I was drunk and didn't know who had stolen the car. I was found in it —

there was no getting around that — and I wasn't going to implicate my friends. By then, I'd done the time for the crime anyway. I knew the parole commissioners would just flip through my record quickly. I could safely say I'd stolen the car to get home in a hurry, even if it said elsewhere on my record that the car had been stolen three days earlier. I admit that most of the stories I told in prison were lies. I always resented the questions. The truth is that I was drunk. If I hadn't been, I would have slowed down when I saw the radio car. The last thing I'd want as an A.W.O.L. soldier and as an ex-con on parole was any contact with the police, much less a car collision with them. Incidentally, I had the right of way." There is nothing in Malinow's record to indicate that he was intoxicated when he was arrested in 1943.

The number that Malinow became when he was brought back to Sing Sing in 1943, three days before Christmas, was 102822. In reception, when he was asked his preference in assignments, he requested — and received — a job as a block porter. "I was only twenty-three, but I already had a different attitude toward incarceration," Malinow says. "I was no longer interested in acquiring a trade. I just wanted an easy job. A block porter spends about twenty minutes a day cleaning." Sing Sing in 1944 was still a grimy, cobwebby prison crawling with insects and rodents, but the old cells down the hill were no longer in use, and Malinow was immediately housed up the hill. Being in Sing Sing was easier for him the second time around not only because he didn't have to spend any time in the old cells but because he had already experienced confinement. There was nothing to adjust to. He wasn't approached sexually, he didn't deem it necessary to carry a knife, he didn't feel tense. He did feel depressed at the prospect of remaining in prison for the next eight years, so he spent only a little of his leisure time shooting the breeze with his friends and a considerable amount of time contriving to escape.

Malinow's first escape plan involved painting two gray prison uniforms green, climbing over an iron fence close to a guard tower down near the waterfront with a friend, and swimming up or down the Hudson — depending on the tide — to freedom. When he dress-rehearsed this escape plan, one spring afternoon, he got over the fence without any difficulty while the guard's back was turned, and waited in the nearby hip-high weeds, with which he blended quite nicely, for his friend to follow him. He waited in vain. His friend chickened out at the last minute. Malinow climbed back over the fence. He told his friend he had just proved the feasibility of the plan, but his friend kept making excuses for not joining him in a second, and real, attempt. Malinow says that the weeds were cut shortly thereafter, so he didn't try that escape route again.

Malinow's second scheme necessitated getting down into one of Sing Sing's underground tunnels from one of the prison shops with several friends and following a steam pipe inside the tunnel to the prison powerhouse, which was outside the prison wall. There were more obstacles between the prison interior and the powerhouse, in the form of granite, brick, and cinder-block barriers, than the men had anticipated. Malinow was still thinking of obtaining crowbars and chisels to overcome the weakest of these obstacles when a third escape scheme presented itself — and misfired.

The third plan — one with which Malinow would entertain his friends in prison for the next thirty years — entailed getting from his cell down to the railroad tracks that ran parallel to the Hudson, by way of the abandoned old cellblock building, and hopping a freight train to New York City. Malinow's scheme involved removing a couple of bars from his cell, a couple of bars from the cellblock window, some bars from a passageway, and some bars from a window of the old cellblock, and leaving dummy bars in their places; getting a duplicate key to a certain tunnel gate; crawling through another tunnel; and climbing over an eight- or nine-foot-high retaining wall, not to mention getting his hands on a freight-train schedule. He acquired a duplicate key, but a friend of his, Fat Teddy, made the mistake of telling another inmate about the existence of the key. The inmate took this information to the prison authorities, who searched for the duplicate key, found it, and correctly surmised that it was part of an escape plan. Suspicion fell not only upon Fat Teddy but also upon his friend Malinow. "It was a case of guilt by association, and in this case they were right," Malinow says. The two men were questioned. They denied everything, but the prison officials decided to send them to Clinton on a disciplinary transfer anyway. On the afternoon of May 24, 1945, when Malinow and Fat Teddy came in from the yard, they were suddenly ordered to pack their belongings. They were put in handcuffs and leg irons and were driven, after dark, to a railroad station several miles up the Hudson from Sing Sing. Three guards escorted them on the all-night ride to Clinton prison, in Dannemora, sixteen miles from the Quebec border. Clinton was in the midst of several thousand densely wooded acres — inhospitable terrain for escapes.

Malinow was momentarily upset over the suddenness of his departure — none of *his* plans for leaving Sing Sing had included an escort of three armed guards or Clinton prison as a destination — but he was still glad to be leaving. He had assumed that even if he were a model prisoner at Sing Sing, he would wind up at Clinton, because in the 1940s few men did eight years at Sing Sing. If he had to stay in prison, he preferred to go to Clinton. Sing Sing was a hard place to do a lot of time; it was too filthy, its food was too bad, it was too temptingly close to New York City, and its population was too transient. Clinton had many old-timers sentenced to "long bids," and was said to be an easier place to do time, cut off as it was from the outside world.

At Clinton, Malinow, no. 28755, met up with numerous acquaintances from Sing Sing and Wallkill. He also proceeded to make many new friends, among them Bernard Czarnowicz and Patrick Halloran with whom he was to be arrested in years to come — again documenting the cliché about the evils of criminal association in prison. Malinow was assigned to work in the tailor shop, which made uniforms for Clinton and garments for other state institutions, and he became a proficient sewing-machine operator. He found the tailor shop's guards to be rather decent and consistent, in contrast to many of their colleagues. Most of the other guards — men of French-Canadian descent who were destined from birth to work at Clinton, Dannemora's principal employer — struck Malinow as clannish and brutal. Like many other men who have done time at Clinton, he insists that some of the Clinton inmates whose deaths there were attributed to suicide or heart attacks actually died of injuries from severe beatings they received.

Clinton had one virtue that Malinow appreciated: it was efficiently run. The men always went to the commissary and to the barbershop on their regularly scheduled days, and were taken care of promptly. They didn't get to the commissary, as men do at Green Haven in 1977, only to find a mob ahead of them, so that they would either have to wait their turn for hours or return on another day. "At Clinton, you always knew where you stood," Malinow says. "You got up in the morning and went through your daily routine like a robot. You even set yourself a precise schedule for your daily chores, like rinsing out your clothes on Tuesdays and Thursdays from four-thirty to five."

Weekdays at Clinton were primarily for work; weekends were for relaxation. The men spent Saturdays and Sundays in the big yard, where they gathered in small groups called courts. Membership in a court was by invitation only. The courts had their own tables, lockers, and stoves (made of fifty-gallon oil drums), where the court members cooked, ate, drank, stored their food, played cards, and talked about the women they had known or dreamed of knowing and about the one big score that would make them rich and really free. The yard looked like a hobo jungle. Each court had its own turf; one trespassed at one's peril. In the mid-forties, the majority of New York State's prison population was still white, and the courts were segregated. Blacks had courts of their own. "We had a much better calibre of men — black and white — in prison in dem years," Malinow says. In the forties, large packages could be sent to prisoners. During his years at Clinton, Malinow received no packages — his mother became critically ill, and died in 1949, and his father was hospitalized for severe arthritis shortly after her death — but some of the other men in his court received fifty-pound and hundred-pound packages from their families and shared them with him.

Clinton's climate was famously cold. It was known as the Siberia of America, and as a place where there were two seasons — winter and July. Even during the fleeting summer, there was no night recreation in the yard, and the men were locked in at 5:00. They listened to their earphones, read, wrote letters, and turned in early. Silent time started at 7:00 P.M. Lights-out was at 11:00 P.M. Some of Malinow's Clinton friends returned to prison in the sixties and seventies, when there were many evening diversions, and lights could be kept on all night, and they stayed up until one or two o'clock. These men say the time went faster in the forties and fifties, because the days were literally shorter. Being cut off from the outside world did make the time easier to do, Malinow says. The men were not permitted to make phone calls. Newspapers were scarce. They had few visitors: Clinton was a long, expensive journey from New York City, where a great many of the inmates were from. According to Malinow, the two saddest days at Clinton were Mother's Day and Christmas. "At Christmas, the chimes of a local church pealed 'Silent Night' across the valley, and you became sort of sentimental," he says. "You thought of people on the outside and wondered what they were doing, whether you really wanted to be thinking those thoughts or not."

During Malinow's first couple of years at Clinton, he kept out of trouble. He was written up just twice for misbehavior — once for being insolent to a doctor (for which he was keeplocked, for fifteen days), and once for having a contraband stove and six yards of shirt goods in his cell. On this occasion, he had to pay for the material, which he had appropriated from the tailor shop so that he could make shirts for some friends who needed them.

On September 17, 1947, Malinow was caught stealing shirt goods and cutting them for coat linings. When material was plentiful, the tailor-shop guards looked the other way and let the inmates help themselves to a few yards. At that particular time, material was in short supply. A friend had asked Malinow to make him a coat lining. Malinow was eager to oblige, so he cut the material he needed from a roll. "It wasn't a big deal, but the guard was afraid there would be a stampede on the material if he let me get away with it, so he wrote me up," he says. This time, the principal keeper, or P.K., not only made Malinow pay for the stolen material but also took away his job in the tailor shop and assigned him to the cotton shop.

There were many places at Clinton where Malinow would have been willing to work. The cotton shop was not one of them. The air in the cotton shop — where raw cotton was spun, carded, and woven into cloth — was so filled with lint that many inmates assigned there had developed lung trouble. It was one of the most dreaded spots at Clinton. Malinow knew that someone had to work there. He thought of the cotton shop as a place for "unfortunates — those who were limited in expressing themselves or those who were meek about sticking up for their rights." He didn't feel that he belonged in either category, and he didn't believe that the theft of a few yards of cloth warranted a transfer to the cotton shop. He refused to work there and asked to be keeplocked. The P.K. told Malinow he would soon be begging to work in the cotton shop. Malinow was determined to prove him wrong. After he had spent a month and a half keeplocked in his cell, the P.K. called him out and asked if he was ready to work in the cotton shop. He said he wasn't. On November 24, the P.K. had him moved to the segregated company. The segregated company occupied the bottom tier of E block, the block closest to the actual segregation building, where men were locked up for offenses more serious than an unwillingness to work.

The inmates in the segregated company, which faced the segregation building, were locked in their cells twenty-three and a half hours a day. They were let out half an hour, for recreation in a small yard of their own; once a week they were also allowed out for showers. They spent the time in their cells playing games like Twenty Questions, they played chess and checkers on boards on the floor between their cells, and they flooded their sinks, taking improvised baths, but they spent most of their time doing legal work. In the 1940s, it was a keeplock offense for two prisoners to help each other with their cases, but that didn't stop the men in the segregated company. "What could they do to us?" Malinow asks rhetorically. "We were locked up anyway." They studied lawbooks, prepared writs, and acted out cases, taking a position and then trying to attack that position from a district attorney's point of view. While Malinow was at Clinton, he wrote to the parole board to request that his year in the army be credited to the delinquent time he owed; the request was denied. He later wrote to the parole board claiming that his 1943 conviction was illegal, because the army had jurisdiction over him then, and not a civilian court. The parole board replied that while Malinow was in the army "parole was merely suspended insofar as making regular reports to a parole officer or to this division," and that "this did not relieve us of the responsibility of declaring you a delinquent for any misconduct while in the service."

One evening in February 1948, after Malinow had been in the segregated company for several months, there was a loud argument over whether the cellblock windows should be open or closed. Three of Malinow's acquaintances were taken to the segregation building for making excessive noise. Malinow's punishment for his share of the noisemaking was only the loss of his earphones for ten days. One night a while later, his three friends in the segregation building called down to him and several others in the segregated company and suggested that they join them up there to discuss a particularly interesting legal case. The quickest and surest way to get to segregation was to hit an officer, so that was what Malinow and the others did. They grabbed the nearest weapons — Malinow's was a tray with a piece of pie on it — and were quickly taken to segregation. On his way to segregation, Malinow received the beating customarily given to any inmate who had had the temerity to assault an officer. When the P.K. read the reports on the men from the segregated company who had gone to the segregation building, he put two and two together and got four. The men who had been dispatched to segregation earlier for making noise were transferred back to the segregated company; the new arrivals from the segregated company stayed in the segregation building. Malinow spent a month and a half in the segregation building. He was then sent back to the segregated company, where he remained for a year.

One day in May 1949, a middle-aged Irishman in the segregated company was telling Malinow and some of the other younger men about the good old Prohibition days. He was describing the silk shirts and the pin-striped suits he had bought with his bootlegging proceeds. The men who worked in Clinton's woodyard locked on E block, one tier above the segregated company. The galleries were open, and conversations carried. DeLorenzo, an Italian inmate who worked in the woodyard, made some snide remarks about the Irishman and his fine clothes. The Irishman cursed DeLorenzo, but DeLorenzo's remarks kept coming. Later that night, after lights-out, DeLorenzo slammed his locker door a few times to make noise. The Irishman didn't want to let the remarks and the locker-slamming go; to do so would be regarded as a sign of weakness. Malinow said he would take care of DeLorenzo for the Irishman, because he was younger and stronger and could do more damage to DeLorenzo. "The old man was a very dear friend," Malinow says. "You only get respect in prison if there are serious repercussions for messing with you." Malinow couldn't take care of DeLorenzo while he was locked up in the segregated company. He asked to see the P.K. — a new man, who had replaced Malinow's former adversary — and said he had decided he was ready to go to work. He requested a job in the woodyard, which he was given. He was assigned to a cell just a few cells away from DeLorenzo's. Malinow worked in the woodyard two days. On the evening of the second day, he caught DeLorenzo unawares on their tier and hit him over the head with an L-shaped piece of iron before a guard could intervene. Segregation was full, so Malinow was taken back to the segregated company. He was let out a short while later, when DeLorenzo went home — "a nervous wreck," Malinow says with pleasure — and he returned to work in the woodyard, where he spent his time sawing tree trunks into small pieces for the tower guards to use in their wood stoves.

Malinow was never in segregation before or after this 1947–49 period in Clinton. "Looking back on those two years, I sometimes marvel at myself and ask myself whether that hotheaded kid was really me," he says. "That was the only time I ever assaulted a guard or an inmate. I was still in my twenties, and I was very frustrated. There were times when that bid at Clinton was really hard — when dinner was bread and jelly or bread and a piece of heated bologna for nights on end. During the four-day Green Haven strike in August and September of 1976, some of the young inmates complained of going stir crazy. I spent two years in a cell at Clinton. I always learned to adjust to my circumstances." Malinow left Clinton only once between 1945 and 1952 — to visit his mother in the hospital in New York City when she was critically ill. She died a year or so after his visit, and he was asked whether he wanted to go to her funeral. He didn't. "I preferred to remember my mother alive," he says. After he had worked in the woodyard for some months, Frenchy, one of the two guards who had escorted him on the hospital visit to see his mother, offered him a job as a block porter. Frenchy, who was in charge of a block, had been very courteous to him on the trip, so he accepted the job. He later returned to work in the tailor shop. "Those seven years at Clinton under rigid conditions went by very quickly," Malinow says of his stretch at Clinton. "Some of the old-timers, men who had been sentenced in the 1920s, when sentences were much longer — thirty to sixty years for first-degree robbery wasn't uncommon — taught me the trick of doing time. They told me never to think of my sentence as a whole but to do it one day at a time. They said that if you concentrated on the day you were up, soon the many days and years ahead of you would be behind you. They were right. The seven years went by like three and a half."

In mid-1951, Clinton's officials began to prepare a pre-parole report on Malinow, just as the Wallkill officials had done a decade earlier. The warden observed that Malinow's conduct during his years at Clinton had varied greatly. "At times he has been easily disturbed, resentful of authority, and even assaultive," he wrote. "At other times, including the present, he has been well behaved. For the past two years his conduct and adjustment have been good. He is working steadily, and he is cooperative and courteous." The P.K. echoed these views and added that his present supervisors in the tailor shop "state that he is a very good sewing-machine operator and that he shows no signs of laziness." The P.K.'s report continued, "On the contrary, he does his own work well and takes it upon himself to help others in their work." The prison chaplain reported that Malinow had "fulfilled his religious duties and obligations," and the prison doctor noted that the twenty / ninety vision in his left eye had been corrected to twenty / twenty with glasses. The prison psychiatrist's diagnosis of Malinow was "without psychosis; neurotic character with psychopathic traits, egocentric, emotionally unstable, and immature." His intelligence now tested above average — 113 — but the psychiatrist gave Malinow, who was about to turn thirty-one, a mental age of seventeen. "The prognosis for a satisfactory socioeconomic adjustment and a positive and consistent change in his patterns of behavior appears doubtful," the psychiatrist concluded. "He has . . . an intellectual insight into his way of life, but has difficulty in curbing himself, in controlling his impulses in emotional situations." (Fifteen years later, when Malinow was tested again, his I.Q. had gone up a few more points; his emotional age had stayed the same as it was in 1951.)

Because of the warrant charging Malinow with possession of the bulldog pistol, on file from 1943, no employment program was submitted to the parole board when Malinow appeared in October 1951. The parole commissioners took less than two minutes to grant him parole, as of November, to meet the warrant only; otherwise, he was to reappear at the January 1952 meeting of the board. In mid-November, the gun warrant was withdrawn by the magistrate who originally issued it. Malinow asked to meet with the board before January, because his father was seriously ill. He saw the board again in late November, still lacking a job, and was told to come back with a job in six months or less. He spent the next few months job-hunting by mail. He had already applied for a job with a rubber company, but when his parole officer got in touch with the manager and apprised him of Malinow's criminal background the manager refused to hire him. Malinow then wrote to the president of the National Maritime Union of America, who wrote back that there was employment for men with seamen's papers provided their records were not too bad. The parole officer didn't consider this letter a definite job offer. In January 1952, a trucking company offered Malinow a thirteen-dollar-a-day job as a platform loader. When the parole officer went to check on it, he found that the trucking company was suffering a post-Christmas and New Year's lull in business and could give Malinow only one or two days' work a week. The parole officer disapproved this job offer because he didn't consider the work enough "to keep the inmate gainfully employed." Malinow kept writing. He received an offer from a man in the building-service-employees union. The parole officer looked into this possibility and learned that the man had two strikes against him: he was involved with an inmate who had recently been discharged from Clinton, and he was involved in loan-shark activities among longshoremen. "I kept getting jobs, and the parole officer kept finding reasons to shoot them down," Malinow says.

In March 1952, Malinow was offered a job for forty-three dollars a week (plus uniforms and two meals) at a restaurant at LaGuardia Airport. When his parole officer went to look this job over, he asked the acting manager, who had written to Malinow, how he happened to know him. The acting manager answered that he didn't know Malinow, he knew one of his friends; he declined to name the friend. The parole officer spotted a bar on the premises and told the acting manager that he would have to apply to the Alcoholic Beverage Control Board for Malinow to be employed there. The acting manager then admitted that he had heard of Malinow from his stepson, who was also serving time at Clinton, and withdrew the job offer, saying he had decided to keep the job for his stepson instead. (Malinow's parole officer advised his superiors to disapprove this offer when it was made, for "the double reason of the sale of alcoholic beverages and the collusion between inmates.") In April, Malinow saw an ad in a newspaper for a dollar-an-hour job as a busboy at the Blue Chip Buffet, a restaurant in the Wall Street area. The parole officer approved this job. Malinow appeared before the parole board again on May 28 and was granted parole. One of the three parole commissioners, who had noted where he was going to be working, said, "I hope you make good at that, because I go in there and eat sometimes." Malinow said he would do his very best to make good. Another of the parole commissioners, who knew where Malinow came from, pointed out that quite a few boys from Greenpoint had done time in prison, and advised him to stay away from Greenpoint. "Yes, sir," Malinow replied.

Malinow left Clinton on June 19, 1952, with $44.37 in his pocket — $11.93 less than he had had ten years earlier when he left Wallkill. He was grateful that the pocket was in a suit a friend had sent him, and not in one of the black suits made in the Clinton tailor shop for men going home. "When you perspired in those suits, the black dye ran across your shirt," Malinow says. "And when it rained, that cheap black cloth smelled to high heaven."

Malinow reached the city on the evening of June 19 and spent some of his money for a room at a cheap hotel in Manhattan. On June 20, he made his arrival report to his parole officer, who told him that under no circumstances was he to associate with Bernard Czarnowicz, one of his Clinton friends. Czarnowicz, who was three years older than Malinow, had a record that went back just as far. In 1934, Czarnowicz was arrested for burglary in the third degree; he pleaded guilty to unlawful entry and was given probation. In 1935, he was convicted of robbery in the second degree and was sent to Elmira; he was released in 1937. In 1938, Czarnowicz was convicted of robbery in the first degree and was sent to Clinton. While there, he got his 1935 conviction set aside on a legal technicality. He was then resentenced on the 1938 case as a first offender and was given time served. Czarnowicz was released from Clinton on April 17, 1952. As soon as he was out of prison, he sent Malinow a money order, using the name of a man who was on Malinow's approved correspondence list. An alert prison censor recognized Czarnowicz's writing and turned the letter and the money order over to the parole division. Czarnowicz's parole officer called him in, learned that he planned to see his close friend Malinow when Malinow got out, warned him against doing any such thing, and held him overnight. On June 20, Malinow had no idea why he was told not to see Czarnowicz — he was unaware of the intercepted letter and money order — but he felt no compunction about disobeying that advice a few days later and going to Czarnowicz's apartment, in lower Manhattan, for dinner. "That rule about criminals not consorting is ridiculous," Malinow says. "How many noncriminals do you know after you've been in prison ten or fifteen years?"

Malinow didn't stay out of Greenpoint, as one of the parole commissioners had admonished. He had no family, so he was let out of Clinton on a furnished-room program. After one night in the cheap hotel and a few nights at a Y.M.C.A., he moved into a furnished room in Greenpoint. Malinow didn't wait on the parole commissioner who sometimes ate at the Blue Chip, either, and he certainly never tried his best to make good there. He took an instant dislike to his busboy's job, and admits that he regarded it simply as a "can opener" — a job that would get him out of Clinton. On his first day at the Blue Chip, Malinow was asked to clean tables, assist the salad man, and help the waiters get the customers their beverages (coffee, iced tea, beer) and their desserts. "Some of the people ordered French pastry," Malinow says. "That pastry has funny French names, and I mixed up the orders. The customers complained. I was ready to throw a tray at them, but that could have been a parole violation. The last straw was when the manager asked me to stay overtime to help clean the silverware. It was slave labor at slave wages. I was tired. I quit. I was glad to take off that silly white hat and jacket." On the subway, riding back to his rooming house, Malinow wondered what excuse he was going to give his parole officer for quitting. Then the felicitous thought came to him that he had had to handle beer at the Blue Chip. The following day, he went to see his parole officer, reminded the officer that he had said a parolee couldn't work in a place where beer or liquor was served, and was given permission to look for another job. He was soon hired to work in the aluminum department of an electrical-appliance factory, but was let go ten days later, although his work had been satisfactory, when the company learned of his prison record. He next took a job at a company that manufactured ship-hatch covers and fireproof doors, but soon quit, because the work was hard and dirty, the pay was average, and he came home at night covered with rust and too tired even to eat. One day in the fall of 1952, some ten years after he had taken out his seaman's papers, he decided to fulfill his boyhood dream of going to sea. In October 1952, he shipped out from Philadelphia on a freighter carrying auto parts and other cargo. He worked in the engine room as a wiper. His ship called at Bremerhaven, Bremen, Hamburg, Antwerp, and Rotterdam, and returned to the United States a month and a half later. Malinow spent most of his shore time in Europe as most seamen have always spent their shore time in Europe — in bars and with women — but he also saw a cathedral or two and did a little shopping: he bought several cuckoo clocks and several blue-gray china vases. Upon his return from his overseas trip, he presented one of the clocks and one of the vases to Louise Drobny, a young woman he had started dating shortly after he got out of Clinton.

Not many people wrote to Malinow while he was at Clinton, but one who did was a boyhood friend named Ralph Drobny. Drobny's parents, who were Czechoslovakian immigrants, owned a bar in Greenpoint a block from the docks. Each weekend while Malinow was growing up, Helena Kanfer gave her husband an allowance, most of which he spent on Saturday night at the Drobnys' bar, on beer, Polish vodka, and kielbasa sandwiches. The Drobnys had eight children. Ralph Drobny was Malinow's contemporary. Louise was nine years younger. When Malinow had last seen her, before going to prison in 1938, she was a child of nine. When he came out of Clinton, she was a pretty young woman of twenty-three. At the age of fourteen, she had hurt her head going through a subway gate; soon after the accident, she started getting epileptic seizures. She had several admirers, but whenever an admirer saw her having an attack of epilepsy he dropped her. The seizures, which occurred every couple of months, didn't frighten Malinow. He took Louise out often before he went to sea. When he returned, she let him know that his traveling made her unhappy. When Malinow is asked what the best times of his life have been, he quickly mentions his early childhood ("before I knew the difference between hot dogs and steak"), his year in the army, and his brief time at sea in the merchant marine. "Seeing dem strange different lands was a thrill," he says, but that first cruise was his last. He decided to remain onshore. He moved back to his furnished room. In January 1953, he got into Local 13 of the Mason Tenders union and started taking construction jobs to fulfill his parole requirements. Doing occasional construction work fitted in nicely with his main occupation — robbing. Malinow had pulled off a few robberies with Bernard Czarnowicz soon after his release from prison in 1952. In 1953, he pulled off some more.

"When I came out of Clinton, I needed money right away," Malinow says. "I couldn't see myself working at a hard job for seventy-five dollars a week and having nothing to show for it. I wanted a car, a home of my own, and some of the better things in life. I didn't want to have to budget or to live on the installment plan. The only way I knew how to get the kind of money I needed to live life the way I considered it worth living was by stealing. I didn't expect to get caught stealing and to be sent back to prison, but I accepted the risk. I knew there was a chance I'd go back. I didn't come out of prison saying I'd never go back. I only came out saying I was never going back for stealing eight hundred dollars. I was thinking in terms of five and six figures." Malinow estimates that in 1952 and 1953 he and Czarnowicz pulled off about fifteen successful robberies. Most of them were payroll robberies. A good score was fifteen thousand dollars, but sometimes, Malinow says, when they were pressed for money they had to pull a three-thousand-dollar job. He once calculated that he and Czarnowicz cleared — and spent — sixty-five thousand dollars the first year or so he was out of Clinton. His legal earnings during that time were $1878.14. Once in a great while, if Czarnowicz was busy, Malinow did a robbery alone, and on one occasion he did a robbery with someone else, but his partner was almost always Czarnowicz. In February 1977, Malinow wrote an account of one of the robberies he and Czarnowicz pulled in 1953. He calls his account "Pick Up and Carry."

During a warm, sunny morning — during the early summer months of 1953, I and my partner were driving in a Queens area, at about 10 o'clock in the morning.

During this drive — we noticed a fairly large new type of apartment complex red brick building, with an outside white sign — reading, "renting agency office," over the entrance doorway on the ground floor level.

There were about 6 to 8 various persons (men and women) walking toward the entrance with some sort of small type white sheet of papers in their hands. My partner and I immediately sized up the situation as possibly being some office where they pay their rents. We drove around the block and parked a short distance away from this said renting office.

My partner went in first by himself — to see how the office and general inside area looked like. He came out and told me that there were about 10 persons paying their rents to the cashier girl behind a counter. We waited about an hour, returned and I went inside by myself. When I entered past the solid wooden door, I found myself in a sorta corridor hallway about 15 feet in length which led into a large office type room with the cashier counter at the far end. There were 2 girls there at the time, taking the rent money receipts from the customers. They both were very busy and no one noticed me at the end of the line of people. There seemed to be about 15 persons in line at the time I was there. I looked over the entire office quickly to see how it was all laid out — (window, doors, position of cashiers, how many — female, male, etc.). I then left.

We did not return until the following month, on the same day of the month that we both checked it out.

It also again was a lovely sunny warm morning when we drove up the second month. We drove into the small parking area, in back of this renting office. We left the car doors shut — but unlocked. We walked up to the doorway in the corridor. We put on our gloves, sunglasses, hats, collars of our work jackets up high and entered. No one noticed us — as all the people were in line — looking straight ahead — opposite direction to where we entered.

There were many people in line at this particular time, I'd say over 20, men and women of different ages. They all had cash bills held in their hands, in view.

My partner stood at the end we entered — I walked by fast toward the counter, past all the people. I did not pull my hand gun out as yet. When I reached the counter — I jumped over it, pulled my gun out. My partner shouted — "don't any body move! It's a holdup!" While he was talking — meanwhile I rushed into the small office at the side of the cashier's counter. There was only one older type office agent sitting behind his desk there.

I told him to come out, it's a holdup! He came out and I told him to face the wall (in the area of the 2 girl cashiers) and don't turn around. I told the 2 girls to do the same thing. Then I said to all the people lined up to pay their rents, listen, we are not here to take your money! We are only taking the company's money. They are insured so don't do anything foolish and you won't get hurt! I then noticed how nervous those people started to act — some were trying to pocket their cash, etc. I emptied out the cash drawers of all the money and put it all into a large paper bag. I then walked fast into the office and pulled out the phone wires — I ripped it off the connection socket.

Then I jumped back over the counter. I again warned all the people — to relax, don't come out that exit door for 5 minutes else they'd get shot! My partner headed out first — started the car. From the moment he walked out — I counted to myself — 20 slowly. Then I walked out. My partner started to roll (drive) the car and I hopped in the back seat. We drove average speed and made it safely to an apartment of another friend in Queens.

The money amounted to slightly over $9000. It was not the type of amount robbery we would go for but we both were low on funds so we pulled this robbery to give us a "breathing spell" so to speak where we could pay our bills, etc., and not be pressed for money in general.

The next morning — the local papers wrote up the events of the robbery. The persons who were in line — all stated that at first, they didn't believe the 2 holdup men would not take their money — as they said they wouldn't. But they were true to their promise. The cashier girls and agent (male) all also stated, that the 2 holdup men did not touch the money in their pocket books, and the male agent said that no attempt was made to take the money from his personal wallet.

The people all stated that whoever they were, they certainly didn't wish to take the working people's money — just only the company's money and they couldn't understand why.

My partner and I laughed after we read the story. My partner said — "George, if some of the guys we both know — knew this about us, they'd say we are fools, for bypassing the other money these people all had as no doubt it amounted to another 1 or 2 thousand dollars!" I replied — "Well — let them live by their code — we'll live by ours! I will not steal money from the working people. I did so as a youngster and I regret it as I didn't know any better. Now I'm a grown man and my parents were poor. I know what it is to be poor. That's why I'll never hurt or steal from the working class. My mother paid premiums on insurance policies for all of us — for coffins and burial plots — for years. Once, during a difficult time, she couldn't pay the premiums for a few weeks. The insurance agent told her the policies had lapsed and couldn't be reinstated. All the money she'd paid in was lost. To me that's stealing, not at the point of a gun but stealing nonetheless. The insurance companies stole from the poor people for years — so now, let them part with some of their such profits!" My partner laughed and said — "George, no one would believe this of us!" I said — "so who the hell cares! I live by my principles and that's all that matters to me. Your principles are identical to mine — that's why we're partners!"

Malinow says that he and Czarnowicz were never caught in

the act of robbing, and that he wasn't afraid of being identified later by someone he had held up. "I was always camouflaged," he says. "Sometimes I just had dark glasses, a workman's cap, and my jacket collar raised high, but sometimes I'd have a fake mustache and nose or wear heavy makeup." He takes pride in the fact that he never hurt anyone during a robbery (although he says he did fire his gun once or twice getting away from the scene of a crime). When he is asked what he would have done if an office agent or a woman cashier had pushed an alarm or pulled a gun, he says he would have shot them. "I always warned people that if they didn't resist they wouldn't get hurt," he says. "Now, if after I've warned them they do something foolish and I have to shoot them, that's their fault." When he is asked how he would have felt if someone had died of a heart attack while being robbed, he says, "I would feel bad any time something happened to someone as a result of something I did, but I have my needs just as other people have theirs, and that wouldn't stop me from robbing. By the same token, would they have felt bad if a cop had come by while I was robbing them and the cop had shot me in the head?" Malinow says that he knows stealing is wrong but that a lot of wrong was done to him when he was sent to Sing Sing "as a child of seventeen." When it is suggested to him that two wrongs don't make a right, he replies, "Neither does one wrong uncorrected make a right."

Not long after the "Pick Up and Carry" robbery, Louise Drobny and George Malinow became engaged. He bought her a diamond engagement ring. Just as Louise's epileptic seizures didn't bother Malinow, his criminal record didn't bother Louise: she felt she could change him after their marriage. Some of her sisters and brothers-in-law had misgivings about Malinow, although he often gave them expensive gifts and sums of money. Louise's parents were pleased that someone wanted to marry her, and were delighted when Malinow insisted on paying for the entire wedding — for the things the bride's family traditionally paid for as well as for the things the bridegroom's side of the family traditionally paid for. Malinow says he wanted to pay for everything because of his independent nature and so that no one would think he was marrying Louise because of the Drobnys' money.

Malinow went with Louise to choose her wedding gown. He liked an expensive dress of French lace. When she hesitated because of the price, and kept looking at less costly gowns, he told her, "Don't take second class. You only get married once. You take the expensive one or I don't marry you." He paid for the bridesmaids' dresses, their lingerie, and their bouquets. Louise and Malinow were married on a hot Sunday afternoon in July 1953, in a double-ring ceremony at a Catholic church in Greenpoint. Malinow had wanted Czarnowicz to be his best man, but when Czarnowicz learned that the best man had to sign the marriage license he declined the honor; he felt it imprudent to supply his parole officer with written proof of the fact that he and Malinow were consorting. Ralph Drobny was the best man. Czarnowicz and another friend, Steve Francisco, who was in the numbers business, were ushers. Louise's younger sister Dorothy was the maid of honor. No members of Malinow's family attended the wedding. He had gone with Marianne Muller to see their father in the hospital once after he got out of Clinton, but she was still drinking heavily, and he had lost track of her. His father had died in late 1952, while he was at sea. There were about one hundred fifty guests at the wedding, including most of Louise's large family.

Limousines that Malinow had hired drove the bridal party from the church to a photographic studio. The Malinows' wedding photograph shows Louise, an attractive woman with dark hair and a sweet smile, looking tiny and trim in her long, lacy white gown. Malinow, his thick hair wavy and black, looks taller than five-eight standing next to her, proud and handsome in a rented white tuxedo jacket. From the studio, they proceeded to their wedding reception, at the Hofbrau Haus in

Queens, where Malinow had rented a private room for the sit-down dinner and dancing. Later that night, the bridal party went to the Copacabana. Louise and George Malinow spent their wedding night at her parents' apartment; they fell asleep counting the money they had received as wedding presents. The next morning, Malinow phoned for a limousine. It took them to the Port Authority Bus Terminal, where they boarded a bus for Pennsylvania. After a few days at a pleasant resort in the Poconos, Malinow decided that being without a car on his honeymoon was inconvenient, so he returned to the city by bus and picked up a secondhand car he had had Louise buy the previous February, and drove it back to Pennsylvania. Louise couldn't drive, because of her epilepsy, and Malinow's parole officer didn't allow him to have a license, much less a car, but he had been driving Louise's car since she got it, sometimes with her knowledge and sometimes without. He occasionally used it on his robberies. The Malinows liked the couple who ran the resort where they were staying, so when Malinow returned to Brooklyn to get the car, he also picked up the cuckoo clock he had brought Louise from Europe and (with Louise's approval) gave it to the couple as a gift. The honeymoon was supposed to last two weeks, but the Malinows had such a good time in the Poconos swimming, riding horses, and playing shuffleboard that they stayed for three weeks.

Louise's parents had moved out of their apartment some time before the wedding. After the Malinows returned from their honeymoon, they lived briefly with the Drobnys in their new apartment while they fixed up the Drobnys' old apartment. The Drobnys' bar was on the first floor of the building they moved into. Louise's sister Vera and Vera's husband, Stanley Novotny, lived on the second floor. Louise's sister Barbara and Barbara's husband, Janos Hodak, lived on the fourth floor. The newly-weds got the third floor, which had one large bedroom for them and one small bedroom for Louise's sister Dorothy. Malinow remembers the fun they had painting the apartment together and choosing blond furniture for it. Czarnowicz remembers that Malinow insisted on the best of everything. "Anyone else would have bought a three-hundred-dollar refrigerator. George bought an eight-hundred-dollar refrigerator. Anyone else would have considered a four-hundred-dollar television adequate. George bought a twelve-hundred-dollar TV. He was always a big spender." Malinow senses that some people don't approve of his high-spending ways, but he thinks his attitude toward money is much more sensible than theirs. "I know people who eat peanut-butter sandwiches for years so that they can put money away for a rainy day or for their old age," he says. "After a few years of that kind of eating, they wind up with stomach trouble and have to spend thousands of dollars on a noted surgeon for an operation. So what did they accomplish? Money isn't for hoarding. It's for spending and for making people happy. Money is just money."

The Malinows' first three married months were happy, although their inlaws gave them little privacy. Malinow, who believes that husbands should treat their wives like queens, brought Louise bouquets of roses and boxes of candy on Sunday, making some of the sisters jealous and some of the less affluent brothers-in-law resentful. If he has any regrets about his brief time with Louise, it is that he was critical of her menu planning. "We'd have steak on Monday, and maybe on Thursday she'd give me steak again, with a different sauce and different vegetables," he says. "I'd ask her if she was crazy, giving me the same meat twice in one week. Later, when I was back in prison, making myself bologna sandwiches, I appreciated all the cooking and cleaning and washing Louise did. There I was, a grown man, in a cell scrubbing T-shirts and rinsing soap out of socks. A man outside ain't going to be doing that." Because of her epilepsy, Louise spent most of her time at home. Malinow was often out. Sometimes he worked on construction jobs. Sometimes he did strong-arm work for the man who had got him into Local 13 of the Mason Tenders, and who was its business manager. Sometimes he was out robbing or planning robberies. Malinow tried not to let Louise see his gun. Once, when she did, he told her he needed it for protection from other criminals. Louise had grown up around men on the waterfront who carried guns, and wasn't overconcerned. Once, when Malinow thought the police were on their way up the stairs to his apartment, he handed Dorothy a large roll of bills to hold for him. She thought it was play money.

Louise believed that her husband was working regularly and earning more than the fifteen or twenty dollars a day he made on a construction job. He told her that he was also engaged in finding buyers for friends who had hijacked cigarettes and whiskey to sell, and that he was getting a percentage for his services as middleman. She was upset when he occasionally stayed out all night, and would call Czarnowicz at six in the morning to ask him if he had seen George. Malinow's parole officer had even less knowledge than Louise of what Malinow was doing. Malinow was making his monthly reports faithfully, and, as far as the parole officer knew, was working regularly. The officer wrote in Malinow's record that he lived in "a very nicely furnished home" and "displayed a very courteous and cooperative attitude." Neither Malinow's parole officer nor Czarnowicz's knew that in October 1953 the two men, both members of Local 13, were working on the same construction site. At that time, Malinow, Czarnowicz, and another friend had their eyes on a half-million-dollar payroll. Malinow often speculates that if that robbery had been pulled off he would have gone straight. "If I had got my one-third share of it, I don't think I'd ever have had to steal again, provided I used the $166,000 wisely in a business venture," he says. "I think I could have run a business successfully, and lived moderately well on the fifteen-hundred- or eighteen-hundred-dollar-a-week profits. Many of my friends are ex-criminals who got a big sum of money, pulled out of crime, and are now doing well in legitimate or semi-legitimate businesses. But it didn't work out that way for me. When the half-million-dollar payroll finally went, Bernie and I were back in jail. Our friend pulled off the job with two other guys. For us, the timing was off."

On Tuesday, September 22, 1953, a warm, sunny day, Eloise Fortune, a bookkeeper for the Devon Industrial Corporation, a zipper company in Queens, came to work at 9:45 A.M. Two of the partners in the company endorsed the weekly payroll check she had prepared the previous day. The check was for $4800.81. Mrs. Fortune's husband, Luther, who worked nights, had driven his wife from their home in Hollis to her place of business, as he had done most Tuesday mornings during the two and a half years she had been preparing the Devon payrolls. Now he drove her a mile or so to a bank, waited for a teller to exchange the $4800.81 check for a manila envelope filled with bills and coins, and drove her back to the factory. By then, it was about 10:30 A.M. Fortune parked his car some twenty feet from the door to the building and waited to see his wife board the elevator safely. The doors to the freight elevator were right on the street. Mrs. Fortune rang for the freight elevator. A man approached the elevator and also rang the bell while Mrs. Fortune was waiting for it to come. In a few seconds, the elevator operator, Julian Maldonado, a long-time building employee, opened the elevator doors. The man stepped into the elevator and asked to be taken to the second floor. Mrs. Fortune waited outside: while she was carrying the payroll she was not supposed to ride in the elevator with strangers. Maldonado told the man that the elevator was for freight, not passengers, and stepped out of the elevator to point the way to the staircase. As he did, the man pulled out a gun and put it in Maldonado's side. He then ordered Maldonado and Mrs. Fortune inside the elevator. He threatened to kill them if they didn't obey. They both stepped into the elevator. The man, who touched Mrs. Fortune's shoulder as he entered the elevator, stood at the edge of the elevator and asked her for the money. She threw the manila envelope containing the $4800.81 to him; it landed at his feet. Her purse slipped off her arm as she threw the envelope. The man picked up the envelope (he didn't touch the purse), backed out of the elevator, tried to pull the cord that closed the elevator doors but couldn't reach it, ordered Maldonado to close the elevator doors, and ran into the street.

Fortune, who had been sitting behind the wheel of his parked car, had noticed the man who had joined his wife outside the elevator. He was about to get out of his car to see exactly what was happening when another man armed with a gun ran up to the left side of his car and told him to stay where he was. The man demanded the keys to his car — which Fortune gave him — and went to another car, parked about fifty feet from Fortune's. The first armed man came out of the building, opened the right front door of Fortune's car, sat down next to him, and told him to get going. "How can I get going?" Fortune asked him. "The other fellow took my keys." With that, the man ran to the second car, which the other man had already started, and they drove off. Fortune tried to pursue the robbers' car on foot. He couldn't keep up with the car, nor could he get its license number, because the license plate was covered by a black inner tube that protruded from the back of the car's open trunk.

When Eloise Fortune, minus the payroll envelope, got upstairs, she explained what had happened to the people at Devon, and they immediately called the police. A number of policemen and detectives from the 108th Precinct responded quickly. Two experienced detectives, Philip Smitt and Kenneth Crosby, were assigned to the case. That afternoon, after the Fortunes had given a detailed account of the robbery, they were taken to the Bureau of Criminal Identification, at police headquarters in Manhattan, to look at photographs in the rogues' gallery. Mrs. Fortune thought the man who had robbed her was about five feet nine inches tall, weighed about one hundred seventy pounds, and had a round face. Fortune thought he was an inch shorter and about ten pounds lighter; he added that the robber had grayish hair. Fortune described the man to whom he had surrendered his car keys as being five feet seven and one hundred fifty pounds, with dark hair. The photographs in the rogues' gallery were arranged according to the type of crime and the height of the perpetrators. The Fortunes were shown files of "inside" and "outside" robbers in various height categories, from five feet five to five feet ten. They were unable to identify any of the men in the photographs as the robbers.

A few days after the robbery, the 108th Precinct received an anonymous letter saying that George Malinow and Bernard Czarnowicz had committed the payroll robbery on September 22. On October 13, Detective Crosby came to Mrs. Fortune's office, showed her a photograph, and asked her if the man who had robbed her resembled the man in the photograph. She said that the man in the photograph was too young to be the robber and that she couldn't identify him. (The photograph, she was to learn later, was one of Bernard Czarnowicz taken in 1938.) Several days afterward, Detective Smitt came to Mrs. Fortune's office with another photograph. This time, she said she recognized a similarity between the robber and the man in the photograph, although the man in the photograph was thinner than the man who had held her up. "I was beginning to feel pretty sure about that picture, but I still would like to see the man," she said. (The photograph later proved to be one of Bernard Czarnowicz which had been taken in 1952, upon his release from Clinton.) On October 21, Mr. and Mrs. Fortune went to the 108th Precinct station house to look at more photographs. One of the pictures that Fortune was shown was a 1952 photograph of George Malinow. He picked it out, saying that it looked like the man who had pointed a gun at him. He felt that the second photograph his wife had seen looked like the man who had robbed her, except that the man was heavier. Both Fortunes expressed a desire to see these two men in person.

On October 14, Victor Miller, who had been Malinow's parole officer since his release from Clinton in June 1952, was informed by Detective Crosby that Malinow was under suspicion for the Devon payroll robbery. Gary Davis, Czarnowicz's parole officer, was informed that Czarnowicz was under suspicion for the crime. As the Fortunes became more certain that the men in the photographs were the men who had robbed Mrs. Fortune (Maldonado was unable to identify the man in the elevator from the photographs he was shown), the detectives decided to take them into custody. By then, the parole officers had learned that the two men were both members of Local 13 of the Mason Tenders, and were working on the same construction site, despite the warnings they had been given not to associate. This in itself was a parole violation. On October 22, at 2:30 P.M., the two parole officers accompanied the detectives to the construction site, a housing project in Queens. They found Malinow and Czarnowicz working in the same room of an apartment in the project. The detectives searched them and then drove them to the 108th Precinct station house, where they questioned them about their criminal records and put them in a lineup, still wearing their work clothes. To appear in the lineup with the two suspects, the detectives selected three of fifty patrolmen who were arriving to work the four-to-midnight shift. The patrolmen were wearing their casual coming-to-work clothes. At 4:30, Eloise Fortune, Luther Fortune, and Julian Maldonado, who had been brought to the station house earlier that afternoon, entered the lineup room separately. All three picked out Czarnowicz as the man who had robbed Mrs. Fortune. Her husband identified Malinow as the man who had taken his car keys at gunpoint. At the conclusion of the lineup, Malinow and Czarnowicz were arrested. They asked what they were accused of, and when they were told about the payroll robbery they adamantly denied participating in it. Czarnowicz was calm. Malinow was hysterical. "I would have to be nuts to do this and spend the rest of my life in jail," he told Detective Smitt. When Czarnowicz was first asked where he was on September 22, he said he wasn't working, because of a lull in the construction business between May and October. Malinow first said he believed he was working on September 22. When Parole Officer Miller checked Malinow's employment record, he found that he had worked on a construction project — a library building in Jackson Heights — on September 17, 18, and 21. He hadn't started on his next job, at the housing project, until September 28. Czarnowicz's first day at the housing project was October 8. Later on the afternoon of October 22, Malinow was handcuffed and taken to his home by Miller and Smitt. His apartment was searched thoroughly. The search didn't turn up a gun, a large sum of cash, or any of the clothing that Fortune said Malinow had worn on the day of the robbery. Louise, who was several months pregnant, appeared bewildered by the proceedings. At the same time, Czarnowicz was taken to his home by Parole Officer Davis and Detective Crosby. A search of his apartment didn't uncover a gun, any of the clothes he was said to have worn on the day of the robbery, or the fruits of any crime. Back at the 108th Precinct station house, where Malinow and Czarnowicz spent the night, they were questioned further. Both were asked whether they either owned or drove automobiles, and both said no. Both were asked whether they owned or carried guns, and both said no.

On October 23, Malinow and Czarnowicz were taken to the Queens jail. A few days later, they pleaded not guilty to the crime. On November 5, Malinow, Czarnowicz, and the Fortunes attended a preliminary hearing at Queens felony court. The Fortunes gave brief accounts of the crime and identified Malinow and Czarnowicz as the two robbers. The judge had the two men held without bail for a grand jury. On December 4, Malinow and Czarnowicz were indicted by the grand jury for robbery in the first degree, grand larceny in the first degree, and two counts of assault (one on Fortune, one on his wife) in the second degree. In mid-December, Malinow and Czarnowicz hired Nathan Cooper, a criminal lawyer, to defend them. Louise Malinow sold many of the Malinows' belongings, including the twelve-hundred-dollar TV set, to help pay his fee. Czarnowicz's family and some of Malinow's in-laws also contributed money to help pay for their defense.

In early February, Cooper brought one of the foremost lie-detector experts of the day to the jail to give Malinow and Czarnowicz lie-detector tests for two days. The expert asked the men certain "critical" questions, of a specific nature — "Did you pull the Devon stickup?" and "Did you have a gun at any time last September?" — and a number of "control" questions, concerning their arrest and their marital status and their prior criminal records, which would elicit emotional responses but to which the answers were no. Czarnowicz's electrically measured reactions to the critical questions were not consistently higher than his answers to the control questions. The expert's opinion was that Czarnowicz was telling the truth in his answers to all the critical questions. There were certain irregularities in the pattern of Malinow's electrically measured reactions to the questions, but the expert concluded that there was no consistent pattern of response which could justify a definite diagnosis of deception, and that he, too, was telling the truth in denying any connection with the holdup.

The trial of the People of the State of New York v. Bernard Czarnowicz and George Malinow began in the Queens County Court House on April 8, 1954, and lasted nearly two weeks. The first thing that Cooper did, after the judge excused the jury for a few minutes, was to ask that the lie-detector tests be admitted as opinion evidence. Cooper pointed out that at least one judge in Queens had previously permitted lie-detector evidence to be admitted. Gerald Vincenzo, the assistant district attorney who was prosecuting the case, opposed any reference to the lie-detector tests, because no appellate court in New York State had adjudicated the subject. The judge ruled against Cooper: the lie-detector tests were inadmissible evidence.

Vincenzo then set out to prove that the crime had happened as the three eyewitnesses said it had happened, and that Malinow and Czarnowicz had committed it. His first witness was the bank teller who had cashed the payroll check for Mrs. Fortune on the morning of September 22, 1953; he said he had given her $4800.81 in bills and coins in exchange for the check. Vincenzo then called Mrs. Fortune to the stand. For the next several days, the Fortunes and Maldonado were questioned at length about the robbery, the photographs they had subsequently been shown, and the lineup in which they had positively identified Malinow and Czarnowicz. Cooper, in his cross-examination of the Fortunes and Maldonado, brought out the fact that there were minor discrepancies in the three accounts of the robbery and its aftermath and a few inconsistencies in each person's testimony. Right after the crime, for example, Fortune had described the getaway car as a light-green 1951 Buick; at the trial, he said it was a bluish-green '47 or '48 Buick. (The car that Louise Malinow owned was a blue 1948 Buick.) Cooper tried to demonstrate that the crime had occurred so quickly — it was over in a couple of minutes — that the witnesses had had only fleeting glimpses of the robbers, and at a time when they were under emotional stress.

One afternoon, Cooper sought to cast doubt on Mrs. Fortune's powers of observation and her credibility. He asked her the height of the court clerk who had sworn her in an hour earlier, the color of his suit, and whether he had worn glasses. She said that he was five-ten or five-eleven, that she didn't believe he had worn glasses, and that she didn't notice the color of his suit but that it "could be gray." The clerk was six feet three and a half inches, was wearing horn-rimmed glasses, and had on a navy suit. Cooper also introduced the fact that Czarnowicz weighed 212 pounds the day he was arrested — 40 or 50 pounds more than the Fortunes had said. He was able to show that there had been photographs of both defendants in the rogues'-gallery files that the Fortunes had gone through on the afternoon of the crime — in Malinow's case, a June 1938 group photograph taken when he was arrested with Giritski, Preniszni, and Stokowski — and that the Fortunes hadn't recognized them. Cooper argued that at the lineup the eyewitnesses weren't identifying the men who had robbed them a month earlier but the men whose photographs they had been shown the week before — and even the day before — the lineup. He also tried to convince the jury that the lineup was unfair. Malinow was five feet eight inches tall and weighed 150 pounds, whereas the three patrolmen who had participated in the lineup were "burly." When the assistant D.A. later put the policemen on the stand, one testified that he stood five-eight and a half and weighed 175 pounds, one that he stood five-nine and a half and weighed 180, and one that he stood five-nine and a half and weighed 200. Cooper also claimed that some of the defense witnesses had been threatened by the D.A.'s office, and that the detective work had been lazy. Although Fortune had testified that Czarnowicz touched his right front car door when he got in and out of the car and that he hadn't been wearing gloves, the police hadn't dusted the car for prints. Thus, he said, the case hinged on eyewitness testimony, notoriously the least reliable of all classes of evidence. The Fortunes and Maldonado were steadfast in their identification of the robbers. They insisted that they had identified them at the lineup not because they had seen the suspects' photographs but because when they were given a chance to see the two men they immediately recognized them as the men who had robbed Mrs. Fortune a month earlier. Mrs. Fortune said that there was "no doubt" in her mind when she pointed to Czarnowicz and Fortune said that there was "no question" in his mind that Malinow and Czarnowicz were the robbers.

After the state rested its case, Cooper tried to prove that his clients couldn't have committed the crime of which they were accused, because they could account for their whereabouts on September 22 between 10:30 and 10:45 A.M., when the robbery occurred. Malinow took the stand first to offer his alibi. He testified that at 2:30 P.M. on Tuesday, September 22, 1953, he had gone with his brother-in-law Stanley Novotny to put a ten-dollar deposit on a bicycle for Novotny's son Andrew, whose tenth birthday was on September 28; the bicycle was to be a joint present from the Novotnys and the Malinows. Malinow remembered that his wife had had an epileptic seizure on the morning of the day he had gone to the bicycle store; the date on the bicycle receipt was September 22, so he was able to determine, when he found the receipt some days after his arrest, that the epileptic seizure had occurred on the morning of September 22. Shortly after Malinow got up that day, at about 6:50 A.M. Louise, who was clearing the breakfast dishes, had an epileptic seizure and lost consciousness. Malinow ministered to her as he did whenever she had an epileptic seizure — by inserting a towel in her mouth to keep her from biting her tongue. He then ran upstairs to get his brother-in-law Janos Hodak. With Hodak's help, he carried Louise to bed. There was no phone in the Malinows' apartment. While Hodak stayed with Louise, Malinow went out at about 7:15 A.M. to call Larry Falcone, the shop steward on his construction job, to say he would not be able to come to work, because of Louise's illness. He then returned to his apartment. Hodak went back upstairs, and Malinow stayed with Louise, who came to around 10:30 A.M. When Hodak stopped in to see how Louise was, at about that time, she and Malinow were having coffee. Hodak joined them briefly. Louise told her husband to try to get half a day's work. Shortly after 11:00 A.M., he left the apartment and drove her car to the library construction site in Jackson Heights. When he got there, around noon, one of the construction workers told him that there was no work that day and would be none until the following Monday. Malinow returned home. Later in the day, he went to the bicycle shop; still later, he went out to a diner to pick up $50.40 in pay that he had earned on September 17, 18, and 21. Louise Malinow, Janos Hodak, Stanley Novotny, and Larry Falcone, whom Malinow had met at Clinton, where Falcone had served time for robbery, took the stand to corroborate Malinow's account of his activities on September 22nd.

If there were certain weaknesses in Malinow's alibi — it was supported only by three relatives and a convicted felon, and the testimony of all of them contained as many small inconsistencies as the testimony of the Fortunes and Maldonado — it rang like a newly minted gold coin after Bernard Czarnowicz, some of his relatives, and a friend had taken the stand and presented his alibi. Although at the time of his arrest Czarnowicz had been unable to remember his activities on September 22, he, too, had been able to reconstruct the events of that day because of a birthday in the family. Czarnowicz shared an apartment with his parents, three of his brothers, and a sister. His brother Raymond's birthday was on September 21. There had been a party for him that night at the Czarnowicz apartment. At the party, which lasted until 1:00 A.M., Czarnowicz and one of the guests — Steve Francisco, his closest friend — decided to meet at 12:30 P.M. the next day to go to a 2:00 P.M. ballgame at Yankee Stadium. Francisco, who was also a member of Local 13 of the Mason Tenders, called the Czarnowicz home at 10:30 A.M. on the twenty-second. Czarnowicz was still asleep. His mother woke him and called him to the phone. Francisco told Czarnowicz that he wouldn't be able to go to the Yankee game that afternoon after all, because he had been called in to work. Czarnowicz went to the bathroom. The door was closed, so he knocked. Alan, his thirty-year-old "baby" brother, was there. He came out. After Czarnowicz used the bathroom, he went back to bed until 11:30 A.M. He stayed home until the late afternoon, watching a ball game on television. Steve Francisco, Bernard Czarnowicz's mother, and his brother Alan took the stand to corroborate Czarnowicz's alibi. On cross-examination, Vincenzo was able to elicit the information that Alan Czarnowicz had been convicted of attempted grand larceny and bookmaking; that he hadn't worked for a couple of years; that he hung around a poolroom; that Alan's birthday was on September 9; and that there had been no party for Alan that night. Vincenzo asked Francisco if it was true that he had two social-security numbers, and used one for employment purposes, the other for the purpose of collecting unemployment insurance. Francisco found it necessary to take the Fifth Amendment several times. Vincenzo then pointed out that there had been no game at Yankee Stadium on the afternoon of September 22. The Yankee–Philadelphia Athletics game on September 22 was a night game. The district attorney's office later claimed that the fact that the Yankees had played a night game rather than a day game showed that Francisco's story of having an appointment to meet Czarnowicz on the day of the holdup was "completely discredited as having been made out of whole cloth."

In the course of questioning Malinow and his alibi witnesses, Vincenzo elicited some other troublesome testimony. For example, Malinow, Louise, Janos Hodak, and Stanley Novotny testified that Malinow and Novotny had brought the birthday bicycle home with them on the afternoon of September 22. The receipt dated September 22 showed that they had only put a ten-dollar deposit on the bicycle that day. No one seemed to know when — if ever — the balance had been paid. Still, Malinow and Czarnowicz were as steadfast in maintaining their innocence as the Fortunes and Maldonado were in identifying them as the robbers. When Cooper asked Malinow, "Did you at any time, from the time of your release from prison in 1952 right on up to today, have a gun?" Malinow answered "No." When he asked him, "Did you at any time go with Bernard Czarnowicz and commit a crime of holdup?" Malinow answered "No, I did not." Czarnowicz made several similar declarations. Today, Malinow and Czarnowicz admit that they may have told "a few white lies" during the trial.

On the afternoon of April 20, after Cooper had finished calling his witnesses, Vincenzo called a rebuttal witness — Mrs. Theresa Malick, who had been Malinow's landlady from

November 1952 (when he left the merchant marine) until July 1953 (when he married Louise). Mrs. Malick's brother owned an eighteen-room rooming house three blocks from Louise and George Malinow's apartment. Mrs. Malick and her husband, Albert, lived there and managed it. One day in February 1954, Victor Miller was making a routine home visit to Albert Malick, one of the parolees on his case load, who had served time for attempted burglary. Malick was out, but Miller had become quite friendly with his wife, Theresa, over the years — the Malicks and the Millers had daughters who were about the same age — and he stopped to chat with her. During their conversation, Miller mentioned that Malinow, her former roomer, had been arrested. Mrs. Malick then told Miller of a strange incident that had happened some months earlier. One morning, after Malinow had married and moved out, he came to her rooming house with a friend and asked if she had a room to rent to the friend. The friend was carrying a small box — it measured about three inches by four by five — but no luggage. She had a room available, for which the man paid a week's rent in advance. Malinow left. Mrs. Malick took the man up to the room. That evening, when she went upstairs to clean, she noticed that the door to the man's room was open. She walked into the room and saw the key on the dresser. She thought the man had forgotten it, and took it downstairs to give to him when he came back. He didn't come back. She never saw the man again. Miller asked Mrs. Malick if she remembered the friend's name or the date he and Malinow had come to the rooming house. She told him that she didn't but that she remembered that the friend had an odd name and was from out of town — she very seldom got out-of-towners — and said she could look it up in her receipt book. She went to the book, looked through it, and gave Miller a receipt showing that she had rented a room to a Bernard Margenau on September 22d. Miller took the receipt to Detectives Smitt and Crosby. Mrs. Malick was called to the D.A.'s office after her encounter with Miller and was asked to testify. At the trial, she said that Malinow and Margenau arrived about the time she customarily made the beds, which was between 10:45 A.M. and 11:00 A.M. She described Margenau as a stocky man, five-eight or five-nine, with unruly gray hair, but when she was repeatedly asked if Margenau was in the courtroom, she looked right at Czarnowicz (who fitted her description of Margenau) and said no. Mrs. Malick also said that she had seen Malinow driving Louise's blue Buick before their marriage, while he was still her roomer, which contradicted Malinow's and Louise's earlier testimony. Cooper called Malinow to the stand for surrebuttal. He denied taking anyone to Mrs. Malick's house on September 22. When Vincenzo asked him the previous week if he had ever returned to Mrs. Malick's rooming house after his marriage, he had said no. He now said he had taken a man named Jackie to Mrs. Malick's house for a room in August or September, a month or two after his marriage. When she was recalled to the witness stand, Mrs. Malick said that she didn't know the name of the roomer Malinow had brought to her house but that the man had cheated her out of a week's rent and had left with the key to his room.

The trial drew to an end with summations by Cooper and Vincenzo. The substance of Cooper's summation was that Malinow and Czarnowicz were the victims of mistaken identity. The substance of Vincenzo's was that they weren't. In his summation, Vincenzo commented ironically on the numerous birthdays required by the defendants' alibis. "He [Czarnowicz] had an appointment to go with Steve Francisco, to go to the ball game the next day. When did that happen? There was a birthday party. Another birthday party. The place was full of birthdays." Vincenzo also expressed anger at Cooper's earlier charge that the D.A.'s office had intimidated Cooper's witnesses, including Janos Hodak, one of Malinow's brothers-in-law. Vincenzo said that Hodak had been "pushed around" and "blackjacked" so much that he had informed the D.A.'s office that Malinow had stuck up the place and that Malinow had said to him, "If you ever tell anybody, I will kill you."

At 10:35 A.M. on April 21, the judge gave the case to the jury. At 3:35 that afternoon, the jury asked to have all of Mrs. Malick's testimony read to them. At 8:47 P.M., the jurors brought in the verdict: they found both men guilty on all counts. Two reporters for the *Journal-American* interviewed eight of the twelve jurors after the verdict was announced. The reporters informed the jurors of the results of the lie-detector tests, which hadn't been admitted as evidence. Five of the eight said that the undisclosed lie-detector evidence could have altered the verdict. "We would have given it prime consideration if it were presented in court, and the verdict might have gone the other way," one juror was quoted as saying. "It certainly would have raised doubt in my mind about the defendants' guilt," another said. Cooper also queried the jurors. One told him he "absolutely would not have convicted" if he had known about the lie-detector evidence. Many of the jurors told Cooper that Mrs. Malick's testimony was the deciding factor. Cooper himself later claimed that, up to Vincenzo's calling of Mrs. Malick, "everyone in the courtroom — including myself and the stenographer — felt we had it won."

A few days after the verdict was brought in, Louise Malinow gave birth to a boy. Malinow received the news of his son's birth in Queens County jail, where he and Czarnowicz were being held until the judge sentenced them. He was glad to have a son, and glad that his son had been born nine months and a week after the wedding and no sooner. "When we got married, many of my in-laws were waiting to see if Louise would give birth before nine months," he says. "They thought of me as a knock-around guy, so they expected me to date Louise, get her pregnant, feel sorry for her, and marry her. After my son was born, I thought to myself, Well, at least one thing they won't be able to say is that she got pregnant ahead of time." Louise named her son Arthur George. She decided not to give him George as a first name, because there were already several Georges in the family and because she thought her husband had had bad luck.

On June 22, 1954, Malinow and Czarnowicz were sentenced, as third-felony offenders, to fifteen to thirty years for robbery in the first degree, five to ten years for grand larceny in the first degree, and two and a half to five years on the two second-degree-assault convictions, all the sentences to be served concurrently. These were the minimum sentences the judge could give them by law. Three days later, Malinow and Czarnowicz were sent to Sing Sing, where, as no. 115874 and no. 115875, they spent four months working as block porters. On October 22, 1954, they were sent to Clinton. Although the crime for which Malinow was convicted occurred on September 22, 1953, his delinquency date reverted to his parole date — June 19, 1952 — meaning that he still owed two years, seven months, and twenty-eight days of delinquent time on his previous sentence, which he had to serve before starting his new term. On February 23, 1957, he would start the fifteen-to-thirty-year sentence. He would be eligible for parole after serving two thirds of the minimum, or about ten years. With the credit he was given for jail time, that meant that he would become eligible for parole on August 30, 1966.

When Malinow returned to prison, he wasn't particularly worried about the amount of time he might have to do. He and Czarnowicz fully expected to win the case on appeal. Malinow was proud that he and Czarnowicz had stood trial together and gone away together. Each had testified at the trial that the detectives had asked him to implicate the other and thereby gain leniency for himself. Each had refused. "With the new element, it's a race to see who gets to the D.A. first," he says now.

Malinow's and Czarnowicz's first move was to try to get the conviction overturned. One of the points in the brief they submitted to the Appellate Division of the New York Supreme Court was that the eyewitness identification of Malinow was incredible as a matter of law and the identification of Czarnowicz was completely against the weight of the evidence. The state of New York in its brief, argued that the jury's verdict should not be set aside. Even if the eyewitnesses' descriptions of the holdup men varied, it said, and even if Bernard Czarnowicz weighed 212 pounds at the time of his arrest, the jury had seen Malinow and Czarnowicz and could judge whether the witnesses' estimates of their height and weight appeared to the ordinary person to be accurate. The fact that the Fortunes didn't pick out early photographs of Malinow and Czarnowicz in the rogues' gallery also didn't render their identifications incredible: the men had changed since the 1930s, and anyway the jury had seen the photographs and could judge whether the Fortunes' failure to recognize them was incredible. Another point in the appellants' brief was that there had been errors made in the trial, including the court's refusal to admit into evidence the results of the lie-detector tests. The state replied that the lie detector had not attained scientific acceptance as a reliable means of ascertaining truth or deception. In early 1956, the appellate division found that the trial had been free of reversible error, and affirmed the conviction. In the fall of 1956, the New York Court of Appeals denied leave to appeal. Some months later, having exhausted all his judicial possibilities in New York State, Malinow tried to take his case to federal district court, on the ground that his constitutional rights had been violated. In 1954, after the conviction of Malinow and Czarnowicz, Cooper had gone to talk with Mrs. Malick, the critical witness. Mrs. Malick told Cooper that the assistant D.A. had put pressure on her to testify. Malinow had heard from people in Greenpoint that Mrs. Malick had been told that if she didn't testify against him her husband would be found guilty of a parole violation and would be sent back to prison. At the trial, while the jury was not present, Cooper complained to the judge that the D.A.'s office had threatened and harassed Louise and some of the other witnesses. One evening, despite the fact that she was in her ninth month of pregnancy, was subject to epileptic seizures, and had another appointment, Louise had been kept in the district attorney's office for three or four hours. She had been threatened, and told that unless she signed a statement she would be held on some charge, on high bail, so that she could not go home. When she was brought to the point of hysterics and tears, she was told to "cut out the sob act," and was allowed to go home only after she had signed the statement out of fear. The next evening, Cooper continued, four police officers had gone to Louise's house and told her they wanted to take a statement from her. They had returned repeatedly during the night, and her family had finally concealed her in a closet to keep her from being harassed. (In court, with the jury out, the assistant district attorney admitted that some witnesses had been visited at night but denied that they had been threatened.)

At first, Malinow says, Mrs. Malick agreed to testify in federal district court that she had been threatened, but at the last minute she backed out. Louise also declined to testify about what had happened at the district attorney's office. Without their testimony, Malinow had no case in federal court. In 1960 and again in 1962, Malinow asked the governor of New York for executive clemency; he was turned down both times. There was nothing more he could do about the case.

Some of the principals in the Devon payroll robbery and the subsequent trial — Mrs. Fortune, Vincenzo — are dead. Some — Fortune, Maldonado — are unwilling to talk about it. Detective Smitt retired from the detective force in 1957, after twenty years in the police department, fifteen of which he had served as a detective. He spent sixteen years as an investigator for an insurance company before retiring from his second career, in 1973. At the age of seventy, looking back on his years as a detective, he says he can think of one case in which he had a little doubt about the verdict. The Devon payroll robbery isn't that case. He makes no apologies for the police failure to dust Fortune's car for possible prints. "We didn't take prints on every larceny or robbery," he says. "We didn't work like Dick Tracy. We had information on Malinow and Czarnowicz that was reliable. I never had any doubts about their guilt, because of their records." Victor Miller recently retired after twenty-seven years as a parole officer. The Malinow-Czarnowicz case stands out in his memory because it was he who unwittingly came across the evidence that clinched it. When he went to see Mrs. Malick in February 1954 and their conversation turned to Malinow, he felt sure she was being truthful when she described Malinow's return to her rooming house and quickly produced the receipt. Miller believes that Mrs. Malick was also being truthful in court when she said she couldn't identify Czarnowicz. "She probably didn't get a good enough look at him, and she was honest enough to say so," he says. "That trial made me lose confidence in lie detectors, because I was so convinced that Malinow and Czarnowicz were guilty. I don't doubt that those guys, with their character disorders, could fool a lie detector."

The 1339-page transcript of the 1954 trial contains some unanswered and perhaps unanswerable questions. Did the robbers know that the Devon payroll, normally three thousand dollars, was eighteen hundred dollars more than usual on September 22, 1953, because it included back pay, or were they just lucky to rob it that day? How could the robber who took the money from Mrs. Fortune forget that he and his partner had a car of their own and get into Fortune's? In 1977, Malinow and Czarnowicz maintain their innocence, the "few white lies" they told at their trial notwithstanding. When friends suggest to Malinow that it is ironic that he got away with fifteen robberies that he cheerfully admits to doing and was convicted of a robbery that he says he didn't do, the irony partly eludes him. "You try to tell yourself that the ones you got away with make up for the one you got wrongly convicted of, but that doesn't really ease the pain of being sentenced to fifteen to thirty years for something you never did," he says. "That ain't supposed to happen in a democracy."

When Malinow returned to Clinton, in October 1954, after an absence of two years and three months, he was given a cordial reception. "It was just like I'd been away on a vacation," he says. "The inmates were glad to welcome back someone they knew. The guards I got along with on my previous bid saw my name on the draft list and came up to the reception gallery. Swifty, an officer whose job I'd helped save on several occasions — he used to come to work drunk, and we'd forcefully put him under cold water and fill him with hot coffee to sober him up — came to say hello. Frenchy said he hated to see me back, but since I was back, would I like to come to work for him again?" After four uneventful years at Clinton — his work and behavior records were satisfactory; he took some courses in English, art, arithmetic, social studies, and typing and did well in them — Malinow felt bored at Clinton and decided that the time had come to sample another prison. He requested a transfer to Green Haven, which he had heard described as "the country club of New York State's maximum-security prisons." On the morning of June 5, 1958, he was Clinton no. 32692; that evening, after an all-day ride, he became Green Haven no. 5296. He was uncuffed, unshackled, and put in a cell on the reception block. Within a few minutes, runners came up to him bringing large bags of groceries and thermoses filled with coffee, compliments of the many friends he had made during his stay at Wallkill, his two stays at Clinton, and his three stays at Sing Sing. "I was very appreciative that people thought of me even before I was in the place an hour," he says. "Old-timers know it can be hard in a new prison the first day or two. Sometimes you don't get your personal property immediately, and you don't get to the commissary right away."

Malinow's first job assignment at Green Haven — a good one, obtained with the assistance of friends — was in the commissary, where he helped truck drivers unload goods, stocked the shelves with groceries, and bagged inmates' orders. He was not unappreciative of the job's fringe benefits. The rest of Green

Haven's inmates could buy groceries only once every two weeks; the commissary workers could do it every day. They could also get some of their groceries without paying for them: the truck drivers gave them jars of instant coffee and other comestibles, and the guards looked the other way when they helped themselves to candy bars, cake, and sundries; the commissary always wrote off a certain percentage for breakage and damage.

In the late fifties, the identification room at Green Haven, where photographs of incoming and outgoing prisoners are taken, was next door to the commissary. The civilian who presided over both the commissary and the ID room considered Malinow a good worker and eventually asked him if he would like to transfer to the ID room. Malinow was ready for a change. He thought photography might be more creative than stocking shelves, and after two and a half years in the commissary he went to work in the identification room as a darkroom technician. He learned how to mix chemicals, develop photographs, and do enlarging and cropping. He enjoyed the work. One afternoon in 1964, after he had spent four years in the ID department, a friend asked Malinow to enlarge two photographs he had. The photographs were of female nudes. The friend liked to draw and paint, and used the photographs in his art work. Malinow took them to his cell, saying he would enlarge them in the darkroom the next morning. That evening, a new block officer unexpectedly searched Malinow's cell and found the photographs. "They were plain pictures of women's bodies, no positions, nothing vulgar, just art," Malinow says. "But the rookie yo-yo insisted on making a big thing out of it. When I came before the P.K., he seemed more amused than anything else. He asked me the purpose of the photos. I didn't want to give up my friend, so I said, 'To admire them.' I was written up for having contraband photos, and I lost my job, but I often helped out in the ID room unofficially when they were really busy or someone was sick." Malinow's next assignment at Green Haven was in the parole-clothing department. Malinow was glad he had transferred to Green Haven. If it was not exactly a country club, he found it more relaxed than Clinton, with more activities for the inmates and milder weather, and by this time he was ready to be closer to New York City. After he left Sing Sing in 1954, neither Louise nor any of his in-laws had come to see him, and he and Louise had also stopped corresponding, as a result of a misunderstanding by mail, but Malinow had one regular visitor at Green Haven, which was one more than he'd had at Clinton. Anthony Mallan, the nephew of a friend of Malinow's at Green Haven whom he had originally known in Greenpoint, came to see him when he visited his uncle; Malinow was Mallan's honorary godfather.

In the spring of 1966, several months before Malinow became eligible for parole, he went through the pre-parole process a third time. The interviews were a little less thorough than they had been in the early forties and the fifties, and were conducted and written up by a parole officer. The parole officer assigned to evaluate Malinow reported that he had not been an institutional problem; in eight years at Green Haven he had only four misbehavior charges, and three of these were even less serious than the contraband photographs. He did his job assignments well and changed jobs infrequently. The parole officer realized that his employment record on the outside was "negligible, due to his various incarcerations," but he said that Malinow had a union card and was certain he would be able to find work again through Local 13. Malinow made a favorable impression on the parole officer, who found him cooperative and courteous, and ended up saying that he thought Malinow could be granted an opportunity to return to the community. "In the past, he has demonstrated irresponsibility and unstableness, but it is felt by the writer that he may have overcome these shortcomings to some degree," the parole officer wrote.

Malinow met with the parole board on June 9, 1966. During his hearing before the three commissioners, he maintained his innocence in the 1953 Devon payroll robbery and brought up the results of the lie-detector tests. When a commissioner asked him if he wouldn't go out feeling bitter toward authority because of his innocence and his long imprisonment, he replied, "If there is any bitterness, it is from my previous record. Who can I blame but myself? If I wasn't a third offender, I wouldn't be in here." One commissioner told him to feel free to say anything that would be helpful. "All I can say, sir, I got approximately thirteen years in, I owe twenty years to the board on supervision now, and the next time if I step out of line, it's a life sentence. I realize this," Malinow said. For the third time in three sentences, Malinow was granted parole the first time he became eligible for it. The board gave him an "Open Date Own Program — August 30, 1966–" to find a job.

Once again (if it is true that history repeats itself, it seems to repeat itself in Malinow's case in unusual detail), Malinow set about looking for a job. By July 8, he had received a letter from his old friend, the business representative of Mason Tenders, Local 13. The letter said that since Malinow was a former union member he would be employed at $5.05 an hour, working thirty-five hours a week. The parole officer decided against this job offer because, according to a confidential file he had been given, some of Local 13's officers were then said to be involved with well-known racketeers. One of the two men in charge of the union had just been killed, on July 3, after several earlier, unsuccessful attempts on his life. By August, Malinow had come up with three other offers of employment, all of them, he later admitted, "obtained with the influence of the criminal element." The first of the three jobs that the parole officer investigated was from a construction company on Long Island. According to one of the firm's owners, Malinow would be employed at $1.75 an hour for a five-day week laying asphalt on parking lots and streets. The parole officer approved the job, so he didn't investigate the two others.

Malinow left Green Haven on the morning of September 6,

1966, with $66.60. This time, he didn't leave prison by bus or train. He left in grand style, which didn't go unnoticed by the Green Haven authorities. They informed the New York parole office that Malinow had been picked up by his godson, Anthony Mallan, in Mallan's black, four-door Lincoln sedan, whose license-plate number they supplied. In 1966, Malinow violated parole even faster than he had in 1952. Mallan drove him first to the parole office, in New York City, where Malinow made his required parole arrival report, and then to his own home, in New Jersey; Malinow wasn't allowed to leave the state without his parole officer's permission, which he didn't have. At Mallan's house, he ate a steak, took a nap, and enjoyed a hot shower. That evening, he, Mallan, and a friend of Mallan's went to a Greenwich Village discotheque, where they had a few drinks. Mallan and his friend had selected a chorus girl for Malinow to spend the night with — a "swinger," Malinow recalls — but his mind wasn't on women, it was on money, so he returned to Mallan's house for the night, alone. The next day, Mallan drove him to Queens. First, Malinow rented a furnished room in Elmhurst, which his friend Steve Francisco, the Fifth Amendment witness in the '54 trial, helped him find. Then he went calling on people to whom he'd been generous in 1952 and 1953, when his pockets were filled with the proceeds of his various robberies and theirs were empty. These friends had prospered while Malinow was in prison, and now gave him large sums of money. Malinow also borrowed a few hundred dollars from Cooper, to whom he still owed a few thousand dollars.

Malinow had never intended to work for the construction company — it was another low-paying "can opener," like the Blue Chip job. He had planned to go to work for Local 13 soon after he got out; he knew from experience that jobs that were disapproved while a man was in prison were often approved once he was on the street. Unfortunately, there was a cement mixers' strike in September 1966. Local 13 respected the picket lines, so the union members were out of work. Malinow's parole officer wanted him to get a job with another union, but Malinow told him that the strike would soon be over and that it wouldn't pay for him to spend the money to join another union. He convinced the parole officer that he had enough money to live on for a few weeks without getting a job. Malinow wasn't in a hurry to go to work anyway; he wanted to relax a little after thirteen years in prison. He spent his time looking up old friends and frequenting the bars-and-grills that some of them owned.

One weekday afternoon, while sitting in a friend's bar sipping a Scotch and playing the jukebox, Malinow took a notion to see Louise and his son, Arthur, who was then twelve. He had told the parole officer at Green Haven that he wasn't interested in a reconciliation with his wife but that he would like to see his son. He had no idea that in June, before his release, a parole officer had called Louise to ask how she felt about seeing him, and that Louise had said she wanted nothing whatever to do with him in the future, and refused to let him see Arthur. Malinow had heard that Louise still lived in the apartment they had fixed up after their wedding. He got into a cab, reached the house around 3:15 P.M., and walked upstairs. He stood in the hallway outside the apartment. At three-thirty, a boy who had to be Arthur — "He looked a lot like me," Malinow says with pride — came home from school. Malinow introduced himself to his son, who recognized him from some photographs he had seen. Arthur had been curious about his father and had often asked his mother and his aunts and uncles about him. He had always been told that his father was "away," and that they would tell him more about his father when he was older. Arthur and Malinow went into the apartment. An older cousin of Arthur's happened to come in and see Malinow. She recognized him and went running out to tell her relatives. The cousin intercepted Louise on her way home from work, at a toy factory. A number of Louise's relatives came up to the apartment with her. They were afraid Malinow wanted revenge because of Louise's refusal to testify at the federal hearing. He assured them that he just wanted to talk to Louise. He and Louise spent an hour in the bedroom and came out arm in arm. Despite what Louise had told the parole officer, she seemed genuinely glad to see Malinow. He seemed no less pleased that Louise hadn't divorced him, hadn't remarried, and still wore her engagement ring and her wedding band. He left the house a few hours later, after shaking hands with his in-laws.

The following Saturday, Malinow returned to Greenpoint in Mallan's car. He brought Louise a bouquet of roses and a box of candy. On his first visit, Arthur had told his father about some Beatles records he wanted and couldn't get in Brooklyn. Malinow had found them in New Jersey and had bought them for Arthur, along with a generous supply of toys and clothes. He took Arthur to a jewelry store, where he let him choose a wristwatch and a ring for himself and a pin for Louise. He gave Arthur a hundred-dollar bill to pay for his purchases. Years later, Arthur remembered the shiny black Lincoln his father had appeared in, and his father's wallet, which contained nothing but fifty- and hundred-dollar bills — lots of them. He also remembered that if his mother seemed slightly more apprehensive with his father back in her life, she also seemed happier: her marriage had been the most exciting thing that had ever happened to her, and she had obviously held on to her memories despite years of listening to her relatives' "I told you so"s about her husband's return to prison in 1954. Malinow stayed at Louise's apartment for several days. He slept on the living-room couch. He was proud of the way Louise had raised Arthur: the boy was polite, obedient to his mother, and truthful; he loved school, did his homework, got good grades, and wasn't afraid to fight if he had to. "He was an ideal son," Malinow says. "I don't think criminals should marry — it's not fair to their families — but if I hurt Louise by making her lead what is essentially a widow's life, I gave her Arthur in return."

Arthur and Malinow took many walks around Greenpoint and had many agreeable father-son chats. Malinow showed Arthur the waterfront pier where he had proposed to Louise and the pier where he had gone swimming as a child — which turned out to be the same pier where Arthur swam. Once, on a walk around his old neighborhood, Malinow passed the display-fixture company that had employed him in 1936. He saw a man he had worked with thirty years earlier. The man had grown old and was just making ends meet. Malinow was glad he had quit that job when he had. "The man proved my point," he says. "There was no future there. I was better off than he was, even if I'd spent most of my time in prison. In that year and a half I was out in 1952 and 1953, I went more places and did more things than most people do in a lifetime, and I spent more on tips in a week than that guy made in a month."

After staying at Louise's a few days — the novelty soon wore off — Malinow returned to his furnished room and to his friends' bars. Czarnowicz was still in prison — he had owed more time on his previous sentence than Malinow, so he had started the fifteen-to-thirty-year sentence later — but Malinow met up with many other prison friends. One was Patrick Halloran, with whom he had once worked in the Clinton woodyard. Halloran, a robber and burglar, had got out of prison in 1961, after spending nearly thirty-four years behind bars. Another was David Balboa, a forger, whom Malinow had met at Clinton and had spent a fair amount of time with at Green Haven. Halloran, who was twelve years older than Malinow, was doing reasonably well. For the past five years, he had gone straight. He had two union books — house-wrecking and metal-lathing — and owned 25 percent of a bar. Balboa, who had been released a while before Malinow, was doing less well. He was a younger man, with a family, and always seemed short of cash. Malinow lent Balboa some of the money his friends had been giving him.

One day, at a bar in Queens, Balboa told Malinow about a

factory payroll that would be easy for him and Halloran to take. He said that he couldn't take it himself, because he had once worked at the factory — the Bingo Machine Company, in the Bronx — but that he could help them by supplying the payroll details and by driving the getaway car. The payroll was delivered from a company office to the factory by an unarmed driver in a station wagon. All that Malinow and Halloran would have to do would be to get into the station wagon, tell the driver to go a few blocks, tie him up, and take off in the getaway car. They wouldn't even have to set foot inside the factory. Malinow was tempted. Czarnowicz needed money for lawyers, Malinow couldn't depend on his friends' largesse forever, Local 13 was still on strike, and he didn't feel like looking for any other work. Malinow told Halloran about Balboa's proposal. Halloran wasn't working at the time, because things were slow in house-wrecking and metal-lathing in September 1966, and, as he later said, "you always want to live a little higher than it's possible by working." As it happened, Halloran had recently come into possession of some guns. He had lent a burglar of his acquaintance three hundred dollars. The burglar had admitted he wouldn't be able to pay back the money and had offered him as payment three guns he had stolen in house burglaries. Halloran took them, figuring that three guns were better than nothing. He gave one to a friend and kept the two others. He and Malinow agreed to do the robbery. On October 24, 1966, the day before a payroll was to be delivered to the Bingo Machine Company, Balboa, Malinow, and Halloran went by subway from Queens to the Bronx (where Balboa lived) to look the area over. They made arrangements to meet the following afternoon. Malinow and Halloran were to go from Queens to the Bronx together. Balboa was to be waiting for them, with a car, several blocks away from the factory. When the three men met on the twenty-fifth, Balboa told them he hadn't been able to get a car. Malinow and Halloran were angry. They told Balboa he had put them in danger, letting them go up there with guns. Balboa made a few excuses and walked away. Malinow and Halloran remained on the street, talking about the crime. Malinow was eager to take the payroll now that he was all cranked up for it, and he tried to talk Halloran into it. They could take the payroll exactly as planned, he said, and escape on foot. Halloran thought that that would be too risky: a car was much faster than his legs. Halloran prevailed. The two men were still standing on the curb talking when three unmarked cars pulled up to them. Ten policemen got out of the cars, surrounded them, and ordered them to stand against the wall of a nearby house. Two detectives frisked them and found a .38 gun with five live rounds in Malinow's pocket and a Smith & Wesson .357 with six live rounds on Halloran. They took the two men to the precinct house and arrested them. When Malinow and Halloran were apprehended, they were confused. They wondered how they could have been the victims of such rotten luck. At the precinct house, Halloran found out from a detective friend that their bad luck was Balboa, who had set them up. Malinow later learned that Balboa had been caught violating parole (he had been forging checks) and had been told by his parole officer and the police that he could either cooperate with them or go back to prison. He had given the parole officer what information he had on the parole violators he knew. When he had no more information to give, he had proposed the robbery to Malinow and Halloran and gone to the police.

Halloran's gun was checked and was proved to have been stolen from a 1964 house burglary. Malinow's gun was believed to have been stolen. When the two men were arraigned in the Bronx criminal court, on October 26, 1966, they were charged with violation of section 1897 of the penal code (illegal possession of a firearm) and section 1308 (receiving stolen property). Halloran was released on ten thousand dollars' bail. Malinow was put in the Bronx House of Detention. When he was interviewed there by his parole officer a few days later, he tried to talk his way out of his predicament, as had long been his custom. He told the parole officer he had done nothing but bring Balboa a gun, as Balboa had ordered him to do. Balboa, he said, had been pressuring him to join him in several criminal ventures. When Malinow rejected all of Balboa's overtures, Balboa had told him that he would "make up a story" and tell it to Malinow's parole officer, and that Malinow would be returned to prison as a parole violator whether or not he had actually done anything wrong. It was only because of this fear that Malinow and Halloran had picked up the guns from their hiding places, as Balboa had directed them, and brought the guns from Queens to the Bronx. When the parole officer pointed out to Malinow that he had gone to prison in 1954 for payroll robbery and that a factory a couple of blocks from the spot where he and Halloran had been arrested had a payroll due on the premises that afternoon, Malinow offered no further statement. In Malinow's violation-of-parole report, the parole officer wrote, "In consideration of this individual's background, it is extremely doubtful that he could be pressured in the manner he describes into becoming involved in the way he did in this matter." The parole officer noted that Malinow hadn't accepted his approved employment with the construction company and hadn't made any effort to find other employment during his seven weeks on the street. Although Malinow had made his weekly parole reports faithfully, it was the parole officer's opinion that Malinow "completely lacked sincerity in regards to attempting to maintain himself by lawful means." According to the parole officer, "his attempt to adjust to parole supervision could best be described as nonexistent."

Soon after their arrest, Halloran and Malinow hired lawyers. The detectives who stopped them in the Bronx had not had search warrants. Malinow and Halloran hoped to beat the gun rap on the ground of illegal search and seizure. On April 20, 1967, at a pre-trial hearing on the defendants' motion to suppress the discovery of the two guns, the two detectives who had searched them testified that on October 21, 1966, they had received a tip from an informer that several men, including Malinow and Halloran, were going to rob a payroll at the Bingo Machine Company on the afternoon of October 25. The detectives had gone down to the Bureau of Criminal Identification on October 22 and had obtained photographs of Malinow and Halloran. They had also studied the rather substantial arrest records of the two men and had decided they were dangerous. On October 24, they had called on the Bingo Machine Company's bookkeeper, who verified the fact that a payroll would be driven from a company office to the factory on the twenty-fifth. They had decided to stake out the area surrounding the factory that afternoon, and they had spotted two men in the vicinity of the factory. They had recognized Malinow from his photograph and had assumed that the other was Halloran. They felt that there was "probable cause" to search them. The judge agreed. He ruled that the police conduct had been proper. The police had corroborated the informer's information, and so had had probable cause to believe that the two men were armed.

Halloran was afraid that his bail would be revoked after he and Malinow lost on the motion to suppress, and he jumped bail on May 1, 1967. He went upstate, where he took a job for seventy-five dollars a week as a dishwasher in a restaurant owned by the Mafia. Malinow remained in the Bronx House of Detention. He realized there was no point in going to trial. "I knew my record," he says. "And I couldn't justify the gun to a jury the way I could justify it in my mind." He told his lawyer he would cop a plea.

On July 18, 1967 (according to a story in the *Daily News* that appeared two days later under the headline BREAK BY 7 FOILED IN BRONX JAIL), a guard at the Bronx House of Detention was leading forty-one men back to their cells, on the fifth floor, after supper. Two men — Clyde Taylor (who was accused of rape) and Timothy Maloney (a convicted manslaughterer) — held up pencils, indicating that they wanted to sharpen them. The guard locked the thirty-nine others up in their cells while Taylor and Maloney went into a utility room to use the pencil sharpener. Taylor and Maloney then slipped out of the utility room, seized the guard, bound his hands with neckties, opened an empty cell, and threw him in it. Next, they opened the cells of five men with whom they had been planning an escape. The men tried to smash a window that separated the prisoners' area from the visitors' area. Before they succeeded, guards and police, armed with shotguns, who had been tipped off about the impending escape a month earlier, appeared on the scene and stopped them. "The prisoners were surrounded as their alleged leader pounded with a metal mop wringer against a screened window separating the prisoners' section from the visitors,' " the *News* reported, citing an account by the Bronx district attorney. "The asserted ringleader, George Malinow, 46, . . . was armed with a metal eyeglass case that had been cut in half and sharpened into a makeshift razor, the D.A. said. As he beat the window, police closed in on him and he 'went berserk.' . . . Malinow raced back into the cell tier where the cons had stashed an unarmed guard . . . into a cell. But the police and other guards reached Malinow first and subdued him. He was treated at Bellevue for cuts. . . . All seven were charged with attempted escape and conspiracy to escape. In addition, Malinow was charged with attempted felonious assault."

Malinow's accounts of the attempt made on July 18, 1967, to escape from the Bronx House of Detention vary from hour to hour, from day to day, and from week to week. Among the recent statements he has made about it are these:

"Had I wanted to escape, it would have been easier for me to escape from the Bronx courtroom where the search-and-seizure hearing was held."

"I wasn't trying to escape on July 18, but I would have gone a few weeks later. I had a better way. My way was to go into a utility room on the sixth floor, pry open two window bars, go out the utility-room window, and drop five stories to the ground."

"I came out of the cell, but I didn't try to escape."

"I became partly involved and went through with the escape because I felt at first there was a possibility of getting away. The doors flew open, everyone was moving, there was lots of confusion, and I soon saw it was hopeless. I had a mop wringer and I had an eyeglass case, but it wasn't sharpened. I wasn't the ringleader."

Whatever the variations on the theme of the July 18 escape, the villain of all of Malinow's accounts is Maloney. As Malinow later learned, Maloney was often used by the district attorney's office as an informer. He was sent from jail to jail to pick up information on various cases — the Alice Crimmins case, among others — in exchange for leniency in his own case. Halloran believes that Maloney was planted in the Bronx house of detention in June 1967 to strike up a friendship with Malinow in order to learn Halloran's whereabouts. Instead, Maloney learned of the escape plan, which Malinow and some of the other prisoners had been working on since February. He tipped off the district attorney's office and then participated in the escape as the secret agent of the district attorney. The *News* did not report Maloney's role as an informer for the D.A.

Malinow refers to the *News* account as "dramatized" except for one passage, which he says was "understated." He received more than cuts in the Bronx jail; he received the worst beating of his life. One of his eyes was badly hurt and all his upper teeth were knocked out by a gun butt. He spent ten days in Bellevue, drifting in and out of consciousness. A month after Malinow got out of the hospital, Halloran was caught while he was visiting the city — he has no idea how the police found him — and was put in the Bronx House of Detention, to which Malinow had been returned. The plea-bargaining process, begun before the escape, resumed.

Malinow was eager to be allowed to plead guilty to a misdemeanor, because he knew that if he was forced to plead guilty to a felony he would be sentenced as a fourth-felony offender, and, according to the penal code in existence in 1966, when the crime was committed, a judge would therefore have to sentence him to fifteen years to life. The Bronx district attorney's office decided against letting Malinow plead guilty to a misdemeanor, because if he was allowed to do that he could be out in four years. The district attorney believed that four years was too short a period of time for a man with Malinow's lengthy record. Although the maximum expiration date on Malinow's fifteen-to-thirty-year sentence was 1986, the parole board did not require him to do all his delinquent time in prison, as he had done the balance of his 1938 and 1943 sentences; he could be paroled from the fifteen-to-thirty-year sentence in two years. He would then have to do, say, only two more years on a misdemeanor. Over the next few months, Malinow's lawyer, the chairman of the parole board, and the Bronx district attorney's office worked out what they thought would be an equitable arrangement. Malinow would have to plead guilty to a felony — attempted possession of a loaded firearm — which would cover all the other outstanding charges against him, including the attempted jail escape. To mitigate the severity of the mandatory fifteen-year-to-life sentence, the district attorney would write a letter to the chairman of the parole board indicating his wish that Malinow serve the minimum time on the violation of his old sentence (two years) and the minimum time on his new fifteen-year-to-life sentence (ten years), provided his conduct in prison was good. The district attorney's letter would be put in Malinow's parole folder, where the parole board would see it. The judge concurred with this recommendation and, on February 6, 1968, sentenced Malinow to the mandatory fifteen years to life. Halloran, a third-felony offender, was sentenced to three and a half to seven years. Eight days later, Malinow was back in Sing Sing, with a new number — 140887. Upon his return to Sing Sing, he went through the usual initial interrogatories. When asked what he attributed the gun charge to, he said he was drunk. "I just wanted to end those discussions," he says.

He asked to be assigned to an idle company. ("I didn't feel like working. I wanted to be left alone.") He listed Auburn as his transfer preference: he had a friend who was there, Auburn was said to be the best-feeding joint in the state, and it was supposed to be a good place to do legal work. Malinow planned to appeal his latest conviction. On March 12, 1968, Malinow was transferred to Attica. He assumes he was sent there because it was considered a "maximum-maximum-security prison," and he now had the attempted Bronx escape on his record. Soon after he got to Attica, he had his parole-violation hearing. The parole board held him two years on his delinquent time and ordered him to reappear in 1970. In January 1970, he was paroled from his fifteen-to-thirty-year sentence to start his new sentence. With a minimum of fifteen years, less a year and three months and twenty-two days' jail time, less four years and six months and twenty-three days' possible good time, Malinow would have to serve a minimum of nine years, one month, and fifteen days. He would first be eligible to meet the parole board on February 27, 1979. When Malinow is reminded of his many broken pledges to the parole board, he says, "There were many times when I was very sincere about what I told the parole board, but future developments caused me to change my feelings." When he is asked what his motive was for the abortive 1966 robbery, he says, "I wanted to accomplish in a few minutes what it would have taken me months to accomplish legitimately." When he is asked why he would risk life imprisonment within seven weeks of getting out of prison after thirteen years, he says simply, "You wouldn't understand."

Malinow took an instant dislike to Attica when he arrived there. "Attica gave me a dismal feeling, a feeling of barrenness," he says. "Many of the guards had stern faces — faces even sterner than the faces of the guards at Clinton — and a very rigid manner of speaking." On March 16, four days after his arrival, he requested a transfer to Green Haven. He was told that his transfer elsewhere would not be considered for several years. He resigned himself to making the best of his situation. As always, he found some guards he liked, and made friends with some of the inmates, who gave him the nickname Popeye because he talked so much about the sea. Spring was coming, so he procured an outdoor job, on the grading gang, which mowed lawns, fixed sidewalk cracks, and did other maintenance work. The grading gang locked on A block and was presided over by a good guard. In November 1968, with winter coming on, Malinow got himself an indoor job, in the state shop, which issued inmates their prison clothes. The state-shop guard was also decent, but the state-shop inmates locked on D block — a block that Malinow didn't particularly care for. He kept the job about a year and a half. In the summer of 1970, he applied for a job as a porter on A block and was made the block's feed-up man: he brought food from the kitchen to the keeplocks and invalids on the block. He preferred A block to D block, he says, but explains, "The main reason I changed jobs was that you always look for a little variety and a little advancement. A feed-up man has to travel around the prison. Guards get to know your face. If your personality is friendly, they let you slide with a number of things. They don't ask what's in the swag bag you're carrying." During his first three years at Attica, Malinow had a perfect disciplinary record. His work reports were all favorable. He pursued his 1968 conviction with as little success as he had had in appealing his 1954 conviction. He got to know and like Leon Vincent, the principal keeper at Attica, and to be known and liked by Vincent. In April 1971, Malinow had his first operation in prison, for a hernia, and was pleased by the treatment he received from the outside doctor who performed the operation in the prison hospital.

In the spring of 1971, Malinow felt that the prison was becoming more and more tense racially. He foresaw trouble between the young black militants, who were coming to prison in ever-increasing numbers, and the Attica guards, all of whom were white. In July 1971, Malinow again requested a transfer to Green Haven. He was told that his name would be added to the list; he would be sent there when the opportunity arose. Before it did, the Attica riot took place.

When the riot began, as a minor incident, on September 9, 1971, Malinow was still a porter, locking on A block. He and his friends, most of whom were white, hoped to isolate themselves within A block for the duration of the trouble, but were forced by other inmates to go to the D-block yard, where they spent the next four days. At first, they thought the riot would be a black-vs.-white confrontation, because they knew that some of the hatred that the blacks felt toward the white guards extended to the white inmates whom the white guards favored. Malinow and his friends therefore climbed up to the roof of a covered passageway in D yard, believing that they would be safer at a high elevation. They stayed there even after it turned out that the riot was not a race riot after all. Although they were sympathetic to many of the demands for change at Attica, they played a passive role during the riot. They didn't serve as spokesmen, they weren't on the negotiating committee, they didn't guard the hostages. They simply ate, slept, and built a wall out of some heavy planks and tried to barricade themselves behind it, in the hope of deflecting the bullets they expected when the prison was retaken, as they knew it would be. When the state police took Attica back, on September 13, Malinow was still on the passageway roof. He says he was blown off the roof by a tear-gas cannister dropped from a helicopter, and fell twenty feet to the ground. Upon landing, he suffered a concussion and went into shock. He was carried out of the yard on a stretcher. His pulse was apparently undetectable, because two doctors pronounced him dead and put a death tag around his wrist. He was paralyzed — he couldn't speak or move, or even blink — but he was able to hear everything, including the information that he was to be taken to the morgue. As he was worrying about suffocating in the morgue refrigerator, a third doctor examined him with a stethoscope, detected a heartbeat, and gave him a shot of adrenalin. He was carried to the hospital.

A month later, Malinow and many other Attica inmates were transferred to Green Haven. In January 1972, he was brought back to Attica under what he claims were false pretenses; he says he was told he would be asked to testify about his riot injuries. When he reached Attica, he was asked to testify against some of the inmates who were being charged with murdering guards. He refused to cooperate, drew up some writs in which he successfully convinced a federal judge that he was being unfairly pressured, and was returned to Green Haven in March 1972, the month in which Leon Vincent became its superintendent.

In 1974, Malinow wrote a long letter to the chairman of the parole board, asking that the time he had left to serve on his fifteen-to-life sentence be shortened by three and a quarter years: he wanted the parole board to let him start his new sentence in 1966 (when he was arrested), rather than in 1970 (when he was paroled from his previous sentence and began the new one). Malinow justified his request for this consideration primarily by recounting his conduct before and during the Attica riot. His letter read, in part:

Approximately five (5) months before the riot broke out, there came a time where a Lt. Matthew Bryant (since retired) approached me while I was working as A-Block porter, and inquired whether I had heard anything definite with regard to the black militants who locked on 5 gallery in A-Block, intending to attack all the A-Block officers the next morning when they came out to go to breakfast. Lt. Bryant had known me for several years at that time and we had a friendly relationship. I stated that I had obtained definite information that that was not any rumor, but true and also, the militants intended to attack the white inmates in A-Block too.

Lt. Bryant was in an awkward position since such rumors had

many times been heard previously and never proved true so he was reluctant to react in haste with respect to the chain of command over him. However, he realized that if it did happen, the lives of the officers in A-Block would be in danger, etc.

Lt. Bryant asked me if I'd agree to gather all the "old-timer" inmate friends of mine locking in A-Block, and speak to them to determine whether we would assist the officers should trouble break out. I did and we all agreed since we also expected to be attacked. Lt. Bryant ordered all the cells I gave him a list of to be opened before any other cell was on the morning of that expected trouble by the black militants. I and my associates, numbering approximately 125 inmates all armed ourselves and assembled ourselves, in groups, in front of every correction officer on duty then in the open areas of A-Block. When the black militants came out to go to breakfast, they surged toward the hall captain's office desk toward about six to eight officers.

As they did so — although they did not display their weapons, we raised our weapons and formed a double line in front of all the officers so that for the militants to reach the officers, they'd have to pass us first. They didn't expect to be confronted by us and were surprised and not prepared to cope with that situation. They gathered amongst themselves and then proceeded to go to breakfast to the mess hall. We remained with the officers all that morning but nothing happened as these said militants returned to their cells and were kept locked in for several days until the situation could be reached as it was later on.

At that time — I can now only recall some of those officers names — as follows: Hall Captain — C.O. Oliver Davies; and Lt. Bryant.

During the time that the riot first broke out early in that morning I was working on my job assignment in A Block. Before we realized what was happening — large fires were blazing all about and inmates chasing and assaulting officers all about the yards, roofs (tunnel) and the blocks and corridor tunnel halls. A large group from the location of the other side of that institution came charging to A-Block cells and C.O. area, assaulting officers, etc. I and my gallery associates grouped immediately and placed ourselves around three A-Block officers we worked for, to prevent any of the assaulting inmates from hurting said officers. I explained to those attacking inmates that we personally knew these officers to have never done anything unjustly to any inmate, during all the years we've known them and we weren't going to let no one harm them. The militants were satisfied with the explanation I gave to them but insisted these three officers had to be locked into empty cells on A-Block. I couldn't prevent that but I and my group of associates insisted we intended to accompany them (militants) to assure that these officers weren't harmed. This was done. Before we had to leave these officers, I and my friends brought them cigarettes, food and soap and towels since the militants took all their personal items they had on them away (wallets, money, smokes, etc.).

Later on — a different group outnumbering my associates and myself by over 10 to 1, and all armed with weapons, knives, gas guns, etc., came to A-Block and demanded we proceed and go to D-Block yard where everybody else was forced to go. Since we were not in any position to resist, we had to comply.

The above can be substantiated by the Supt. here at Green Haven Facility — Mr. Leon Vincent, as Mr. Vincent was Principal Keeper at Attica Facility, at the time of the Attica riot.

When Lieutenant Bryant was recently apprised of the contents of Malinow's letter, he said, "The first incident Malinow relates is made up. I worked with inmates for thirty-five years. I'm an old-timer. I know inmates. I'd never encourage inmates to take things into their own hands like that." Bryant couldn't recall the second incident, either, and didn't remember Malinow. Oliver Davies had no recollection whatever of the first incident that Malinow described, although he remembered Malinow well and regarded him as a good inmate, one whom he had liked, and who he believed would try to help an officer if he could. Davies, who was working on A block on September 9, 1971, was one of the first two men hurt at Attica. He, another guard, and a lieutenant barricaded themselves into a cell on A block. Davies was later taken hostage, blindfolded, and led to D yard, where he stayed until September 13. "No inmates protected me in any way," he says. As for Malinow's letter, Davies says that there were any number of men who wanted to get out of prison and who wrote letters to the parole board describing their heroic deeds during the Attica riot, in the hope of receiving early-release consideration. In 1974, Leon Vincent wrote a short letter to the parole board and sent it along with Malinow's letter. "The statements he is making concerning his role prior to and during the Attica uprising are true," Vincent wrote. When he was asked in 1976 about Malinow's conduct during the riot, Vincent said he didn't remember anything about it. "Vincent probably just took Malinow's word for what he had done," Davies says.

Malinow isn't disappointed that Bryant's and Davies' Attica memories don't coincide with his. "They'd be hurting themselves too much with all their prison cronies if they admitted I'd helped them," he says. "And why would they jeopardize their pensions for me? I'm just an inmate. I know what happened. I wouldn't have written the parole board if it wasn't true." Malinow has never told any inmates at Green Haven that he helped any guards at Attica. "They wouldn't approve," he says. In any event, the chairman of the parole board denied his request.

When Malinow was transferred from Attica to Green Haven in early 1972, he was evaluated by a counselor. On an inmate admission form, the counselor described his future outlook as "very poor . . . strictly a recidivist." The counselor's custodial recommendation was, "Suggest extreme security." Leon Vincent disregarded the custodial recommendation. To work outside the wall at Green Haven in the early seventies, an inmate had to be within a year or two of meeting with the board or being released. In 1972, Malinow still had seven years to go before meeting with the board. Superintendent Vincent gave him a job working outside the wall — at his house. Many guards disapproved of Malinow's work assignment; he claims that several placed bets on when he'd take off from the superintendent's house. Vincent didn't worry. "Malinow was an old-timer," he says. "When an old-timer gave you his word, it was his bond." Malinow admits that there were times while he was standing outside the house, watching the cars streak by, when he was tempted. He says he didn't run — as another man assigned to Vincent's house later did — because Vincent was the first official in all his years in prison who had really gone out of his way to show him consideration, and he would never have let him down. "I loved that man," he says. Vincent took Malinow along with him to the dock where he kept his houseboat, and allowed him to attend services at a local church with a civilian who worked at his house, and no guard. Vincent was a prankster by nature, and liked to tease Malinow. "It's too quiet in the prison. Let's have some excitement," he said to Malinow one day, tossing him the keys to his car. A guard who was in the room reached into his pocket and handed Malinow some bills. "Here, you'll need some cash," he said. Malinow returned the keys and the money.

After a few months at the house, Malinow asked to go back inside, because he couldn't get along with one of the guards assigned to Vincent's house, a man of Polish ancestry, whom he described as "a stubborn Polack — just like me." Malinow became a superintendent's runner, doing assorted errands for Vincent in the Administration Building and all over the prison. The female clerical workers in the area outside Vincent's office liked Malinow; one brought him a bottle of hair dye, so he could blacken his graying hair. He was always polite to the women, and dressed neatly, often with an ascot under his shirt, to please them. One of his tasks as a superintendent's runner was to set the lunch table for the parole board commissioners during the week each month when they met at Green Haven. Once, a few minutes before the board's lunch was to begin, Vincent grabbed a pitcher of water and threw it at Malinow, who was standing near the table. Malinow ducked. The water landed on the table. Malinow hastily reset the table. He enjoyed Vincent's clowning around. Many of the officers, sergeants, and lieutenants at

Green Haven did not approve of a superintendent who indulged in such antics with an inmate.

Life at Green Haven between 1972 and 1975 was more agreeable for Malinow than life in prison had ever been for him before, partly because of his relationship with Vincent, and partly because of some of the changes in prison that came about after the Attica riot. As a superintendent's runner, Malinow was housed on J block, the prison's honor block at the time, where the inmates lived in tiny rooms rather than in cells. Because of the liberalized correspondence regulations, Malinow could write freely to his pen pals and his girlfriend, Liwayway Ona.

After corresponding with Malinow for a few months, Miss Ona — a poor salesgirl who lived in a small town lacking electricity — wrote to Green Haven to ask about Malinow. She wanted to know who this man was who was sending her photographs of himself and letters that all sounded the same, who gave her to understand that he was very rich and that he wanted to come to the Philippines to marry her and spend a large sum of money on the wedding. "Jesus. Is George sane or otherwise?" she inquired. A Green Haven Service Unit counselor replied that Malinow was serving a sentence of fifteen years to life after pleading guilty to possession of a gun, and that he was scheduled to meet with the parole board in February 1979, for release consideration. Malinow was told about Miss Ona's letter, which didn't upset him. "You have to understand, she's a foreigner," he says. "They have a different culture. She felt she had to check to see if I was giving her a line." Nor did the Service Unit's reply trouble Miss Ona, who continued writing to Malinow and sending him photographs of herself and her family. Instead of spending the money from Halloran and a couple of other friends on himself, Malinow sent it to Miss Ona. On one occasion, he sent her three hundred dollars, and on other occasions fifty or a hundred dollars. He also sent many gifts — jewelry and pocketbooks for her, basketballs for her nieces and nephews. Miss Ona now signs her letters "Liwayway

Ona Malinow," which pleases Malinow. When she recently received a photograph he had sent her of one of his inmate friends holding his child, Miss Ona wrote back to say that she was looking forward to holding their first child. She said she wanted at least six children with Malinow. "That made me feel real good," he says. His friends think Miss Ona is taking him for all he is worth. Only a few of his friends know that he has a son; those men wonder why he has never done anything for Arthur.

Leon Vincent retired in May 1975. Several months later, Malinow lost his job as a superintendent's runner. The new superintendent, a straitlaced man, didn't like the idea of inmates working around women. Malinow was also implicated in a romance that had flourished in the Administration Building between an inmate and a female civilian employee. He was later absolved of complicity in the romance by the Inmate Grievance Committee. He was given a job as a clerk in the parole-clothing department, in the basement of the Administration Building, in December 1975.

Whoever chanced to meet George Malinow at Green Haven in January 1976, met a man who had resigned himself to being in prison until he first became eligible for parole, on February 27, 1979, and who was keeping as busy as he could in the meantime.

Late one night in mid-February 1976, Malinow was in bed, reading a parole newsletter that many inmates receive. He came across an article that seemed to say that a certain law he had known of and had never believed to be applicable to his case might apply to him after all: under specified circumstances, section 70.30 of the penal code allowed the time a man had served on a previous sentence to count toward the minimum of his next sentence; he could, therefore, be eligible to see the parole board right away. Malinow got out the box in which he keeps his legal papers and did some arithmetic. He figured out that he had served nine years, six months, and thirteen days

— from February 23, 1957 until September 6, 1966 — on his fifteen-to-thirty-year sentence for the Devon payroll robbery. With jail credits and good time, he had nine years, one month, and fifteen days (from January 13, 1970, to February 27, 1979) to do on the current sentence. The nine years, six months, and thirteen days was greater than the nine years, one month, and fifteen days, so he should be a PIE — a Parole Immediately Eligible — case. He was so excited he couldn't sleep at all that night. At 7:15 the next morning, when his cell door and the gate to his tier opened, he bounded down to parole clothing and phoned a sergeant of his acquaintance who worked in the superintendent's office. He reported his findings to the sergeant, who agreed with them and helped him get his papers into the hands of Green Haven's head clerk. On February 19, the head clerk classified Malinow as a PIE case and put him on the list of men who would meet with the parole board the next time it came to Green Haven — the week beginning March 22.

The next four weeks were busy ones for Malinow as he once again got caught up in the pre-parole crash program. He went to see a prison doctor and had a physical examination. The doctor found him in "excellent condition." He went to see a psychiatrist for a pre-parole psychiatric interview. After talking to Malinow for five minutes, the psychiatrist decided he was a "moderately poor" parole risk because of his recidivism. He also said — Green Haven's psychiatrists are given to hedging their bets — that his age and "recent devotion to positive humanitarian activities" (Malinow had told the psychiatrist he was involved with the financial adoption of children abroad) were "good signs." Malinow was also interviewed by his parole officer, who described his attitude as "cooperative yet guarded in thought and information." He refused to discuss his 1966 crime with the parole officer, "due to the possibility of reopening the case," and wouldn't say whether he was guilty or innocent of it. When he was asked about his friendships at Green Haven, he said he had "hundreds of associates . . . but no real

263

friends." He did admit to "a great need for material possession." Green Haven's chief parole officer sent a form letter to the Bronx district attorney inquiring whether the district attorney had any recommendations to make in Malinow's case. Unknown to Malinow, the chief parole officer received a form letter back from the district attorney's office which read, "Please be advised that this office makes no recommendation regarding the inmate's possible release on parole."

In late February and early March, Malinow was happier than he had been in a decade. He had his shaggy hair neatly trimmed by a friend. (He later insisted that the haircut wasn't for the parole board's benefit.) He obtained a place in a halfway house for newly released prisoners in Manhattan. In parole clothing, he selected a pair of dark-blue pants, a gray-blue blazer, and a gray-blue-and-white plaid tie to wear home. He tried on a light-blue leisure suit in his size and put it aside, along with some other clothes, to mail home to a friend: he would need an up-to-date new wardrobe after his release. Malinow had given up smoking in 1975 and had taken to popping candy into his mouth whenever he got the urge to smoke. He had gained a few pounds, and the leisure suit was snug. He started smoking several packs of cigarettes a day and eating only one meal. He wrapped up some of his many personal possessions and took them down to parole clothing, so that he wouldn't have too much packing to do after he made parole. He was absolutely certain he would be released. A promise was a promise, and he had a copy of the district attorney's letter to the chairman of the parole board asking that he be granted parole the first time he met with the board if he had behaved himself in prison, which he certainly had. He hadn't had a misbehavior report for almost four and a half years.

Malinow went to the parole board on Monday, March 22, 1976. His five-minute hearing was similar to the hearings of most of the other men who met the board that month and every month at Green Haven. New York State has twelve parole commissioners, who travel in threesomes to the various state prisons. In 1976, they usually spent five days a month at Green Haven. The three parole board commissioners divide the cases they are scheduled to hear, each member taking every third case. While one commissioner questions a subject, the two others riffle through the parole folders of their next subjects, which they haven't had a chance to look at ahead of time.

The commissioner who had Malinow's folder didn't seem to like what he read, and gave Malinow what Malinow considered a contemptuous look: an inauspicious beginning. He asked Malinow how much time he had in and what he had done to better himself during that time. Malinow answered concisely and courteously. The commissioner then asked him why he thought the board ought to let him out. Malinow mentioned his good behavior record, his good work record, and his involvement in many prison programs. He also said he had changed his whole way of thinking since 1966. To his dismay, the commissioner started to lecture him, in an angry tone. "Look at this record," he said. "Prison, prison, nothing but prison. You keep promising to stay out, and you keep coming back. You're a threat to the community. Nothing you've said justifies your going out. You've got a criminal record that goes back to your childhood."

Malinow fought to control himself. Without raising his voice, he told the commissioner that if people had taken an interest in him as a child and had gone out of their way to help him he wouldn't be in the situation he was in today. As soon as the words were out of his mouth, he realized that they hadn't sat well with the commissioner, so he returned to the matter of his lengthy record. He told the commissioner that both the district attorney and the sentencing judge were fully aware of his long record when he was sentenced and yet both had agreed that he should be released the first time he met the board. Why should the commissioner think otherwise? The commissioner didn't react. "I can't undo my record," Malinow said. "I've got over

265

nine years in for carrying a gun. That's twice as long as many men get today for a string of robberies and muggings. I've paid my debt to society. I don't owe society nothing."

The commissioner asked Malinow about his future plans. Malinow said he hoped to go into the construction business in the Philippines. The commissioner thanked him. Malinow left the room.

Some men leave their parole board hearings not knowing whether they have made parole. The questions and answers are usually routine, and the atmosphere is fairly polite. A few months earlier, however, a good friend of Malinow's had gone before the board. The commissioner asked him what he had done for himself in prison. The man, a robber with three convictions, said he had taken some college courses, had earned his two-year degree, and was working on his B.A. "You were a pretty good thief before you got an education, so you'll be an even better thief when you get out," the commissioner said. Malinow's friend was not surprised when he received a fifteen-month "hit," after which he promptly abandoned work on his B.A. Malinow knew when he left the room that he would be turned down for parole. The commissioner had been hostile. The parole board can hit a man with as little as a month, as much as two years. A short hit (three or six months) is regarded as a sign to the next board to let him go if his behavior has remained good. Malinow thought he would get a short hit — perhaps three months, perhaps six. The board's decisions aren't given to inmates until the end of the week, after the commissioners have left Green Haven. On March 22, Malinow asked an officer in parole clothing to find out the results of his hearing; two Green Haven parole officers and a guard are in the room when the parole board commissioners dictate their decisions on the cases they have heard. The following morning, Malinow was stunned to learn from the parole-clothing officer that he had been hit with twenty-one months. He was officially notified of the board's decision on March 26. On March 27,

Malinow received a list of the board's reasons for denying him parole. The board is required to give reasons. In Malinow's case, it gave six:

1. You have had nine (9) convictions and four (4) felony convictions.
2. You do not learn from experience.
3. You have violated parole and probation in the past.
4. You were on parole when present crime was committed.
5. You have unrealistic plans for the future.
6. You need more time in institutional programs to prepare to live within the laws of society.

Although Malinow had made parole the first time he met with the board on every other occasion, he seems, like many prisoners, to hate parole even more than he hates prison. He knows of too many cases in which men with similar records have gone to the board and one has been granted parole, the other denied it. Often, one man draws an easygoing commissioner or a commissioner who is in a good mood, another a tough commissioner or a commissioner in a bad mood. The parole system makes most men feel helpless, because they know that no matter how exemplary their work and behavior records are in prison, if their crimes are serious the board will simply decide they haven't got the time in, and keep hitting them. Thus, Neil Shea, a cop-killer, knew after the board had hit him twice that "they ain't never going to let me out," and escaped from Green Haven. As for Malinow, he thought that most of the reasons for denying him parole were either inaccurate or beside the point. He did have four felony convictions, but by his reckoning he didn't have nine convictions. It was true that he had violated parole and probation in the past, but although he had violated parole, he had still been re-paroled, and he personally knew hundreds of men (and had heard of thousands) who had violated parole many times and had been re-paroled. He didn't consider his plans to go to the Philippines unrealistic; he had written a letter to President Ferdinand E. Marcos of the Philippines, and he had received a reply from the Philippine consulate, a copy of which had been put in his parole folder, for the parole commissioner to see, inviting him to call the consulate to discuss his plans when he could. And, goodness knows, eight years in institutional programs at Attica and Green Haven was long enough to prepare anyone to live within the laws of society.

For a few days, Malinow appeared a defeated man. He sulked, he brooded, he was unusually quiet. He didn't accept defeat long. In April, he was busy fighting the adverse parole board decision. In May, he decided to go to court to contend that he had been denied parole for insufficient reasons, as many other inmates have done in recent years. Judges have often ruled that the board's reasons were inadequate and have ordered inmates back to the parole board for rehearings, especially when, as in Malinow's case, the board didn't give specific suggestions on how an inmate's behavior in prison had been deficient or how he could improve it to meet the board's standards.

Malinow had also decided to fight his battle to get out of prison on a second legal front. He had taken a plea based on the fact that a district attorney and a judge had made a recommendation that he be released the first time he met with the board if his conduct in prison was good. He had kept his part of the bargain, but for some reason their recommendation hadn't been followed by the parole board. He filed what is known as a 440 petition — a motion to vacate judgment — in which he contended that promises made by a district attorney to induce a plea must be fulfilled. The wheels of justice, such as they are, grind slowly, but in late 1976 Malinow learned that the district attorney's office had sent the form letter to the chief parole officer at Green Haven in error, and in early 1977 he had the district attorney on his side. On January 10, 1977, a member of the district attorney's appeals bureau wrote to the office of the chairman of the parole board to say that the form letter had been sent by mistake and that the district attorney's office stood by its original recommendation. The district attorney requested that a determination be made whether in reaching its March 1976 decision the board had relied upon the form letter that had been erroneously sent, and whether the board had before it the original letter of recommendation. The letter concluded:

> Since the Board is required by statute to consider any recommendation made by the District Attorney in reaching its decision, the position of the District Attorney is obviously material to the Board's decision-making process. Due to the promise made by us to Mr. Malinow upon his plea, we feel obligated to pursue the possibility that our error affected the Board's decision adversely to Mr. Malinow's interests.

In January 1977, Malinow felt certain that he would get out when he saw the board, no doubt in February. In February, he felt certain he would get out when he got back to the board, surely in March. And if not in March — well, no one could keep him from meeting the board in December 1977, twenty-one months after his March 1976 hit.

After Malinow met with the parole board in March 1976, he began to talk a great deal about his post-prison plans. He knows he will need a job after he is paroled, to satisfy his parole officer. His old friend is still the business representative of Local 13, and Malinow has written to him. He expects he will get a job through Local 13, because of "past favors" (an expression he prefers to "strong-arm work") that he has done for the union. Local 13's members are currently earning $315 a week — $9 an hour for a thirty-five-hour week. Should Local 13 be on strike when Malinow gets out, as it was in 1966, he is considering other jobs. Perhaps his nephew, William Muller, will help him get a job in his field, bridge painting, which also pays very well. Or perhaps, through friends in another union, he will be offered a job as a doorman. "Doormen only get two hundred a week, but I hear the tips are good," Malinow says. "You take an old lady's snooty little poodle around the block and she tips you twenty bucks." He is sure his friends will give him some money, as they did in 1966, to help him get started. He would like to buy some furniture for a three-room apartment he plans to rent in Brooklyn or Queens. (He has no intention of staying in a halfway house.) He doesn't expect to keep a salaried job long. "A conventional, stagnated life isn't for me," he says. "If I had thought that would bring me happiness, I could have done that at seventeen. I'm still interested in big money."

Once he is out, he plans to buy two books. One, entitled "How to Rob Banks Legally," is a book he first heard about in 1975, when he took an economics course taught by an inmate at Green Haven. Under the guise of teaching economics, the inmate gave lessons in such subjects as how to get a number of simultaneous loans from banks by bending but not quite breaking the law. Malinow believes he can go to five different banks, all in an hour's time, and obtain five ten-thousand-dollar loans. "Each bank will ask if I have any other outstanding loans, and I'll say no, which is unethical but not illegal, so each will give me ten thou, and by the time they check up on me — if they even bother to do so — it will be too late," he says. He will put the fifty thousand dollars in a commercial bank and borrow more money against that. With the four hundred thousand dollars he thinks he can borrow against the fifty thousand, he will invest in an apartment building. He has been receiving brochures from the Department of Housing and Urban Development during his last couple of years at Green Haven, and knows of many apartment buildings with theoretically attractive rent rolls which H.U.D. is trying to sell. With the rent money coming in, he will be able to make his mortgage payments and his loan payments, and will clear a few thousand dollars a month. "I'll be a millionaire within three years," he says.

The second book he plans to buy is a biography of the late gambler Nick the Greek. The book gives Nick the Greek's winning formula for playing dice. Malinow once read it but has forgotten part of the formula. Once he has the book and has mastered the system, he will fly to Las Vegas and clean up at the dice table. After Malinow has piled up some money in real estate and gambling, he will go to the Philippines — with a forged passport, if necessary — and marry Miss Ona. When his friends remind him that she is thirty years younger than he is, Malinow says, "Look at Charlie Chaplin. Look at Justice Douglas." He has already sent away for plans for a Spanish-style villa he intends to build in the Philippines for himself and Miss Ona and their future children, and is looking into generators, for he does not fancy living without electricity. He talks about going into the construction business in the Philippines, and perhaps into the import-export business, too. Before he flies out there, he says, he will get some upper teeth — not cheap false teeth but expensive dental implants. He will also try to find his son, Arthur and go to see him once — only once — to tell him his side of the story. It will be easy for Malinow to find Arthur, who is still living with his mother in the apartment that Malinow and Louise fixed up for themselves in 1953. The eight-hundred-dollar refrigerator is still working. Louise hasn't divorced him. Arthur has served in the marine corps, is engaged to be married to a pretty, blond childhood sweetheart, and works as a security guard. Arthur has spent the last ten years wondering about his father's whereabouts and has always planned to find him. After Malinow left the house one day in the fall of 1966 and didn't come back, Louise and Arthur had no idea if he had been rearrested, if he had moved away, or if he had died.

Malinow's most important project once he gets out of prison on parole is to get himself off parole. He knows he would find parole too restrictive. He wants the freedom to travel and to make a lot of money with no questions asked. Once he is paroled, he will hire a good lawyer and attack his fourth conviction on the ground that he was induced to take a plea, kept his part of the bargain, and was betrayed by the district attorney, who had made a promise he hadn't kept; Malinow didn't get out on parole the first time he saw the board, in March 1976, as he should have. He will then retract his plea, as many men have successfully done. He will replead to a shorter sentence — probably the three and a half to seven years that Halloran got. That will remove his life sentence. He has more than enough time in prison on the three-and-a-half-to-seven-year sentence, so he will get "time served." Even then, he will still owe a few years on parole for the fifteen-to-thirty-year sentence he got in 1954 for the Devon payroll robbery. Since he doesn't want to do any time on parole and has exhausted his appeals on that conviction, he will attack his first conviction — for the 1938 Dillard-Scott robbery — on the ground that he had no counsel when he entered his plea. "I was a seventeen-year-old youngster, processed by the court in unseemly haste," he says. "I pled, I was sentenced, and I landed in Sing Sing all within five days. That's Southern-style justice." If he can eliminate his first conviction, his second conviction becomes his first, and his third becomes his second. He can then be resentenced on the Devon payroll robbery. As a second offender, he would not have to be given the mandatory fifteen to thirty years. A judge cannot touch the fifteen-year minimum, but he can change the maximum. He could, for example, give Malinow fifteen to sixteen years — which he has long since served — and Malinow would be free and clear and off parole.

When Malinow is asked if his plans include seeking revenge on David Balboa, the man who set him up in 1966, he says no. He doesn't even seem particularly angry at Balboa, and is interested only in accounting for Balboa's successful deception.

"Balboa was an inmate I trusted," Malinow says. "He had reached a point in his mind where he couldn't do any more time. He was told that if he wanted to stay out he'd have to give information. There came a time when he had no more to give. That was right around the time I got out. I regarded Balboa as a friend. He'd proven himself trustworthy on other occasions. He'd stood up to pressure for fifteen years, and broke during the sixteenth. You can't anticipate that. The best of us are going to get fooled. It's the same thing with a husband and a wife. The husband is faithful for fifteen years. The sixteenth year, he strays."

Malinow says that his future plans do not include robbery. Sometimes, he says jokingly that, at fifty-seven, he is past the retirement age for robbers. The two men with whom Malinow was last convicted did not retire from robbery in their fifties. Bernard Czarnowicz was paroled from Green Haven in 1969, at the age of fifty-two, after serving his sentence for the Devon payroll robbery. A few months later, he married for the first time. In 1971, "completely broke, unable to find a job, and desperate for money," he was caught in the act of robbing a bank on Long Island of $6530 with a loaded gun. He pleaded guilty and was sentenced to seven years in federal prison. While he was imprisoned, he developed heart trouble. He was released in 1976. Czarnowicz's release made his wife — a widow whose first husband had been a law-abiding citizen — nervous. She fell ill the day he got home. The Czarnowiczes are living in a small apartment in Queens, on welfare. Czarnowicz recently had to borrow some money from his stepson-in-law to install a phone in his apartment. Patrick Halloran, a lifelong bachelor, was fifty-eight when he set out to rob the Bingo Machine Company with Malinow in 1965. Since his release from prison in 1971, he has been working for a beer company, loading beer bottles onto trucks, and living in a small apartment in Brooklyn with an Irish setter. He also works as the superintendent of his building, in exchange for free rent and a hundred dollars a month. He says he is just getting by.

George Malinow has seen only a few of the pieces of paper that make up his eight-hundred-page record — the letter from the district attorney to the chairman of the parole board and the letters of recommendation that most prisoners ask for (and usually get) from the guards who have known them in prison, for the benefit of the parole board. He has not seen the eight-page account that the Green Haven parole officer wrote after talking to Malinow and reviewing his record in March 1976, which the parole board commissioner who hit him with twenty-one months later that month almost certainly did see. In that account, the Green Haven parole officer enumerated Malinow's four crimes, three sentences, and three previous failures on parole. Malinow "could not stay out of trouble for any too long a period of time while on the streets in the city of New York," the parole officer wrote. What seemed to worry him particularly was the fact that Malinow had been arrested for his fourth crime seven weeks after his third release, having "obviously derived no benefit from institutional and parole experiences." He concluded by saying, "One does not have to be a prophet of any sort to predict that this inmate will if released again be in trouble with the law." He also wrote that Malinow is "a man with an extremely long criminal past who cannot by any reasoning stay out of trouble while in a civil environment. . . . Since inmate adjusts extremely well behind bars and extremely poorly on the outside, it is the opinion of this writer at this time that this inmate be considered as a guarded parole risk."

If Malinow had read his parole officer's report, it wouldn't have caused him a minute's anguish. He has never put any credence in other people's opinions of him. He doesn't believe in rehabilitation, but *he* knows that since he was last sent to prison people have responded to him with kindness and love, and that he has a different outlook, and that is what counts. He is convinced that he can obtain the money he wants by legal or semi-legal means rather than by altogether illegal means. He doesn't care that even some of his closest friends predict that he will get out of prison, stay out for a while, and eventually do something that will result in his being sent back to prison. "No one knows more about me than myself," he says. "I know I ain't coming back."

Lewis and Clark College - Watzek Library
HV9475.N72 G737   wmain
Sheehan, Susan/A prison and a prisoner

3 5209 00319 9979